1000 beautiful garden plants

and how to grow them

1000 beautiful garden plants

and how to grow them

BY JACK KRAMER

DRAWINGS BY ROBERT JOHNSON

WILLIAM MORROW AND COMPANY, INC., NEW YORK

DESIGN BY CRAVEN & EVANS, CREATIVE GRAPHICS / KAY WANOUS

Printed in the United States of America.

1 2 3 4 5 80 79 78 77 76

Library of Congress Cataloging in Publication Data

Kramer, Jack (date)
    1000 beautiful garden plants and how to grow them.

    Includes index.
    1. Plants, Ornamental.   2. Landscape gardening
3. Vegetable gardening. I. Title.
SB407.K7   635.9   76-984
ISBN 0-688-03025-4

contents

AUTHOR'S NOTE

This note is for my artist, Robert Johnson, who did the fine drawings for this book. It was a voluminous task to draw details of one thousand plants, and he approached it with enthusiasm and stuck to it with perseverance while putting up with my many changes and revisions as we went along. So to Robert Johnson I owe a special thanks indeed. He may not have started out a gardener when he took on this book, but he surely is one now.

And also a special thanks to Judy Smith, who typed and retyped the many lists in the book; her patience and good nature were indeed appreciated.

PART ONE:

your garden

This small garden is a handsome combination of trees, shrubs, bulbs, and colorful marigolds; a beautiful landscape plan that creates a happy oasis. (Photo by Ken Molino)

1. what have you got?

Gardens can be large or small, formal or informal, opulent or simple. But no matter what the size or style of your garden, flowers will be a major part of it because color is what creates the dramatic impact for a total garden, and trees and shrubs will be the backbone of the garden that sets the stage for the seasonal color of annuals, perennials, vines, and bulbs.

I have seen lovely gardens in notoriously small lots in San Francisco, vast gardens in Illinois suburbs, and elaborate gardens in Europe. Just what kind of garden you have depends on the amount of land available, type of plants, soil, climatic conditions, and one other most important factor: your own personal taste. But whether it is small or large, you can have a garden. Space is not as important as what to use where. Proper *planning* and proper *planting* of *plants* make the difference. Keep these considerations in mind, and your garden will sing rather than sulk in mediocrity.

HOW MUCH LAND?

This question is not superfluous because these days land is at a premium. We must learn to use intelligently whatever space we have. No longer can we afford to use just a portion of the property and let the rest go; now we must utilize all the space. But you can have several types of gardens within one area—cutting, vegetable, border—if you plan it properly.

Generally, the average suburban house and accompanying land occupies approximately a quarter-acre. The house usually is on half this space (one-eighth acre), which leaves you approximately 4000 square feet for a garden. This is plenty of space, but not so much that you can have all kinds of gardens with all kinds of plants. First determine the priorities, such as what you want to grow for what reasons. Then consider your land, and start your plan. Decide whether you want a vegetable garden and a cutting garden, or an ornamental garden with a few vegetables and herbs, or perhaps only a garden of seasonal flowers. No matter what suits your land and your fancy, a well-maintained garden enhances the property and is lovely to look at. Feeding the body is important, but equally important is soothing the mind and soul. Gardens can do both. They can be practical and aesthetic at the same time. Invariably space limits your choices, but even the smallest property carefully planned can be a garden paradise. You must choose a landscape plan that uses your property to the fullest no matter how small.

In order of importance, consider the following types of gardens when planning your property:

Ornamental garden. An ornamental garden is a pretty way to greet guests. This is a tree and shrub garden with masses of flowers; it needs space.

Vegetable garden. A vegetable garden needs only a small area, saves you money, and is fun to grow. Generally the vegetable garden can be tucked away within another garden.

Formality is the keynote of this garden, with clipped boxwood hedges accented with irises and other bulbous plants. The character is formal, the plan symmetrical. Plants have been used with restraint here to make a handsome, low-key garden. (Photo by Barr)

Cutting garden. If at all possible, plan for a cutting garden; you need only a 5- by 10-foot area. This area can be part of an ornamental garden. Cut flowers are a joy in the home and, again, save you money.

Border garden. This is a highly formal and special type of garden.

Herb garden. Not much space is needed and again this can be part of another garden.

Secret garden. Cultivate this happy sanctuary if any space is left over. It is nice to have a place really your own. This garden may be a rock garden or perhaps a special place for roses.

HOW TO PLAN THE GARDEN

Most plants, especially flowering ones, need sunlight (vegetables, too); some plants can tolerate shade. Other factors, such as humidity and watering, you can take care of, but how sun strikes your property deserves much consideration because it governs what you can grow. For instance, if you plant a flower garden in the shade, you will not have the kind of flowers you want, so you

There is really more to this small garden than meets the eye. The plan is ingenious, with a relatively small border of alyssum, geraniums, and primroses beautifully balanced with the handsome Dutchman's-pipe vine. (Photo by Molly Adams)

Dicentras and primroses mingle with flowering shrubs in this very attractive ornamental garden; there is a woodsy feeling and yet enough colorful garden plants to delight any eye. (Photo by Molly Adams)

This vegetable garden of beans, chard, lettuce, and tomatoes occupies a space only 20 feet by 15 feet and yet provides an abundant harvest for the family. (Photo by Jerry Bagger)

must carefully consider exposures as you outline your garden. Know the limitations of your property, and then work within that realistic picture.

North exposure. If all you have is a north exposure, grow shade plants (there are several flowering kinds).

East, south exposure. If your garden has an east or south exposure, you have a choice of many kinds of gardens.

West exposure. A west exposure allows for many but not all kinds of growing.

The kind of soil you have also governs what you can grow. Soil can be reconditioned, but that is a costly and laborious procedure. Know your soil. Is it sandy? Clayey? Whatever, plant those plants that will survive in your type of soil.

Do not be afraid to run your garden right up to the house. The era of expansive lawn and meandering paths is over. Use every inch of space to bring the outdoors indoors. Forget about foundation plantings and all old-fashioned garden planning "rules." Try to keep the garden natural so there is little actual planting work. Do not ever plan on those artsy predetermined spring, autumn, summer garden plans you see in books and magazines; they can drive you crazy, and I guarantee you will never attain that picture-book perfection. Just plant annuals and perennials at the proper times (this is necessary if you want any flowers), but forget elaborate plans. Enjoy your gardening, and you will enjoy every little flower. Worry and fret about your garden, and you will fret each flower into the ground in desperation.

Some alyssum, a few azaleas, roses mingle happily in this modest garden; trees and shrubs furnish the vertical accent. (Photo by Barr)

A very informal garden where flowering shrubs are the keynote and where maintenance is minimal. (Photo by Molly Adams)

KNOWING PLANTS

Half the battle of a good garden is getting to know the plants (the other half is planning). And knowing the plants is not that difficult. It is okay to know common names, but remember that they differ from place to place, and some flowers have three or four common names. Learn the botanical names. This is a bother, but today's handsome plant catalogs make learning the botanical names fairly easy. (Common-name/botanical-name charts are given at the ends of Chapters 6 and 7.)

Do get and study the various catalogs that make such good winter reading: Wayside Gardens, White Flower Farms, Park Seed Co. Get to know the popular annuals and the favorite perennials, and do not forget the wonderful world of flowering bulbs. Bulbs are bought all ready to burst into bloom and need only planting and water. You will also need some trees and shrubs as accents to give scale to your flower plantings; see the dictionary in Chapter 6 for recommended trees and shrubs.

If possible, buy from local nurseries at seasonal times. Annuals, perennials, vines, and vegetables are available then as prestarted plants, trees, and shrubs ready for seasonal planting. Buying from a local dealer means those plants will generally flourish in your area. You do not have to worry yourself unnecessarily about weather-zone maps. However, when you buy from mail-order houses, you will have to do some studying of the zone maps in Chapter 5 to know what you can safely grow in your area.

This garden combines the formal with the informal to create a pretty picture. Day lilies and other bulbous plants are featured with manicured privet to furnish just the right amount of elegance. (Photo by Molly Adams)

2. design, planning, and color

Whether you have a lot of land or a little area, you can have a garden. Generally you want your garden to be a place of beauty and relaxation, full of lovely color. But your retreat from the busy world can be more than that: it can also be a place to grow vegetables, a spot brimming with flowers, a cutting garden, or a patio with a sun area. Just how you allot your space and evolve your garden depends on your priorities, good design, and intelligent planning.

There is no need to get bogged down in the design rules of proportion, scale, line, and form. True, these factors are somewhat important, but nothing is rigid in garden planning—what suits you may not suit someone else. Go ahead and plan your own garden, but do it wisely, concentrating on such things as site, weather, and the uses you want to make of the space you have.

A plan on paper (a sketch is fine) is very useful in creating your own garden. You do not have to be a landscape architect or an artist to plan on paper; more important is some basic information about plants, types of gardens, and color. Basic care of plants is discussed in Chapter 5; full *descriptions* of plants are in Chapters 6 and 7. First let us consider garden styles.

TYPES OF GARDENS

In colonial America the garden was utilitarian, a place to grow vegetables and herbs with a few spots of flowers for color. Today this kind of garden still makes good sense. Certainly lovely ornamental gardens have their place, but because of dwindling land space and the rising costs of food, smaller, functional gardens are a definite asset to your property.

Any garden can have a particular feeling or character. It may be stark and simple, almost Oriental in character, imparting a feeling of serenity. An English garden will be a potpourri of vividly colored flowers, lending a cheery feeling to your home. A formal garden strongly separates in the middle of the design. That is, one side of the garden mirrors the scene on the other side, creating perfect symmetry. This type of garden needs a great deal of space because proportion and balance are absolutely necessary. The informal or "natural" gardens rely on asymmetrical balance. There are no pairs of trees or straight lines or rigid flower borders. There is a continuous row of plant material. An informal garden will make you feel relaxed and comfortable. (The true natural garden can be achieved only if your land has old trees and shrubs.)

Most of today's gardens are a mixture of a little formality and a lot of informality. The result is a pleasing picture as well as a functional garden where you can cut flowers, raise vegetables, and grow herbs.

PLANNING

No matter what your site is like or how much land is involved, certain general principles must be applied when you plan your garden. One principle involves the location of the sun (exposure) as it applies to the land. Get directions in mind as to east, south, west, and north. Try to determine which way the prevailing wind strikes the property. For example, is there more wind at the northwest corner than at the southwest? Observe the boundaries; you want to use as much of the property as possible. Visualize where you might want walls or fences. Take advantage of what natural conditions exist. These would include a rolling hill, a backdrop of stately trees, or, on the contrary, a nearby neighbor or an unsightly view that will have to be screened. Note existing trees and shrubs; decide whether they will stay. As a final check, walk the property several times. Look at the house from the grounds and then view the property from the inside of the house. Now you are ready to draw a rough plan on paper.

HOW TO PLAN ON PAPER

The first general ground plan for the property does not have to be drawn exactly to scale. Make a sketch using the boundary lines as the outline. Your builder or former owner may have a plot plan to help you if you don't. Using this as a guide, transpose the location of the house and the boundary lines onto graph paper. Let each square represent one foot. Draw the outline of the house and all existing man-made objects such as steps, walks, and driveways. Show existing trees and shrubs.

Determine the ground slope; this can make a difference in placing flower beds, fences, and patios. A flower bed in a gully is hardly in the best place; water will not drain properly and flowers will suffer. To determine where the hills and valleys are on your property, place a wooden stake at the highest corner of the lot; tie a string around the stake. Now walk the property to the opposite corner, running the string out as you go. Tie the string to a wooden stake at the corner. Use a mason's level on the string to be sure it is horizon-

This lovely rock garden shows the beauty of rocks and plants used in perfect harmony. Cerastium, dusty miller, rock roses, and azaleas are all part of this well-proportioned, harmonious garden. (Photo by Molly Adams)

tally level. Now measure the distance between the ground and the string to determine just how much of a grade there is. Find whatever other high and low places there are and mark these on the graph paper. You will need another person to help you make these measurements, so do it on a day when help is on hand.

Next, mark the graph paper with the sun and shade areas and indicate the north point. Use any kind of symbol to delineate these areas. When all existing features are present, you can start to plan the garden.

Over the graph paper, lay a sheet of tracing paper. Sketch traffic patterns first; then draw rough sizes and shapes of objects you want outdoors such as terrace, garden beds, raised beds, new trees and shrubs, and whatever else is necessary to the overall plan you have in mind. The irregular shapes you have

Masses of chrysanthemums are used in this patio garden. There is a continuous flow of plant material to delight the eye. (Photo by Ken Molino)

drawn should start to relate to each other. If you are not pleased with the layout, start over again on a new piece of tracing paper. First arrangements are rarely satisfactory. Consider all things carefully and make several plans so that all members of the family have a chance to agree.

Once you have a rough sketch that is agreeable to all and solves most of the problems, a detailed drawing is necessary. Exactness counts now, so be sure to have proper measurements of the house and lot, objects, and existing plant material.

Here are some ideas to help you plan.

Rectangular or square patterns are simple and most natural to use. They are usually projections of the house form. Working with a uniform module (that is, a space repeated again and again) simplifies a plan. The module can

A mass of gazanias is the color accent in this handsome landscape plan; the color scheme is monochromatic to provide dramatic statement. (Photo by Ken Molino)

be 3 by 4 feet or 5 by 5 feet, or almost any block size that fits your needs. Planting islands and beds can relate to the same module. In this way every design line in the plan is in proportion and pleasing to the eye. There will be simplicity, and yet there will be concise organization of space.

Acute or obtuse angles or triangles reflect the angular form of the house and site, and they lead the eye to a focal point and give a sense of space and direction.

Circular forms add interest to the pattern, and in proper balance with straight lines can give a pleasing composition.

Free curves are curving lines with a constantly changing radius. These are sweeping natural lines of nature and, skillfully used with geometric forms, produce richness and motion.

The simple basic forms we have mentioned are responsible for all linear patterns that develop in the garden. From these any number of combinations of patterns can be drawn.

COLOR AND YOUR GARDEN

Using color properly in landscape design is almost an art form because it is placing and combining plants to make an eye- and soul-pleasing picture. It is creating a visual impression. The relationship of one color to another is the key to beauty in the garden.

To some degree many of us are familiar with color—its harmony and combinations—in interior decoration, paintings, and fashions. We all know that color is vitally important in creating an attractive entity. And so it is in outdoor planning. But outdoor color compositions are much larger in scale and always changing, depending on the time of day, the seasons, and the distance plants are from the eye. Also, outdoor color schemes are influenced by green, which is both prevalent and variable in nature, and by the blue of the sky and the brown of the earth.

Because color is so vital in the garden, it is wise to know color basics. A little knowledge saves much time and money because hit-and-miss color planning is rarely attractive and invariably has to be redone.

We see color through light. Color is the result of sunlight, light being reflected or absorbed from any surface. The color *not* retained by an object is the one we see. For example, if an object neither reflects nor transmits light, we see black. On the other hand, white is the reflection of all color wavelengths. Any gardener should be concerned with the psychological aspect of color, how we react to the colors we see. For example, red flowers tend to create excitement in people, but green has a soothing effect.

Elements of Color

Value. Value (also called tone) is the lightness (tint) and darkness (shade) of color, as in a black-and-white photograph. The color value of one plant in your garden must harmonize with the value of another plant. In other words, your plants' colors must graduate from one tint or shade to the next. Without a related sequence of color value, your garden will be spotty in appearance, assaulting the eye rather than pleasing it.

Hue. Hue is the name of a color, such as orange or red. Hue is generally the term a gardener means when he says he wants red flowers. Hues are classified as warm—yellow, orange, and scarlet—or cool—blue, green, and purple. We'll discuss warm and cool colors and their psychological effects further on.

Intensity. Intensity is the purity of a color, its vividness, and the amount of chroma (pigment) in it. Intense colors are vivid red, orange, yellow, green, blue-green, blue-purple, purple, red, and magenta. Intense color is harsh, and too much of it produces a jarring effect in the landscape. Yet adjacent colors of the same intensity can produce a breathtaking garden, as evidenced by magenta and scarlet flowers next to each other or scarlet and red-orange blossoms together. This placement of intense color creates depth: the colors are pulled together so that the eye sees them as a concentrated mass.

To use the elements of color—value, hue, and intensity—intelligently in the flower garden is the basis of a good color scheme. First decide if you will feature tints or shades. Then use this value quantity in rhythmic sequence. If you decide on light-valued flowers of, say, the hue pink, start with a great quantity of them—light pink, for example. Then use a smaller amount of dark-pink flowers. Or start at the dark end of the value scale and progress to small quantities of light values for a handsome color scheme. Either way, the combination of tints and shades will create carrying power for the eye and a definite visual impression. Your garden picture will be constant, even at a distance, and it will never be splotchy. And always consider the intensity of your hues. You want to create certain effects, certain moods.

Flowers of light color value running in a sequence to dark values in the landscape will produce a soft mood, while darker colors (values) running to light values will be dramatic. Wavelengths reaching the eye from light values are easily seen and there is a natural blending of blue sky and green, while the blue of the sky and the green of the foliage with dark-valued flowers is a shock to the eye, a dramatic effect.

Once you decide whether you want your flowers to go from pale to dark or vice versa, pick the actual colors (hues) you want. Consider all the psychological aspects of warm versus cool colors. The warm colors—yellow, orange, and scarlet—and all their tints and shades make muscles tense. This psychological aspect contributes to your psychological mood: as your muscles tense, you get a feeling of excitement. The cool colors—blue, lavender, and purple—create relaxation in the muscles, giving you a feeling of serenity.

You must also consider the time of day in your garden. Warm colors are dulled and diminished by shade and shadow.

Using Warm and Cool Colors

A warm color scheme will obviously impart a sunny, cheery note to your garden. Select a large area for the flowers for an effective picture, and use the colors in rhythmic steps. For example, start with red; work into orange-scarlet; advance to orange, orange-red, and yellow; and, finally, finish with white. Or start with white and work down the color scale: white, yellow, yellow-orange, orange, and so on. The gradual sequence of color is necessary to promote a flowing line of color. If you jump the sequence too rapidly, from, say, white to red, the effect will be formal and austere. If your property is small, about 20 by 20 feet, the same gradation can be used with only one-third of the whole warm-color sequence. Do not forget that warm colors like orange and scarlet in association with green foliage will impart an informal look because green is a cool color. But yellow is one of the complements of green; complementary colors impart a formal look.

Use the cool colors—blue, lavender, and purple—to create a serene garden or an illusion of space in the small garden, because cool colors move away from the eye. You can also use cool colors as contrasts to warm colors. These cool colors should relate in both value and intensity to the warm colors they will accent. For example, pale blue can be used with a pale yellow. But do not use a dark blue with a pale yellow because the difference in intensity will cause the colors to pull apart and break the unity of the scheme.

Placement is vital when using flowers in combinations. Colors side by side or near each other on the spectrum will combine and mix; disharmony is a likely result even if the colors in themselves are beautiful. Complementary colors—red and yellow—make strong accents and are deep and vivid; try vivid red pyrethrums next to yellow black-eyed Susans, for instance. The further apart the colors in the color wheel, the more severe the contrast.

The primary colors are red, yellow, and blue, and the secondaries are orange, green, and violet. Warm colors are red, orange and yellow, as men-

All kinds of garden plants abound in this natural garden setting; there is much beauty and color in a relatively small area. (Photo by Molly Adams)

Agapanthus with dramatic blue flowers and clematis in dazzling white are the high points of this garden area, set off with trees and shrubs. (Photo by Ken Molino)

tioned, and their tints and shades. These colors are said to advance toward the eye for they affect the eye quickly and attract attention even at a distance. The cool colors push the color to the background. This advancing and receding of color vitally affects how the composition will appear as a whole.

You can intensify color in the landscape by placing contrasting colors such as orange and blue or red and green side by side. Such unrelated colors placed side by side in the landscape produce some distortion.

The colors of the flowers will also be affected by the time of day; warm colors are dulled and diminished by shade and shadow. Red flowers will appear brilliant in daylight (because of the yellow of the sun) and, after sunset, blue light will make the same red flowers appear almost violet. Daylight contains all wavelengths so all but red will be absorbed. Further, the eye sees one color one way against a specific background, red against green grass for example, and another way when red is placed against blue, as it often is in gardens. The eye seeks balance and so balance of contrasts is necessary for good color harmony.

The best color harmonies can be based on one hue and its tints and shades—yellow flowers, light-yellow flowers, and dark-yellow ones—or with three hues with one of them predominating. If you use more than three different colors in a garden, then harmony must be achieved by gradation or quantity or both with the use of a predominating color to tie it all together.

Do not think of a group of flowers as one color but rather of what the color does to another group of flowers.

This is the author's cutting garden, where asters, hollyhocks, and marigolds grow profusely and gloriosa daisies furnish vertical thrust; it is a space-saving garden and a money-saving one, too. (Photo by Barr)

3. personal gardens

Your garden should be just that—yours; it should be pleasing to you in all respects. Rigid rules about planning your garden are not necessary, but some basic suggestions will help you select your own kind of garden and also help the plants. As mentioned, light and weather will dictate what kind of garden you can have and where it will be located. For example, cutting gardens, a joy indeed, can thrive only in south or east light because most of the annuals and perennials need lots of sun.

Most people prefer a natural landscape. A natural garden means less work and more beauty, but *small* touches of formally manicured hedges or symmetrically laid out shrubs (repeating some shrubs on one side and the other) are often most effective. For people with small properties, this is an ideal garden layout.

Personally, I like secret gardens, those little oases of greenery you unexpectedly come across when you suddenly turn a corner. Even a secluded nook full of rock-garden plants can become a lovely secret garden, a place you can retreat to.

If you prefer your garden to be a productive one, grow vegetables along with flowers because growing your own food saves acres of money and provides really good eating (and kids love having their own vegetable patch).

So as you can see, there is a choice as to what style of garden you can have, and what you finally plan as a total garden will depend on space, light, weather, and your own personal taste. For the rest of the chapter we will consider different types of flower gardens and recommend plants suitable for each garden. (*Complete* descriptions and requirements for 1,000 plants are in the plant dictionaries in Chapters 6 and 7.)

CUTTING GARDENS

There is something infinitely enjoyable in having cosmos and snapdragons, lupines and such in a garden area where you can snip and cut to your heart's content. The cutting garden provides you with a closeness to nature, a way to communicate with your plants. You grow your plants and nurture them to bloom. And the more flowers you cut, the more you get, because in most flowers the cutting encourages new buds and new blooms.

Your cutting garden need not be extensive. I have grown dozens of annuals and perennials in an area no larger than a planter bin of, say, 5 by 10 feet. From this bed I had Salpiglossis and Alstroemeria, stock, and cosmos to cut for the house. Of course, some flowers are better than others in the cutting garden, and these are the ones you want to concentrate on (see the list at the end of this section).

If space is at a premium (and it usually is) consider a step or terrace garden. These gardens utilize space to the fullest and also allow you easy access to your plants. Make the beds not more than 3 feet wide or they will be hard to tend. For your cutting garden, include a rich blend of soil at least 12 to 16 inches deep. If you start right and use good soil, flowers will flourish. Of course, select the spot in your garden where sun is abundant, which means a south or east exposure. Feed and water to keep plants in peak health.

Native plants and cultivated ones are combined handsomely in this natural garden; the result is pleasing and colorful. (Photo by Barr)

In the beginning, spacing is important because plants must have enough room between them to grow. Crowded conditions will not yield a bountiful harvest of flowers. So do space plants, not as closely as most books indicate, but with ample space. A cutting garden acts as both a cutting and ornamental garden (you will not be cutting *all* your flowers). For a vibrant display, plant lots of one kind of plant in one area, and plan in drifts or arcs rather than straight lines. Rows of flowers are not half as attractive as graceful arcs and curves of flowing color. Do not stint on the number of plants. You want enough to really bring abundant bloom, so use at least a few dozen plants of one kind here, another arrangement of plants in another area, and so on.

Do not try to keep up with spring, summer, and fall displays of flowers because it just is not worth the effort and it takes so much time. You will never really get a spring-summer-fall garden in one hunk of dirt. It is best to plant as the plants come in season, that is, as they are available at your local nursery. Put them in then, and forget the time-chart garden.

For your cutting garden I suggest you try the following annuals:

Antirrhinum (snapdragons)
Arctotis
Browallia
Calendula officinalis (pot marigold)
Callistephus (Chinese aster)
Chrysanthemums
Cosmos
Delphiniums (many kinds)
Dianthus (pinks) (many kinds)
Dimorphotheca (cape marigolds)
Helianthus (sunflower)
Lathyrus (sweet pea)
Salpiglossis sinuata
Scabiosa atropurpurea
Verbena hybrids
Zinnias (many kinds)

For perennials try:

Achillea (many kinds) (yarrow)
Anemone japonica (Japanese anemone)
Asters (many kinds)
Chrysanthemums
Gaillarda grandiflora (blanket flower)
Lilium (lilies)
Paeonia (various) (peony)
Pyrethrum (painted daisies)
Rudbeckia gloriosa (gloriosa daisy)

(Plant descriptions are in Chapter 7.)

A fine garden of roses for cutting and loving; note that the yard is quite small and yet hundreds of roses are seen. (Photo courtesy Star Roses)

BORDER GARDENS

If you have an expanse of lawn or a group of shrubs, bordering these areas with annuals and perennials can create a handsome if somewhat formal effect. This kind of gardening takes more time and care than perhaps any other planting plan, so be prepared to devote sufficient energies to it.

As with cutting gardens, borders should be planted in large arcs or curves rather than in straight lines, and use one kind of flower in one area and another kind of flower where a natural definition is needed. Color is a predominant factor in border gardens and must be used with care. If you mix too many colors you get a rainbow effect that, although pleasing in the sky, is not so on the ground (See Chapter 2.)

If the border garden is your thing, pay close attention to color. This means choosing plants by color rather than primarily the plants you personally like. Sometimes this can be enjoyable, but at other times it is frustrating, especially if the particular plant is not available at your nursery.

The cutting garden can be a mixture of colors, but the border garden, as explained, cannot. The border garden is strictly for looks, so use for it a small area near the house to impress the guests.

Annuals and perennials for borders include:

Achillea tomentosa (woolly yarrow)
Ageratum
Bellis perennis (English daisy)
Brachychome
Calendula officinalis (pot marigold)
Celosia (dwarf)
Dianthus sinensis
Iberis umbellata (candytuft)
Lobelia erinus
Lobularia maritima (sweet alyssum)
Phlox drummondii
Phlox subulata (moss phlox)
Tagetes (marigolds)
Tropaeolum (nasturtiums)
Verbenas
Veronica incana (woolly speedwell)
Viola (violets) (many kinds)

SECRET GARDENS

If you have a small space anywhere in the yard, whether in sun or shade, you can make it a fine secret garden. These spots should be small to make them intimate. My favorite secret garden is at the north side of my house. This area, only 5 by 5 feet, is full of lovely shade plants—shrubs and flowers—and always looks cool, even on hot days. Once established, shade-loving plants require little care other than sufficient watering and an occasional feeding to make them prosper.

ROSE GARDENS

Roses are popular flowers that have been with us for a long time and continue to be much grown and admired. A well-designed and properly cared-for rose garden is a stunning sight in bloom. And it seems that roses, because of their special requirements, do need a place of their own.

In planning the garden, select a place that has good air circulation but is still protected from wind. Choose a natural background so the roses will be seen to their best advantage. Light shade during part of the day is not objectionable, but in general give roses all the sun possible. Install paths of brick or flagstone to enhance the beauty of the garden, and decide upon a definite pattern for the beds.

Design

Traditionally, a rose garden is a formal design: a geometrical repeat pattern of a definite form. In other words, the garden itself has a beauty independent of the flowers. But today the strictly formal rose garden is not popular, and with good reason: most lots are small, and the space needed for a formal plan is prohibitive. Somewhat more casual and more varied rose gardens are what we see today. Whatever design you choose—and draw several arrangements on paper before making up your mind—do not make the beds too wide, because then it becomes difficult to reach the plants from the paths and spraying and pruning them become chores.

For a successful rose garden, choose an open area that is sheltered on the north and west sides, provide a good soil, and install adequate drainage provisions to carry off water. When you buy plants, select vigorous ones. Put them in the ground properly, then follow with good cultural practices—pruning, mulching, fertilizing, and protecting them from insects. A rose garden does not grow by itself; it needs attention and daily observation.

Soil

While roses need a fertile, slightly acid soil with a pH range between 5.5 and 6.5, the actual structure and content of the soil are not as important as its drainage capacity and its fertility. Roses require large quantities of water for maximum growth and simply will not thrive in soil which does not drain readily. To assure good drainage in the beds, put in a 6-inch layer of crushed gravel in the bottom of the site.

The more attention you give to soil preparation, the less trouble there will be later on. If the soil is very sandy, improve its water-holding capacity with compost, peat moss, and other organic materials. If it is a heavy soil, add sand and compost. The soil must be porous and somewhat rich (see Chapter 5). Dig the beds at least 20 inches deep; rose roots are long and need depth to grow well.

Planting and Care

Planting distances depend upon the type of rose being grown. For hybrid and tea roses a distance of 18 to 24 inches apart is fine. Floribundas and grandifloras need more space, about 18 to 36 inches between each plant. Trim the roses before you plant them; remove broken or injured roots. As I have mentioned, plant roses deep and place them in position so that the crown (point of union between the stock and scion) is between 1 and 2 inches below the surface of the soil. In mild climates the bud union should be just above the surface of the soil. After planting, pack the soil firmly around the roots. Keep the roses very well watered the first few weeks until they are established.

Roses need pruning to produce strong roots and shoots; without proper cutting they get leggy and dense. In spring, before growth starts, prune plants just above a node (bud); cut in a slanting direction and leave 3 to 5 buds on each stem. Only light pruning is needed for rambler roses that bloom on old wood. The ramblers that bloom on new wood from the base of the plant need pruning after flowering.

The time to plant roses depends upon your climate. In cold-winter areas early spring is best for setting out dormant bushes. In the midpart of the country, early spring or late fall is suggested, and in all-year mild climates, roses can be planted from November to January.

Bare-root plants are most often selected by gardeners. These are dormant and ready to start a new cycle of growth when you get them. If you cannot plant them immediately, keep them cool and be sure the roots are kept moist. Never allow rose roots to become dry before they are planted. Put them in water until you can get the plants in the ground. Packaged roses are often seen, and if they have been stored in a cool place they are satisfactory. If the branches look dry and shriveled, chances are they have been kept in a hot location. Don't buy them. Container-grown roses are already started for you. They cost more than dormant ones, but for beginners they are the best buy.

In cold regions plants should be protected for the winter. Place mounds of soil about 10 inches high around them. Do not scoop the soil from around the plant; bring in fresh soil. Remove the covering gradually in spring when growth starts.

Numerous kinds of roses are available today. See the plant dictionary, Chapter 7.

Masses of agapanthus are the backbone of this garden for cutting or for viewing; trees and shrubs complete the setting. (Photo by Ken Molino)

This ornamental garden at the front of the house has been well landscaped with colorful plants: dianthuses, roses, irises, and bright marigolds. (Photo courtesy Theodore Brickman, L.A.)

ROCK GARDENS

A rock garden is not the easiest landscape to simulate on your property, but it is certainly a worthwhile undertaking. This garden requires labor, patience, and careful construction, but when finished it is a picturesque, highly desirable feature. The secret is to build it slowly and with care so it will become a permanent landscape asset.

The rock garden takes you into the world of alpine plants, which are among the most attractive of hardy subjects. These are intriguing cold-weather plants that blaze with color in their season. The garden can take many forms; it can be a many-pocketed structure in a small area—a few rocks and plants—or it can be a large landscape scene where the plants are placed at intervals throughout the area.

Whatever form it is, the garden must be a true representation of natural rock scenery. Find just the right place for it; in the wrong location it becomes an eyesore rather than an attractive picture. A woodland setting is, of course, the most convincing background for the garden, but many times the perfect setting is simply not available. In general, keep rock gardens away from walls and buildings and avoid constructing them on a level site; a natural slope is an ideal place.

An important part of assembling the garden and how it will eventually look depends on the individual shapes of the stones used. Plan different levels so that there is constant interest. It is easier to work with a slope or a bank that naturally lends itself to rock treatment than with a flat piece of ground.

The placement of rocks is hard work even if lightweight stone, such as featherock and lavarock, is used. The rocks should be used like a retaining wall—each one set in place with a slight tilt backward. This gives stability to the structure and allows rain to run into the rock bed behind. Set the stones firmly in place. Most of them should be buried with one-third of their height in the ground and placed in a natural design of ledges and abutments.

Designing the Rock Garden

The site for a rock garden should preferably face south or southeast on an irregular slope with natural outcroppings of rocks. This is the ideal location. But ideal conditions are rarely found, and often we must settle for second-best places—perhaps a corner where there are some big trees, or even a bare slope that will in time require background plantings to show the rock scene to its best advantage.

While the garden is an arrangement of rocks, it is essentially a place to grow alpine plants, those species that grow at high altitudes in cool conditions with lots of sun and with an active but short period of growth. These plants are highly colorful and infinitely charming. To grow well they need some approximation of their natural conditions—shade, coolness, moisture. The emphasis in rock gardening is not so much on soil as on location and a place where water continually runs off rather than settles. There must be plenty of moisture in the soil, but it must be moisture in motion that constantly drains through. The soil can be dry on the surface but must be damp below.

A rock garden is three-dimensional, and elevations and depressions are vital to the total design. The design itself is a study in heights with appropriate paths and steps to give adequate access to the plants. The paths can be steppingstones or gravel. The ultimate appearance of the garden depends on the kinds of stones available and the way they are placed to create masses and slopes. Many rock plants are small and require little space; others grow rampant and should be placed within rock barriers. Rocks must be firmly in place without air pockets behind them, which will cause the soil to dry out and the plants to die.

New England areas and the cooler regions of the Great Lakes have favorable conditions for rock gardens. In warmer climates this special landscape is difficult to create.

This curving rock garden abounds with cheerful plants and is also an effective accent for the total landscape plan. Arabis, Achillea, lavender, and poppies vie for attention. (Photo by Molly Adams)

In the first year only grow a few plants rather than dozens of them. Rock gardening requires patience and skill that comes from experience. You are growing alpine plants from high altitudes quite unlike other flowers. However, the flower bed and the rock garden do have one thing in common—good composition. The rock garden should have harmony, unity, and balance.

Soil

Provide soil for the garden that is porous so that excess water will drain away quickly and yet, at the same time, hold moisture to keep plants growing. I use a mixture of 3 parts loam, 2 parts crushed stone, 1 part sand, and 2 parts humus. You can deviate from this soil mix somewhat, but you cannot deviate from the principle of perfect drainage for these small plants. Without adequate drainage, they simply will not survive. Provisions must be made to carry excess water away from plant roots. A 4-inch layer of cinders under the soil works well in keeping water running below the plants. Or you can use small stones or broken pieces of clay pots as a drainage bed.

After the drainage material is in place, three-quarters of the soil is spread over the excavated site, the remainder left for filling in behind and between rocks as they are put in place. In the planting area use soil to a depth of 18 inches. Start at the lowest point and place each rock on its broadest side. Sometimes it will be necessary for you to dig out soil to make space for a stone, or you can leave a freestanding stone and fill in and around with soil.

Care and Maintenance

Most alpine plants need bright light or partial sun, and during the hot summer months will need frequent waterings, for moisture is the key to success. In long hot summers, keep alpine plants as cool as possible. Exposed to wind and sun, they dry out quickly. While they can stand drought if necessary, there will be a better harvest of flowers if ample moisture is supplied.

Because most plants are small, they can get lost in weeds, so keep the rock garden free of weeds; cover bare places with stones to discourage weeds from growing. Nothing destroys the appearance of this garden more than a crop of weeds.

Plants are set in place in fall or in very early spring. In winter many alpines can go without protection, but others require protection against dampness (not cold) and the ill effects of freezing and thawing. Mulching the plants will conserve moisture and keep the soil cool. Plants that form heavy mats of foliage need no protection, and species that are deciduous can withstand winter, but plants that have rosettes of leaves need some mulching. Use a mulch that affords some air circulation. You do not want a wet decaying mat around the plant. Evergreen boughs, salt hay, and oak leaves are satisfactory mulches. Remove them gradually rather than all at once in the spring when danger of frost is over.

Plants for rock gardens:

Achillea tomentosa (yarrow)
Ajuga repens (bugleseed)
Alyssum saxatile (golden tuft)
Aquilegia vulgaris (columbine)
Campanula carpatica (bellflower)
Dianthus deltoides (maiden pink)

There are dozens of bouquets in this yard; hundreds of snapdragons and petunias grow lavishly for seasonal color and for cutting. (Photo USDA)

Geranium grandiflorum
   (cranesbill geranium)
Gypsophila repens (creeping
   gypsophila)
Iberis sempervirens (candytuft)
Iris pumila (dwarf bearded iris)
Linum perenne (flax)
Myosotis scorpioides (forget-me-not)
Phlox subulata (moss pink)
Primula polyantha (primrose)
Sedum album (stonecrop)
Sempervivum (many)
Veronica incana (speedwell)
Viola cornuta (Viola)

For descriptions see plant dictionary (Chapter 7).

HERB GARDENS

You can buy dried herbs in jars from your grocer, but harvesting fresh ones from your own garden is a more satisfying experience. Homegrown herbs have more flavor and taste than those bought in stores. Not only are there herbs for flavoring, but there are many—lavender, geranium—for fragrance.

Herbs are attractive plants that are easy to grow in average conditions, take little space, and can be grown directly in the ground or in pots. Put them near the kitchen so you can snip fresh herbs you want quickly for a stew or salad or stroll outside for a refreshing scent whenever you want.

You can buy small herb plants or start seeds that germinate easily. Grow them in a somewhat sandy soil that drains readily, and where they will get at least 3 hours of sun. Keep the soil moist and divide and prune the plants occasionally to keep them within bounds and to prevent them from crowding out other plants.

Cut herbs just as the flowers are about to open, as this is when the essential oils are the most plentiful. To save the herbs for future use, properly cure and store them. Wash the leaves or stems in cold water, and then dry them thoroughly by spreading out leaves over a wire mesh in a warm place. Or put them on a baking sheet in a 200-degree oven with the door open. When they are dry, strip the leaves from the stems and put them in airtight containers. Do not overdry the leaves; they should barely reach the crumbling stage. Or tie stems in bunches and hang them from the ceiling in an attic or other dark place until it is time to use them.

Herbs that can be used as needed; plant after last frost.

Plant	Depth	Spacing	
		Plants (inches apart)	Rows (inches apart)
Basil	¼″	9″	9″
* Chives	—	4″	4″
Dill	¼″	9″	18″
* Mint	—	Keep contained	
Parsley	¼″	6″	12″
* Rosemary	—	36″	36″
° Sage	¼″	9″	9″
° Thyme	¼″	9″	9″

* Buy prestarted plants
° Buy prestarted plants or sow seed

GARDENING FOR KIDS

Children have an insatiable curiosity, and the miracle of plants growing can lure them into the garden for an education with earth. The drawback is that children demand instant results; they do not have the patience to wait for flowers to bloom. But there are some very good plants that will provide this miracle of nature. Vegetable gardening is perfect for children because pumpkins and squash, carrots and lettuce grow so quickly that children will always be in the garden marveling at this rapid growth.

The kids will be somewhat reluctant to wait for lovely annual and perennial flowers. But once plants have produced blooms, blooms can be used in dried arrangements and pressed-flower pictures to get the children enthusiastic about this phase of gardening.

Collecting small native plants such as ferns and mosses from your garden for terrariums is another way to bring nature to children or children to nature. The instant lilliputian garden under glass, which can be made in a day, brings kids to the garden.

Putting a few annuals and perennials in pots and growing them at the window is another almost surefire way to pique children's imagination. All these things can be done easily, but you must remember to let the *kids* do it, not do it yourself.

The Garden Patch

If you want your kids to garden, give them their own patch of ground. It is fine to help them get started by preparing the soil and making boundaries, but let them do everything, including starting the seeds or putting in prestarted plants (best for kids), watering, feeding, and harvesting.

Most vegetables grow quickly, but squash, zucchini, and such grow the quickest, so they are good choices for fledgling gardeners. Show the kids how to dig the hole for the new plant and how to get the plant in the ground, and then let them do it. Also, let kids tend their garden. If this means that plants die from lack of water, let them, as unbearable as it might seem to you. Youngsters must realize that water is the source of life for their plants; they will realize this only if they see the actual process taking place.

Besides fast-growing vegetables, let the children grow some sunflowers. These grow rapidly to great heights that kids enjoy, and later the seeds can be dried in the oven for good nutritional eating.

Some easy vegetables for kids are:

Lettuce
Carrots
Beets
Radishes
Squash
Tomatoes

(For more on vegetables, see next chapter.)

4. vegetables

Years ago, vegetables were usually grown in a hidden place in the garden, a separate plot. Today vegetables are being grown in all areas of the garden, almost everyplace and anyplace, and with success. You can have a few vegetables even in tubs or bushel baskets if you have a little land. Fresh produce from your own plants beats any vegetables you buy at supermarkets, both in taste and price. Besides the fun of gardening, growing your own vegetables makes a great deal of sense in these days of high inflation. Hybridizers have provided us with an array of vegetable varieties, including some midgets suitable for tub growing and some strains that are far more disease- and insect-resistant than those available a few years ago.

You can start your own vegetables from seed or from prestarts. Prestarts are young plants already through the crucial stage of germination; they are all ready for planting. Prestarts are sold at nurseries at seasonal times.

SOWING SEED

Starting your own vegetables from seed is an easy way to get lots of plants for little money. Each seed packet contains many seeds and some are bound to sprout even if ignored. It makes good sense to start easy vegetables such as lettuce, radishes, and carrots from seed; other vegetables that require more care to germinate can be bought as prestarts at nurseries.

Some seeds can be sown directly in the ground where they are to grow; others are started in flats or containers indoors to be transplanted to the garden later. Do not buy special containers to start seed because you can use almost any throwaway household item such as the aluminum trays frozen rolls come in or milk cartons cut lengthwise. The important thing is that the container have drainage holes so excess water can escape. Put a small layer of pea gravel on the bottom of the container to facilitate good drainage. Sow seed

An inexpensive way to have lots of plants for little money is to start seed in peat pots for your vegetable garden. (Photo by author)

on standard seed-sowing mediums—perlite, vermiculite; these come in packages at nurseries. Some seeds can be placed on top and then covered with a thin layer of soil, but larger seeds have to be buried into the starting medium (or soil, if outdoors) to the depth of the seed. See the chart that follows.

If you are starting plants in containers, once the seeds are in place and watered, put four sticks, about 4 inches high, at each corner of the container, to hold the plastic tent (a Baggie) that should now be put over the container to ensure good humidity so seeds can germinate. Place the seed container in a bright warm place and do not water the seeds again until they sprout. Check daily to see if the growing medium is too moist; too much moisture causes mildew. If the soil is too wet, remove the plastic and let the seeds dry out in a bright place for a few hours.

When seedlings sprout first true leaves (and you will see this), it is time to thin out the small plants so there is ample space for growth. The thinning-out process is absolutely necessary, and when seedlings are 2 to 4 inches high transplant them into larger containers. Always keep soil moist and in another few weeks (when the weather is warm outside) you can transfer the seedlings to the garden.

Seed tapes (the seeds are inbedded in the tapes) can be used to sow seed directly into ground as with lettuce and carrots; easy to do and fast. (Photo courtesy George Park Seed Co.)

If you are sowing seed outdoors, prepare the soil bed by turning soil and adding organic matter. Sow seed when weather is good and there is no longer any danger of frost. Some people merely sprinkle seed on the ground, but the better method is to sow seeds in rows, spacing them as directed on the package. Always keep seedbeds evenly moist and when seedlings show their first true leaves, thin the smallest out so the larger plants have room to grow.

VEGETABLES FOR YOU

What to grow? You have an unlimited choice, so the best way to decide on a few vegetables is to ask yourself, "What does the family like?" Perhaps you just want some greens and tomatoes for salads, or maybe you have a special fondness for carrots and beets. You can grow what you want because today there are varieties suitable for all climates; it is simply a matter of getting to your local nursery at seasonal times, buying plants, and putting them in the ground at the right time.

For the small garden or the beginning gardener, I think some varieties of lettuce, a few tomatoes, beets, carrots, and spinach make a nice bit of produce. Here is a planting chart to help you decide:

Vegetable	Depth (inches)	Distance Between Plants (inches)	Germination (days)	Days to Maturity	Remarks
Beans	1½–2	3–6	7–14	60–80	Many kinds
Beets	½–1	2	7–10	55–65	thin out
Cabbage	½	8–10	4–10	65–95	Use prestarts
Carrots	¼	1–2	10–17	60–80	Thin out
Cauliflower	½	8–10	4–10	55–65	Use prestarts
Cucumbers	1	12	6–10	55–65	Train on trellis
Eggplant	½	18	7–14	75–95	Use prestarts
Endive	½	4–6	5–9	60–90	Grow as lettuce
Lettuce					
head	¼–½	4–8	4–10	55–80	Keep moist
leaf	¼–½	8–12	4–10	45–60	Keep moist
Peppers	¼	6–8	10–20	60–80	Prestarts good
Radishes	½	14–16	3–10	20–50	Early spring or late fall
Spinach	½	10–12	6–14	40–65	Many kinds
Squash (summer)	1	4–6	3–12	50–60	Pick early
Tomatoes	½	—	6–14	55–90	Use prestarts

CARE

Do not waste time meticulously preparing soil for your vegetables. Do some preliminary work, but do not knock yourself out. Rake the soil, turn it over, and add some topsoil. If the soil is very clayey or sandy, add compost (in

Eggplant grows lavishly in this garden. (Photo courtesy Burpee Seed Co.)

packages at nurseries). How much? Enough to make the soil porous and loamy, almost mealy, like a well-done baked potato.

Remember that for seed to germinate successfully, it should usually (but not necessarily) have warm soil, so do not rush the seasons. Wait until the climate is dependable before putting seeds or prestarts into the ground. Vegetables must be grown quickly. To grow fast, along with a fairly decent soil, vegetables need lots of water; this means a thorough soaking, down to at least 6 inches or more. As an example of how much water soil needs, consider that a 25-square-foot plot of soil 24 inches deep requires 30 gallons or more of water to be thoroughly soaked. Hand sprinkling won't do. Under normal water conditions a hose runs about 5 gallons of water a minute. Thus it takes at least 15 to 20 minutes to really soak soil.

Plants need about fifteen essential elements for adequate nutrition. The three most important elements are nitrogen, phosphorus, and potassium (potash). These are also the most likely elements to be missing from cultivated soils. Nitrogen stimulates leaf development and promotes the healthy growth of stems. Phosphorus is needed in all phases of plant growth, particularly in the development of fruit and seeds; it also helps promote good root development. Potassium promotes the general vigor of the plant, making it resistant to diseases, and has a balancing influence on other plant nutrients. Trace elements such as copper, zinc, iron, boron, manganese, and sulfur are also important to the welfare of the plant.

All commercial fertilizers are labeled as to the percentage of nitrogen, phosphorus, and potassium they contain, and there are many formulas: 5–10–10, 10–10–5, 20–10–5, and so on. There are also time-release fertilizers, fertilizers for specific vegetables, and foods in the form of pellets, granules, liquid, and on and on. What to use? Use a suitable plant-food formula such as 10–10–5 in granular form. Apply it to the soil and then water it in. Use the plant food once plants are actively growing and then about three times during the season. In other words, take it easy. Too much can kill the plants, but moderate amounts will help produce good crops. Try the following organic fertilizers (they are much better than the chemical ones): blood meal, cottonseed meal, bone meal, or manure (packaged). (See also Chapter 5.)

Remember to keep your vegetable garden free of weeds. Every weed that grows saps nutrients from the soil. You can mulch the soil to keep down weeds, use plastic over the soil, or simply get down there and pick weeds out as soon as you see them.

A well-planted vegetable garden in a small space; easy to tend, delicious eating. (Photo by Jerry Bagger)

Carrots and beets ready for harvesting. (Photo by Barr)

If space is limited, by all means consider growing some vegetables such as squash, peas, and cucumbers on wooden trellises (available at nurseries). This allows a copious garden in a small area and makes tending plants much easier for they are at a convenient height for tending and harvesting. Trellises can be inserted in planters and containers if you have a container garden or, of course, can be built to install in the ground in the garden. Climbing vegetables such as those mentioned adapt well to this kind of growing.

Also remember to thin out vegetables such as carrots and beets; this is *essential* if you want good crops. When you grow vegetables it is important that you do thin out seedlings once they have started growing. This simple but important procedure allows the strongest young plants to grow without crowding. Too many carrots or beets in a crowded situation simply will not produce a bumper crop. There aren't enough nutrients in the soil to support all the plants. Thinning remedies this condition and makes for vigorous, healthy plants that will bear heavily. Proper spacing of vegetables varies after thinning and is usually indicated on the seed packet.

THE SPOILERS

You like vegetables, but so do insects, so be prepared. Generally, if you run a healthy garden, troubles will be few and far between. Yet no one is perfect, and insects may take root along with crops. Following is a list of the garden vegetable pests, their description, and what they love to eat.

Insect	Appearance	What They Attack
Aphids	Small and oval; many colors	Almost all vegetables
Leafhoppers	Tiny, long insects	Lettuce, potatoes, beans, carrots
Whiteflies	Small flying insects	Tomatoes, beans, others
Cabbage loopers	Look like caterpillars	Broccoli, brussels sprouts, cabbage, cauliflower
Cucumber beetles (striped and spotted)	Beetle-shaped body	Cucumber, squash
Blister beetles	Long and large	Peppers, tomatoes
Cutworms	Invisible	Tomatoes, cabbage, peppers, beans
Squash bugs		Cucumbers, squash
Corn earworms		Corn
Snails, slugs (not really insects)	Recognizable on sight	All vegetables

If you discover any of these bugs in your garden, first try nonchemical remedies to eliminate the invaders. Plant marigolds and nasturtiums between crops (these flowering plants repel insects), or use onions (a so-so remedy). If all else fails, try chemical warfare. If you use chemicals, select those that are

Squash ready for harvesting in the author's garden. (Photo by author)

nonaccumulative in the soil, such as rotenone and pyrethrum (see Chapter 5). These are natural insecticides and will not harm the ecology. By the way, the odds are 100 percent that your vegetables will be bothered by snails. Use a snail bait such as *Snarol*, one that does not contain metaldehyde.

DISEASES

Years ago diseases in vegetables were commonplace and it was difficult to control them. But today's disease-resistant varieties have lessened the problem. For the most part, disease will not strike your plants, but if it does, you should be prepared. Here are the most common diseases and the vegetables they attack:

Disease	Vegetables They Attack
Fusarium wilt, verticilliosis	Tomatoes
Mosaic, scab, powdery mildew, anthracnose	Cucumbers
Mosaic, powdery mildew	Snap beans
Virus, yellow	Cabbage
Blight, downy mildew, mosaic	Spinach

Local nurseries sell effective chemical fungicides. Always pay strict attention to the labels and instructions, and stop application the specified number of days before harvesting.

The reddish brown areas on these bean leaves show rust at work. (Photo USDA)

5. basic gardening

Basic gardening techniques have gone almost full circle in the last hundred years and the natural garden of Grandmother's time is very much with us today. But so are the newer techniques of garden protection and growing of plants, and among them is a mind-boggling array of foods and fertilizers, insecticides and chemicals, mulching materials and soils, and many other assorted horrors. The manufacturers of these products have tried to convince us that gardening is highly scientific and involves constant and fussy attention. Happily, however, gardening is still quite basic, consisting merely of a good soil and good watering, the proper selection and planting of plants, and the cultivation of those plants. We have to pay a bit more attention to our gardens than Grandmother did because we now know a bit more (feeding, insect prevention, and so on), but gardening is still fairly easy and rewarding.

The commercial products cost money. I prefer to let nature help me for free—if I lose a few plants from lack of nutrients in the soil, from not mulching at proper times, or from insects, so what? Most plants (except annuals) will come back by themselves when they should, no matter how much food I give them or how many chemicals I use. If you prefer to use all the commercial gimmicks and time-consuming devices, go ahead (you can still follow this book). But I am not going to push you into such drudgery; beautiful gardens are beautiful if you do not have to kill yourself cultivating them.

SOILS

Today we hear so much about soils, what is and what is not a good soil, that it is a wonder people have enough courage to just start a garden in the plain old dirt that exists outside their homes. But be courageous—I have started many gardens on spent soil, adding to it as I went. Eventually (although never overnight) I created a lovely garden.

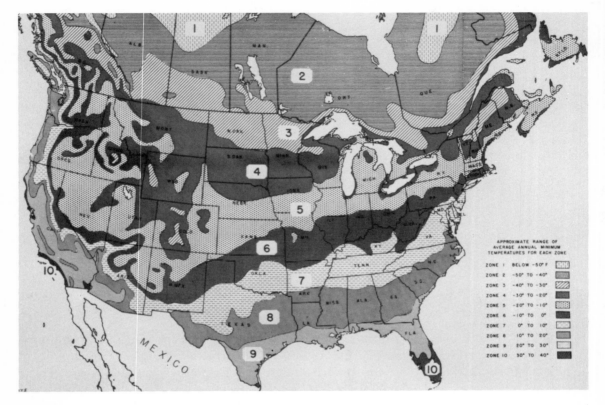

Weather zone map. (USDA)

First, break up whatever soil you do have, whether it is good or bad, mud or clay. That is, spade and turn it, push and pull, crumble it so it has porosity (tilth). Plants *must* have a porous soil so water can get to the roots. So get the soil action moving; there are chemicals you can use if you shy away from muscle power, but they take the real joy out of gardening. After you have done your own earthquaking (or have had the soil rototilled), determine whether you must add humus to the soil to make it plantable.

If your soil is sandy, add humus; if the soil is clayey, add humus. Humus is decayed vegetable matter. You can gather humus from the forest (if you are near a forest), or buy it by the bag. Humus is damned expensive but worth its weight in gold because it gets the soil action going so all those microorganisms can start working to make good nutrients for plants.

To determine if you have added enough humus, feel the soil. It should be porous and mealy, like a well-done baked potato. Let the soil run through your hands. Also, smell it; good soil has a nice earthy smell. You can also have your soil tested by the local agricultural extension service or test it yourself with a soil-testing kit. In any case the results will rarely be to your satisfaction. So forget the soil-test jargon and just add the humus; that cures just about everything.

If you want to buy soil, remember that there are dozens of kinds; you want a screened soil with the necessary additives (it will be costly). Buy soil from a *reputable* dealer and buy it by the truck. Soil comes in 6-yard trucks and is delivered "tailgate" to your home, which means you have to spread it yourself.

If you want to buy only small amounts of soil, buy it in 50- or 100-pound sacks and hope for the best. Buy soil as you would any other item: with caution and after shopping around.

While most plants do fine in what is called a neutral soil (neither too alkaline nor too acidic) some do prefer an acid soil; a few, alkaline soil. The pH scale is a designation for acidity or alkalinity in soil. Soil with a pH of 7 is neutral; below 7 the soil is acid; and above 7 it is alkaline. (There are soil-testing kits at suppliers.)

To lower the pH of soil (increase the acidity), apply ground sulfur at the rate of one pound to 100 square feet. This lowers the pH symbol about one point. To raise the pH of soil (sweeten it) add ground limestone at the rate of 10 pounds per 150 square feet. Do this in several applications at 6- or 8-week intervals.

Good soil is black in color, mealy to the touch. (Photo by author)

Feeding

Most gardeners love their plants, so they pour out affection in the form of plant foods, and in some cases too much feeding can cause plants not to bloom. (Nasturtiums are a prime example.) Use plant foods with discretion. First, if the soil is good and has necessary nutrients, there is not a whale of a lot of feeding necessary. Basically, annuals or perennials require little additional feeding, about twice a month (trees and shrubs require even less feeding). Too much food will not kill the plants, but it will kill your pocketbook—the excess food will just wash away with your money.

The innumerable plant foods on the market all contain percentages of nutrients; these percentages are marked on the package, for example, 10–10–5, 20–10–5, and so on. The first number denotes the amount of nitrogen, which makes plants grow. The second number indicates how much phosphorus the food contains. Phosphorus promotes strong stems and leaves. The last number is the amount of potash, which helps plants resist disease. Generally, a 10–10–5 food formula will do for most plants. This is not too strong or too weak (I have used it for years).

Plant foods come in granular and spray form and as foliar foods that are applied to leaves. I lean toward the granular type because you can conveniently sprinkle it on the soil and just water it in.

Fertilizers are offered in five forms:

Powdered. Good, but blows away on a windy day; may stick to foliage, and if stored in a damp place will cake.

Concentrated liquids. Used for all fertilizing.

Concentrated powders. Diluted in water and applied to foliage and plant roots.

Concentrated tablets. Used mostly for houseplants. Dissolved in water and are applied in liquid form or put in soil and allowed to dissolve gradually with water.

Pelleted or granular. Easy to spread. Some granular fertilizers also have insecticides; others have weed killers.

In addition to the man-made fertilizers (most often used), there are nitrogen materials to help plants grow.

Quickly available nitrogen materials are water-soluble and the nitrogen becomes available to the plant immediately. Results are quick, but they do not last long, and frequent light applications are necessary to obtain uniform growth over a long period of time. These materials include ammonium sulfate, ammonium nitrate, urea, nitrate of soda, ammonium phosphate, calcium nitrate, and others.

Slowly available nitrogen materials release their nitrogen over relatively long periods. These materials depend upon soil bacteria to decompose and transform the resultant compounds into the nitrogen forms that then become available to the plant. There are two groups of slowly available nitrogen materials: (1) organic matter, which includes sewerage sludge, animal and vegetable tankage, manures, cottonseed meal, and others; (2) ureaform compounds, which are synthetic materials made by chemical union of urea and formaldehyde. Do not confuse urea (quickly available nitrogen) with ureaform.

There are also fertilizers for specific plants—roses, azaleas, camellias. These are especially prepared and are perhaps more valuable for certain plants than the general fertilizers. You can choose them the way you choose the best dog food for your dog.

Because there are so many plant foods, know which ones will do what for your garden. For example, if you want to feed a lawn, use a high nitrogen food like 20–20–10. For flower beds and to make plants bloom, select a food with high phosphorus content like 12–12–12 or 5–10–5. If you want something to improve the soil structure and to release nutrients slowly, choose an organic food like blood meal or bone meal.

Plant food used wisely greatly aids a plant in producing better growth and flowers. Used with abandon, it can kill a plant.

Difference in soil is seen here: on the left is sandy soil; the right shows rich porous soil. (Photo USDA)

Compost is a vital ingredient of good soils; here soil is added to help decompose organic matter. (Photo USDA)

WATERING

Water, water everywhere and not a drop to drink. I imagine this is what plants would say if they could talk because most people water and water—but they water only the surface of the soil, and the roots never get the water. When you water, really do it. It takes at least 3 hours for water to penetrate soil a few inches. Plant roots are many and generally deep and they require sufficient moisture; intermediate sprinklings simply will not do. Regular routine watering during spring and summer is necessary to get those flowers growing. Annuals and perennials can and do absorb buckets of water, so if you are not energetic, get a good automatic watering system.

Mechanical Watering Devices

More than anything else, watering depends on mechanical devices such as sprinklers and sprayers. Do not even think of hand watering—even a small plot—because it simply takes too much time. Automatic watering systems that go on and off at the flick of a switch are not magic; they are just costly. So the best thing is to use good sprinklers. The highway departments of many states use the Rain Bird waterer. This is the one you have seen throwing a wide, revolving (360 degrees) arc of water. This is an excellent way to get the soil moist. Less expensive and just as satisfactory as the Rain Bird are the sprinklers that can be set at different degrees (front, rear, center). Of course, placement is the key to the sprinkler watering method. You must place the sprinkler properly to get the most out of it. This is somewhat of a hit-and-miss arrangement until you find the right spot to water the particular area you have in mind. Undoubtedly you will get wet trying this helter-skelter method, but it is the best way (short of automatic watering) I know of. (On my half-acre of gardens I use five sprinklers in various areas.)

When to Water and How Much

Most garden books tell you to water early in the morning before the sun is too hot. I suppose this is good advice, but I have watered almost all times of the day without harming my plants. The one exception is late evening, when soil gets too moist; if you have cool weather, some fungus problems could result.

How much do you water? Naturally this depends on local rains, but generally plants, especially annuals and perennials and vegetables, will require water every day during June, July, and August if they are to really grow. Sure, you can miss a day now and then, but too many missed days will result in too many missed flowers. If the soil has good tilth, you can water to your budget's limit.

MULCHING

Mulching, spreading various materials (usually organic) between and around plants to cover the soil, decreases the amount of moisture lost from the soil surfaces through evaporation and keeps the soil cooler than when it is fully exposed to the sun. Mulches also help (after the soil has frozen) to minimize the thawing and freezing effects that can harm plants. (It is the fluctuating thawing and freezing that kills plants rather than freezing itself.) Finally, mulching also helps to control weed development: under a protective coating, many weeds fail to develop, or, if they do, they are weak and easily removed.

You can keep plants mulched all year, or apply a mulch after the soil has warmed up in spring and growth has started. Do not put mulches in place too early or growth will stop because the soil will stay cool. In fall, apply mulches after the ground has frozen.

Mulches can be such nonorganic materials as aluminum foil, roofing paper, stones, and gravel. But for best results, use the following organic mulches:

Leaves. Old oak leaves and pine needles are perfect for acid-loving plants.

Hay, straw. The perfect organic mulch, because it decomposes slowly and is weed-free.

Grass clippings. Mix clippings with a coarse material to prevent matting.

Cocoa beans, pecan shells. Cocoa beans and pecan shells decompose slowly and make a satisfactory mulch. Do not use for acid-loving plants.

Ground fir bark. Fir bark, available in several grades, is an extremely good mulch because it decomposes slowly, is attractive, and stays in place.

Sawdust, wood chips. Use these mulches alone, or mix with peat.

Wood chips make a good garden mulch and are sometimes free for the asking. (Photo USDA)

CLIMATE

The climate of your specific region dictates how much water and food plants need and what you can and cannot grow. The warmer the weather, the more sun. The sun's intensity determines how much food plants can assimilate and thus how much water is needed. That is, if the weather is hot, plants will need more water. So it behooves you to know your weather. After you have lived in an area awhile, you will be able to determine more or less just how the weather usually is in each season. If you are new in a neighborhood, do ask neighbors about the climate and look at their gardens. Note, too, that nearby areas can have climatic differences. For example, in California, areas 3 or 4 miles apart can have completely different climatic patterns.

It is a good idea to get the rainfall maps of your area (available through the U.S. Department of Agriculture) to get some indication of the moisture pattern. You can also get maps of your area's average sunlight percentages. Rainfall and sunlight maps will tell you more than pages and pages of written information. The point is that climate does make a difference in how plants grow, so you should be aware of your climate if you want to be a successful gardener.

CULTURE

Not all plant problems are caused by insects or disease (we discuss insects and disease in Chapters 6 and 7); sometimes you are the culprit. Cultural conditions have not been tended to as they should have been. Are the plants getting enough water? Enough light? What about wind—is it harming plants? Before you suspect bugs or disease, check for the following conditions.

Plants that develop leaves with brown or crisp edges may be getting too much heat and fluctuating soil temperatures. New growth that quickly withers may be caused by the same conditions. If new leaves are yellow, there may be a lack of acidity in the soil. Leaves turning yellow and dropping off may be a natural condition. If leaves develop brown or silvery streaks, they are getting too much sun. If leaves appear lifeless, they are not getting enough water.

Buds suddenly dropping off plants is a complaint of many gardeners. This is caused by fluctuating temperatures, and there is no remedy. If plants are not blooming as they should, they are not getting enough sun. On the other hand, if stems turn soft and leaves wilt, the plant is in too much shade with too much moisture.

Healthy plants are rarely attacked by predators and are not prone to disease because they are just too strong. When you buy new plants, inspect them carefully before you put them in the garden. Be sure there is nothing wrong with them.

In conclusion, if you want to keep plants free of insects, keep the garden clean. This simple step goes a long way in assuring healthy, robust plants. Throw away trash where insects can hide, pick faded flowers that can cause bacterial disease, and cut and burn dead wood.

Control Methods

There are several ways of applying insecticides to control pests. Decide which of the following methods is the best and most convenient for you.

Spraying. This is a satisfactory method because with it you can reach all parts of the plant, either with a sprayer that attaches to a hose or a portable sprayer. The equipment you choose depends on how much soil you have to cover. Before you spray, be sure the ground is wet. Try to do the job in early morning or late afternoon; hot sun on treated plants sometimes harms them. After spraying, clean all equipment thoroughly. Wash the sprayer with soapy water, rinse it with clean water, and force water through the nozzle before you use it again.

Dusting. Dusting is a messy procedure. If you do not do the job on a calm day, you are in for trouble—your lungs will get more insecticide than the plants.

Spreading. Spreading is the easiest way to eliminate insects. It is fast and clean, and merely requires sprinkling insecticide on the ground and watering the soil.

Systemics. Systemic control is a popular method of killing insects. The poison, in granular form, is sprinkled on the ground and water is applied. The soluble liquid-type poison must first be mixed with water. Either type of poison is absorbed by the plant roots, and all parts of the plant become toxic to many (but not all) insects for 4 to 6 weeks. The trade names in this group of chemicals are Benomyl (liquid) and Meta-systox-R (granular). These poisons are popular with gardeners because they are so easy to apply, but their high toxicity affects human beings. Use them only if absolutely necessary, and then with extreme caution, according to directions on the package.

Biological means. This method fights nature with nature and involves using natural enemies of insects rather than poisons. It also includes using plants such as onions and marigolds which naturally discourage insects. Ladybugs, praying mantises, and lacewing bugs are all part of the organic gardener's weapon force. This control method also involves mulching plants and using a great deal of compost in the soil. It is gardening without poison. Biological control is *not* disturbing the balance of nature and, as such, has much to recommend it.

Insects

Before you start fighting insects, you should know specific facts about them. Insects are divided into two types: sucking and chewing. The sucking types pierce plant tissue and the chewers bite off and eat portions of the plant. The first group can be controlled by applying contact poisons to their bodies. Control the other group by applying poisons to the plant parts attacked; the insects will then die of internal poisoning.

Some insects attack any plant, whereas others have a preference for specific plants, such as azaleas. Many insects can be seen easily. Other insects are so minute that they are almost invisible; these are the most difficult to control. Hard-to-see pests include root lice, mites, and stem borers.

The ladybug is a friend in the garden, but poisonous sprays will eliminate this aphid-eating insect. (Photo USDA)

Timing is important when applying insecticides. Many insects are more vulnerable in the early stages of their life or after they have hatched from their eggs. For instance, scale are more susceptible to chemicals when they are right out of the egg than when they start maturing.

Not all insects harm plants. Indeed, many insects maintain a balance of nature. There are many beneficial insects, so when you spray to kill aphids you might also be killing the larvae of the lacewing fly, which is a voracious exterminator of plant lice and other insects. Ladybugs, too, eat many times their weight in aphids and keep the insect population under control. Tachina flies live on cutworms and caterpillars. The praying mantis can devour hundreds of insects a day. Digger wasps and wheel bugs are other beneficial insects that eat larvae of various detrimental insects.

Another good guy in the garden is the praying mantis, scary to see but horrifying also to many harmful garden insects. (Photo USDA)

So before you start killing insects, think about it. There is more involved than meets the eye; often when you spray to kill a few attacking pests, you may be killing off hundreds of beneficial insects that are actually friends of the garden. See Chapters 6 and 7 for a summary of how to identify insects and how to control them. Also check with your local agricultural station for further information on insects in your area and suggestions on eliminating them.

Insecticides

There are numerous insecticides on the market, and although packages list the active ingredients, they are not readily distinguishable by most people. Often insecticides are listed by chemical rather than generic name and thus are

This handsome insect is not beneficial to the garden; it is a tree borer and can cause havoc in trees. (Photo USDA)

impossible to decipher. By all means, question your local nurseryman about insecticides, whether they are inorganic, botanical, or synthetic. Arsenic is inorganic but generally no longer in use. Pyrethrum and rotenone are botanical preventatives because they are derived from plants; they are coming back into use. The synthetic chemicals derived by man include chlorinated hydrocarbons, carbonates, and organophosphates. DDT, chlordane, lindane, and aldrin are hydrocarbon-type insecticides that should not be used; they are highly poisonous.

Read all instructions carefully before applying chemicals, and always use less rather than more. Handle poisons with care. Keep them out of reach of children and pets. Repeated applications may be necessary (this information is given on the package).

Beneficial Birds

The most common birds in the garden are likely to be helpful ones. True, some birds eat fruit and berries, along with their basic diet of insects. But preventing occasional damage from birds is not difficult compared with the problem of checking the work of chewing, sucking, and blight pests.

Swallows are fine, insect-eating garden friends. These birds sweep back and forth in the sky in early evening as nocturnal bugs begin to swarm. Using their large throats and open mouths, swallows scoop insects from the air with amazing speed.

Purple martins are invaluable garden helpers that stay with you if you give them a birdhouse (martins nest in a community house). Martins feed on wasps, flies, and other unwanted summer pests.

Kingbirds are members of the flycatcher family. They eat aphids and caterpillars at ground level or catch insects on the wing. The Baltimore oriole will consume caterpillars, pupae, and adult moths. Wrens, titmice, and bushtits are other friendly birds that can help keep your garden almost insect-free.

Some birds are undesirable, including English sparrows, linnets, and house finches; and very often mockingbirds can be detrimental in the garden because they feed on berries and other fruits.

To attract birds to your garden, give them sprays or mists of water, not just water in birdbaths, because many birds love a light shower. Supply them with food and birdhouses. Birds are not only lovely to watch; they in turn watch your garden and help keep it free from insects.

PLANT DISEASES

Many destructive plant diseases are caused by bacteria, fungi, and viruses. Diseases are generally named for their dominant symptoms—blight, canker, leaf spot—or for the organism causing the disease—rust, powdery mildew. Many times unfavorable conditions and poor cultural practices open the way for these agents to cause trouble. A poorly grown plant, like a human being in poor health, is more susceptible to bacteria and virus. Insects, too, spread diseases from one plant to another.

Environment also plays a part in the development of bacterial and fungal attacks because bacteria and fungus are responsive to moisture and temperature. Moisture is particularly important because it is necessary for the termination of the spores of the disease organisms. Excessive moisture in the soil can lead to root rot. Frequently, plants in shade are more apt to develop disease than those in light.

Following is a simple explanation of the organisms that can cause plant disease:

Disease-causing Organisms

Fungi. Fungi are familiar to us because we have seen old bread and fruits on which fungi have developed. There are thousands of different kinds of fungi, some of which can cause serious plant damage. Rot, wilt, rust, and powdery mildew are basically caused by specific fungi.

Bacteria. Bacteria are microscopic organisms that survive in soil or plant parts and cause blights, rot, galls, or wilting. Bacteria are the causative agents of fire blight and iris rhizome rot.

Virus. Many of the most serious diseases of ornamental plants are caused by a virus. We are still trying to decipher viruses in human beings, and viruses are as much of a mystery when they attack plants.

See Chapters 6 and 7 for specifics on plant diseases.

the plant dictionaries

Trees and Shrubs

Annuals, Perennials, Bulbs, and Vines

how to use the plant dictionaries

PLANT NAMES

Plant names may be confusing or simple, depending on how you approach them. Each plant family is divided into one or more families called genera (singular, genus), and in each genus there are usually several species. For example, Centaurea is the genus. In this genus there are several centaureas, so the species name *rutifolia* makes it specific: i.e., *Centaurea rutifolia.* So far plant names seem fairly easy, but more is involved. Many nurseries specialize in plant breeding, that is, mating the best with the best to bring you a superior plant—one that blooms abundantly or has larger flowers than the species. These plants have special names such as *Centauria rutifolia* 'Snow Ball'. You can identify this improved-variety name because it is in 'single quotes' while species are *italicized.*

Many plants have common names (some do not). In the case of *Centaurea rutifolia* the common name is dusty miller. The plant dictionary includes the common names of those plants listed. Common names are fine except that they vary throughout the country, while botanical names are universally the same.

THE DICTIONARIES

Our plant dictionary is divided into two separate sections. In Chapter 6 is the dictionary that covers trees and shrubs, alphabetically. The dictionary in Chapter 7 covers annuals, perennials, bulbs, and vines. This arrangement was chosen to make it easy for you to find a specific plant quickly in either broad category.

In the case of trees and shrubs, varieties are designated by single quotes and a description of the variety is given. For annuals, perennials, vines, and bulbs, the varieties are listed after the species description, under the heading "suggested variety." Descriptions are not included for varieties because most varietal names are self-explanatory: i.e., 'Pink Glory', 'Red Star', and so forth.

The annual and perennial, bulb and vine dictionary is arranged with botanical names of the plants alphabetically at the left and common names and types of plants at the right. Categories of Light, Water, and Bloom are expressed as follows: Light: Sun, Bright, and Shade. (In some cases you will find both Sun and Shade under the "Light" category, which means the plant will tolerate shade but prefers sun. The other categories (Water and Bloom) are self-explanatory. Where necessary, soil conditions are designated as sandy soil or loamy garden soil (also acid soil where required).

If you do not know the Latin name of a plant, after each plant dictionary there is a common-name/botanical-name cross-reference chart.

In the plant dictionaries there are 1,000 drawings, one of each plant, to help you identify them. If your favorite plant is missing, that is a matter of page space, not of my personal preference. It is impossible to list all the many plants available to gardeners today.

Insofar as possible, *Hortus Second* and the *Dictionary of Gardening* (Royal Horticultural Society, 4 volumes) were used as sources for plant names.

6. trees and shrubs

Like all plants, trees and shrubs need their share of attention, but not as much as other plants. Once planted and established, trees and shrubs can fare very well for themselves. The first year or so is the critical time when you must give these plants some extra attention.

If possible, plant trees and shrubs in early spring; the next best time is in fall. You can buy plants at nurseries in various stages of growth: bare root, balled and burlapped, or in cans.

PLANTING TREES AND SHRUBS

When planting trees or shrubs, you want to disturb the root ball as little as possible. Handle plants carefully when you lift them; never pull or drag them on the ground or pick them up by the trunk. I usually try to cradle plants in my arms, unless they are very large.

We have already discussed soils in the previous chapter, so, assuming the soil is cultivated and ready for the plant, proceed as follows: If the plant is bare root, dig deep wide holes. Remember that the hole must accommodate the roots when they are spread out; the hole should be half again deeper than the root system and twice as wide at both top and bottom. At the bottom of the hole insert some rich topsoil—enough to elevate the plant to the proper collar depth. Insert the plant; if it is too high in the hole, remove soil. If the plant is not high enough, add soil.

Now fill in and around the plant with fresh, friable soil. When you have filled up the hole halfway, get the hose and thoroughly soak the plant several times. Finish adding soil until the hole is filled. Now make a shallow-dish formation around the plant; tamp down the soil with your feet to eliminate air pockets in the soil. The soil level should be no higher than the original soil line on the trunk. Soak the tree or shrub again with water. For the first few months be sure the plant has ample water—at least twice a week—if there is no rain.

Plant trees and shrubs that come in cans the same way as described above; just make sure you have the nurseryman cut the can first or you will have to buy a can cutter and do it yourself. Plant balled and burlapped trees as they are; that is, do not remove the wrappings. In time the burlap decomposes.

If you plant in a windy location, stake trees and shrubs. Drive a stake about 2 inches in diameter 3 inches from the trunk of the plant on one side; insert another stake on the other side. Anchor the tree or shrub to the stakes with nylon string. Or buy the special staking devices; these are wires with short lengths of hose that protect the tree from the wire cutting into it.

WATERING AND FEEDING

More than any other plants, trees and shrubs when initially planted must have thorough soakings of water. A little dab will not do; indeed, it can be harmful. It is much better really to saturate the soil and allow it to dry out before watering again than to apply a daily 15-minute sprinkle. You can mulch trees and shrubs with organic mulch to conserve water (this is explained in Chapter 5).

A good all-around fertilizer for trees and shrubs is one marked 12–6–6 or 10–10–5 as previously explained in Chapter 5. It is best to apply the first feeding about one month after planting the tree in the spring. If you plant the tree in the fall, wait until the following spring before feeding. Immediate feeding when you plant the tree or shrub can harm roots; transplanting is enough of a shock at the beginning, so do let the tree recover before you start the feeding program. In midsummer apply another dose of plant food. Some gardeners add still another feeding in early fall, but I do not. Late fall feeding can result in accelerated growth, affecting the plant's natural cycle of slowing down for winter.

Tree stakes coated with plant food are a new form of feeding that has been much advertised on television. The plant food is a slow-release type especially made for trees. I have not used it myself, so I cannot recommend it.

If a tree or shrub is not doing well despite all your efforts, you might want to give it a midsummer boost by using the "hole" method. Punch holes about 2 inches in diameter around the tree at a distance of several feet from the trunk (depending on the spread of the tree). Insert food directly into the holes; the food will go right to the roots.

PRUNING AND TRAINING

Pruning is an essential part of good gardening and yet it is often neglected. Trees and shrubs require some (but not drastic) pruning and training as they grow to keep them attractive and healthy. The problem with pruning is that people often do too much or not enough. You want to maintain a healthy tree with open limbs and a beautiful shape. Cutting and removing a few branches here and there a few times a year is all that is necessary in most cases. And you can do it yourself, except if trees are grossly overgrown or if storms have battered them, in which case you should have professional people do the pruning.

Diseased and dead branches should be removed for the health of the tree, and branches that rub against each other also should be eliminated. Prune plants that flower in spring right after flowers fade; prune all other plants in very early spring. You will need only a good pair of pruning shears and a pruning saw—I have used just these two tools for years on all sorts of small pruning jobs.

When you prune, do not butcher. Make a cut only above a bud, a small side branch, or a main branch. If you leave a small stub, it will wither and die and be an invitation to decay. Cut branches in the direction you want the new growth to take, and when you cut the branches, cut flush with the trunk. Trim away twiggy and unattractive growth so that branches can be seen. Study the skeleton of the tree first, and then prune to open up the tree so that light can reach all parts of the tree. Cover all wounds with tree-seal solutions.

Shade trees especially need pruning to help them develop strong frameworks to resist windstorms. Remove unwanted branches before they become so large you cannot handle them. Watch for branches that cross; remove one to allow the other to grow.

DECIDUOUS FLOWERING TREES AND SHRUBS

Many deciduous trees and shrubs bloom on old branches, but others have flowers on current wood. The plants that bloom in spring or early summer on previous years' wood should be pruned immediately after they flower. Cut away weak shoots, unattractive branches, and old flowering stems. The objective is to open the tree or shrub to light so that the new flowering branches will grow readily. Do not do any drastic pruning, just thin out. If the trees are too large, of course get a professional tree service to do the job. Prune plants that bloom on current wood in winter or early spring.

TREE AND SHRUB AILMENTS

Will your garden trees and shrubs be bothered by pests or disease? Generally, no. Plants are usually quite robust once they are growing and can by themselves fend off most invaders. However, insects or disease will attack occasionally, so it is well to know what to expect just in case. I can only generally touch upon these ailments; a comprehensive section is not necessary because nine times out of ten, if trees are attacked by insects, you should contact a professional tree service—spraying insects in a 50-foot tree is not a job for the average homeowner.

Most important is to keep abreast of general insect conditions in your region. Pests in your trees or shrubs usually will be a regional problem. The county agriculture department (listed in your phone book) can advise you of what is going on. For example, one of my shade trees started dying back for no apparent reason. I consulted the local agricultural department and they had the answer. A particular weevil had invaded much of the region. The department's solution did the trick. Remember, too, that insects 50 feet above the ground are impossible to detect unless you are an excellent tree climber. Your agricultural department most likely can tell you what the insect problem is without having to see the bug. So in this section the problems covered for trees and shrubs are general ones; for specific help consult the agricultural service of your area.

Spraying is perhaps the most widespread way to cope with garden insects and diseases. Manufacturers are well aware of this, and thus there are dozens of sprayers on the market, each supposedly better than the others. I have never used anything more than the standard hose sprayer. Some of my friends have the compressed can sprayer, but they rarely use it. So forget elaborate and expensive spray equipment.

The hose sprayer can reach areas about 25 to 30 feet; any trees larger than this should be handled by professional tree services.

INSECTS

Trees and shrubs, like other plants, occasionally have insect problems. Here is an insect chart for trees and shrubs so you can battle the bugs.

Insect	How to Recognize	Symptoms	Control
Aphids	Black or white soft-bodied insects	Leaves and new growth eaten	Use ladybugs or praying mantises.
Bagworm	Caterpillars; bags with dead foliage	Foliage eaten	Pick off bags, or use light traps for moths.
Budworm	Red-brown "worms"	Chewed buds	Use Diazinon just as buds open.
Canker	Cankered areas on branches	Dipping of lower branches	Prune out and burn infected branches.
Gall aphid	Green growths	Attack on terminal shoots	Destroy galls before insects emerge.
Lace bug	Lace-winged bugs on underside of leaves	Whitish mottling of foliage	Use botanical sprays or nicotine sulfate.
Leaf miner	Caterpillar; larvae within foliage	Foliage tips white	Prune back infected branches. Spray with soapy solution in June.

Insect	How to Recognize	Symptoms	Control
Mite	Tiny red spiders	Gray-speckled foliage	Spray heavily with water or Malathion.
Nematode	No apparent evidence	Stunted growth	Use sterile soil.
Pine-shoot moth	Light-brown, black-headed worms	Dead buds	Prune lower branches that would be snow-protected (here larvae find protection from killing temperatures).
Red mite	Tiny and red	Foliage gray-streaked	Blast with water or use Dimite.
Sawfly	Variously colored "worms"	Needles marred	Use parasitic wasps (from suppliers).
Scale	Brown or gray small bugs	White waxy coating; eaten leaves	Use ladybugs or spray with Malathion.
Taxus weevil	Grubs near roots	Yellowed needles	Birds eat grubs.
Thrips	Spindle-shaped insects	Grayish foliage	Control with insects. Spray with soapy solution.
Tube moth	Greenish yellow worms	Needles eaten	Use Diazinon.
Webworm	Yellowish worms	Foliage skeletonized	Use Diazinon.
Whitefly	Tiny white flies	Speckled foliage	Control with insects or Diazinon.
White-pine weevil	Pale yellow grubs under bark	Young growth eaten	Plant in shade; destroy infested tips.

DISEASES

The common diseases affecting trees and shrubs are difficult for the novice gardener to identify or control. Fortunately, disease is not a major problem in home gardens, so I will just briefly list a fraction of the diseases that can attack evergreens. Your best prevention is observation and contacting your local agricultural department if you see anything amiss in trees such as rot, decay, and so on.

Disease	Symptoms	Control
Anthracnose	Gray, brown, or black spots on foliage	Spray with Zineb.
Chlorosis	Leaves turn yellow	Apply iron chelates.
Fire blight	Leaves blacken and die	Spray with Fermate
Leaf spot	Dark-edged foliage	Spray with Zineb.
Powdery mildew	Powdery blotches on leaves	Cut away infected areas; dust with wood ashes.
Rust	Orange residue on leaves or bark	Spray with Zineb.

PLANT DICTIONARY—
trees and shrubs

ABIES Fir

Evergreen

Generally, these evergreen trees are pyramidal in shape and have rigid horizontal branches, making them a decisive accent in the landscape. Use them sparingly. Needles last about 5 years before they fall; cones are ornamental but do not appear every year. The trees have few insect or disease problems, but as they mature the lower branches become unsightly, and once removed they do not grow back, so a mature specimen lacks symmetry. Firs need a cool, moist climate to grow well or they deteriorate rapidly. Firs are Christmas favorites.

A. alba (European silver fir). Hardy to -20 F. Pyramidal to 150 feet. Dark-green needles.

A. concolor (white fir). Hardy to -20 F.; narrow, pyramidal in shape, to 120 feet. Bluish green needles; rapid grower.

A. nordmanniana (Nordmann fir). Hardy to -30 F. Grows to 50 feet, with glossy green needles. Quite handsome, but if attacked by gall lice (to which it is susceptible) tree will possibly die.

ACACIA

Evergreen

Evergreen shrubs and trees suitable to temperate areas, acacias differ widely in foliage and growth habit. Some have feathery divided leaves, but others have flattened leaves. Acacias are short-lived (to about 25 years), yet they are useful and lovely in the garden, especially in very early spring (February–March), when they are covered with clouds of yellow flowers.

A. baileyana (Bailey acacia). Hardy to 30 F.; grows to 30 feet. Feathery, fine-cut, blue-gray leaves and clusters of light-yellow blooms.

A. cyanophylla (blue leaf wattle). Hardy to 30 F., grows to 30 feet. Bluish, narrow leaves; clusters of orange flowers.

ACER Maple

Deciduous

Maples are popular deciduous shade trees; and there are many kinds for many uses. Varied in habit and rate of growth, size, and leaf shape, some maples (for example, Japanese maple) are low and squatty; others, like the Norway maple, are round at the top and quite tall. Smaller varieties are ideal for landscaping where there is limited space. Some maples have interesting and colorful bark, but it is the autumn color of the foliage—brilliant red or yellow—that makes them popular. Maples grow in any good garden soil and are generally not bothered by pests or diseases.

A. campestre (hedge maple). Hardy to -5 F. Rounded habit; grows to 25 feet. Yellow foliage in autumn.

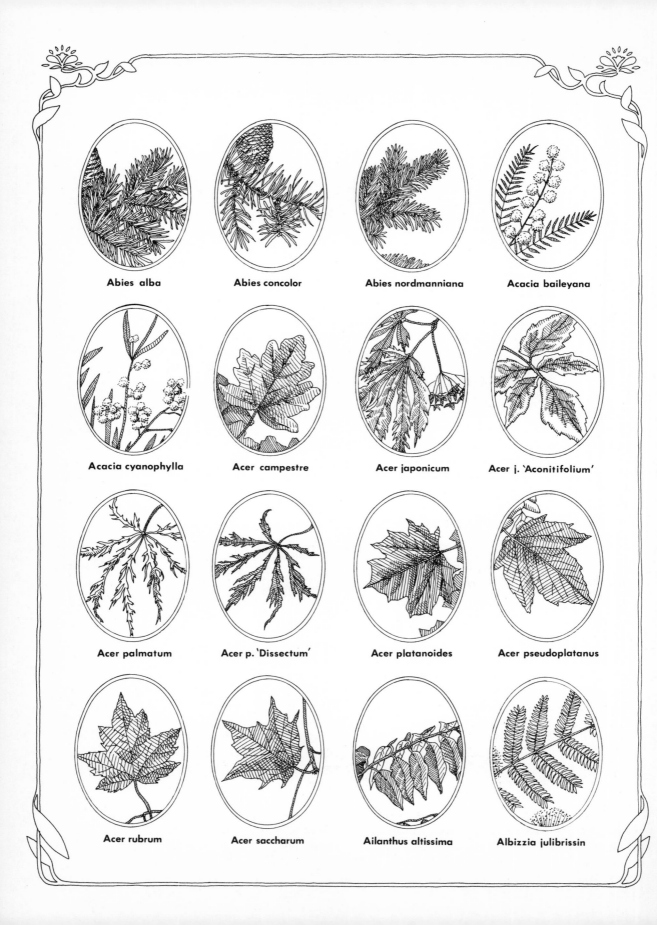

Abies alba

Abies concolor

Abies nordmanniana

Acacia baileyana

Acacia cyanophylla

Acer campestre

Acer japonicum

Acer j. 'Aconitifolium'

Acer palmatum

Acer p. 'Dissectum'

Acer platanoides

Acer pseudoplatanus

Acer rubrum

Acer saccharum

Ailanthus altissima

Albizzia julibrissin

A. japonicum (full-moon maple). Hardy to -5 F. Can reach 25 feet, with lobed leaves. Good bright-red fall color.

'Aconitifolium' (fern-leaf maple)—Leaves deeply lobed.

A. palmatum (Japanese maple). Hardy to -5 F. Rounded habit to 20 feet. Dense, handsome tree, with scarlet autumn color

'Dissectum' (laceleaf Japanese maple)—Leaves cut into threadlike segments.

A. platanoides (Norway maple). Hardy to -20 F.; broad-crowned to 90 feet. Leaves turn yellow in fall; greenish yellow spring flowers.

A. pseudoplatanus. Similar to above; better form and more robust.

A. rubrum (red maple). Hardy to -20 F.; fast grower to 120 feet. Brilliant red autumn twigs and buds. Profuse red flowers.

A saccharum (sugar maple). Hardy to -20 F.; fast grower to 120 feet. Silver-gray bark; yellow to orange and red fall color.

AILANTHUS ALTISSIMA
Tree-of-Heaven

Deciduous

A tree that grows in almost any situation with open foliage; leaves divided into leaflets. Rather graceful when young, eventually becoming rounded in shape. Fast-growing, the tree-of-heaven can tolerate almost any soil and seems to thrive in untenable situations. Hardy to -20 F.

ALBIZZIA JULIBRISSIN Silk tree

Semi-evergreen/Deciduous

An overlooked good, small tree with delicate fernlike foliage and charming summer flowers. With arching stems and compact growth, Albizia is a stellar landscape subject. It likes sun and a good garden loam somewhat on the sandy side. In the north the silk tree is likely to die down to the ground in winter; remove dead stems early in spring to encourage new growth. Hardy to 5 F.

ALNUS Alder

Deciduous

Fast-growing trees that thrive in moist situations; multiple-stemmed with coarse-toothed leaves. Trees have a dense character and can tolerate most soil conditions and still survive. Not the best of trees but good for most areas where little else will grow.

A. glutonusa (European alder). Hardy to -5 F.; grows to 75 feet. With canopy habit and dark-green leaves this tree can tolerate wet soil if necessary.

A. incana (speckled alder). Hardy to -50 F.; grow to 60 feet. This is the hardiest of the alders; rather shrubby with dense habit and dark-green leaves.

AMELANCHIER Serviceberry

Deciduous

These shrubs and trees are delights year-round. The white spring flowers are followed by edible fruits in summer. Serviceberries have pretty autumn foliage. The best of these plants are trees.

A. bartramiana. Hardy to -35 F.; grows to 6 feet. Flowers in May, purple berries in September.

A. canadensis (shadblow serviceberry). Slender tree that grows slowly. Foliage rounded, yellow to red in fall. Fruit dark red. Hardy to -20 F.

A. humilis. Hardy to -20 F.; grows to 3 feet. Oval leaves; low-growing.

A intermedia (swamp Juneberry). Hardy to -35 F.; grows to about 15 feet. Dark-purple fruits in fall.

A. laevis. (Allegheny serviceberry). Hardy to -20 F.; grows to 15 feet. Upright growth; white flowers and bluish purple fruits in July.

A. obovalis (coastal Juneberry). Hardy to -10 F.; grows to 4 feet. Vertical grower; purplish black fruits in June.

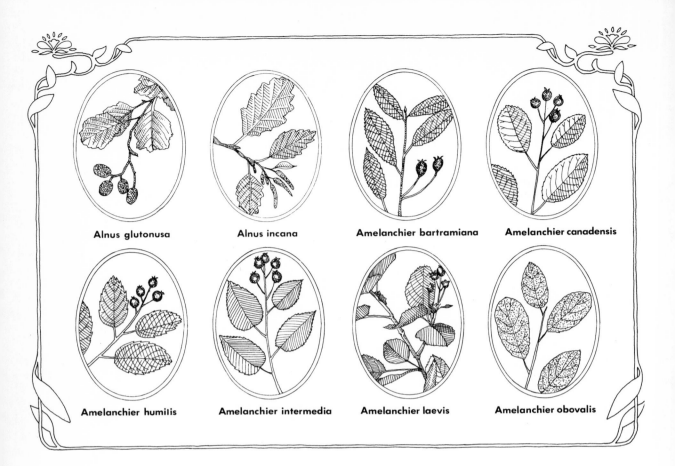

Alnus glutonusa **Alnus incana** **Amelanchier bartramiana** **Amelanchier canadensis**

Amelanchier humilis **Amelanchier intermedia** **Amelanchier laevis** **Amelanchier obovalis**

A. sanguinea (round-leaf Juneberry). Hardy to -10 F.; grows to 8 feet. A straggly shrub; purple berries in August.

A. spicata (running Juneberry). Hardy to -20 F.; grows to 4 feet. Oval leaves, spreading habit.

BERBERIS Barberry

Deciduous / Evergreen

A group of dense, thorny shrubs, deciduous and evergreen, with small, bright flowers. Barberries are effective as barriers, and they can also be used as landscape specimens because many species have a lovely branching habit. Small bright-red or purple-black berries appear in autumn. Most barberries lose their fruit quickly after it ripens, but the Japanese barberry holds its color through winter. These shrubs grow in almost any kind of soil, in sun or light shade. A very useful group of plants.

B. buxifolia (Magellan barberry). Hardy to -10 F.; upright growth to 6 feet, with small leathery leaves. Orange-yellow flowers and dark purple berries. Evergreen.

B. julianae (wintergreen barberry). Hardy to 0 F.; grows to 6 feet. Very leathery, spiny-toothed, dark-green leaves. Red fall color; thorny. Evergreen.

B. koreana (Korean barberry). Hardy to -5 F.; grows to 6 feet. Deep-red autumn color in fall and winter, and yellow flowers in May. Deciduous.

B. thunbergii (Japanese barberry). Hardy to -10 F.; grows to 7 feet. Graceful in growth, with arching stems. Deep-green foliage and fiery-red berries in fall, yellow flowers. Deciduous.

B. verruculosa (warty barberry). Hardy to -5 F.; neat habit, and grows to about 4 feet. Leathery dark-green leaves and golden-yellow flowers. Evergreen.

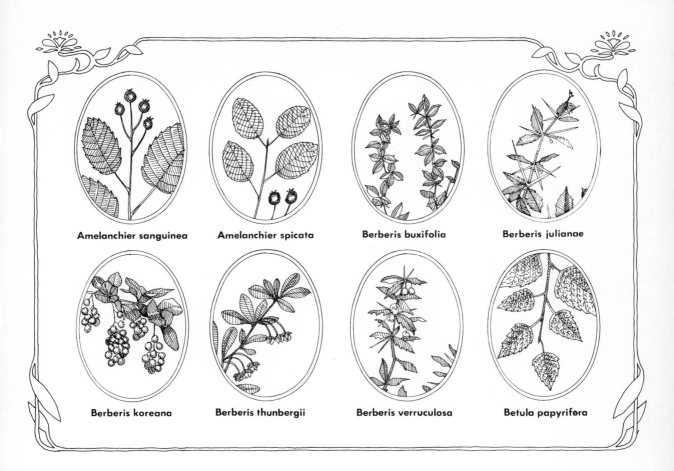

Amelanchier sanguinea

Amelanchier spicata

Berberis buxifolia

Berberis julianae

Berberis koreana

Berberis thunbergii

Berberis verruculosa

Betula papyrifera

BETULA Birch

Deciduous

Birches, favorite ornamental deciduous trees, are graceful in appearance; the most popular birches have handsome white bark. Somewhat short-lived, these trees are difficult to transplant unless they are balled and burlapped. You *must* move them in the spring. Once established, most birches are easy to grow and will thrive in wet or dry soil. The bright-yellow autumn color is certainly desirable in the landscape. All in all, these are worthwhile garden subjects.

B. papyrifera (canoe birch). Hardy to -35 F.; grows to 90 feet. White bark peels off in thin sheets.

B. pendula (verrucosa) (European white birch). Hardy to -50 F.; pyramidal in shape. Grows to 40 feet; white bark.

   'Youngii' (Young's weeping birch)—Pendulous branches.

BUDDLEIA Butterfly bush

Evergreen/Deciduous

The buddleias are valued shrubs because they produce such beautiful flowers through the summer months. Even though classified as hardy, the plants generally die back to the ground in winter but come back the following spring. These floriferous shrubs need good sun and a loamy garden soil. Usually not long-lived plants, buddleias still are worth their space in the garden.

B. alternifolia. Hardy to -20 F.; grows to 12 feet. Large spikes of light-purple florets in clusters. Deciduous.

B. colvillei. Hardy to -20 F.; grows to 30 feet. Small rose florets in June. Very handsome.

B. davidii (orange-eye butterfly bush). Hardy to -5 F.; grows to 15 feet. White, pink, or red flowers.

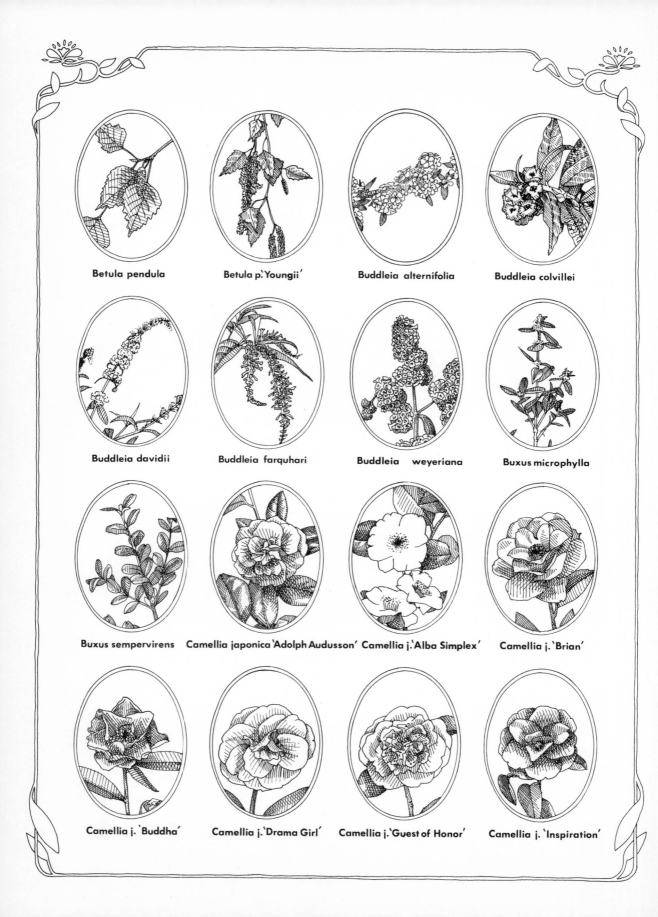

Betula pendula

Betula p. 'Youngii'

Buddleia alternifolia

Buddleia colvillei

Buddleia davidii

Buddleia farquhari

Buddleia weyeriana

Buxus microphylla

Buxus sempervirens

Camellia japonica 'Adolph Audusson'

Camellia j. 'Alba Simplex'

Camellia j. 'Brian'

Camellia j. 'Buddha'

Camellia j. 'Drama Girl'

Camellia j. 'Guest of Honor'

Camellia j. 'Inspiration'

B. farquhari. Hardy to -10 F.; grows to 5 feet. Fragrant lavender florets in pendent clusters in July.

B. weyeriana. Hardy to -10 F.; grows to 6 feet. Handsome clusters of golden-orange florets.

BUXUS Boxwood

Evergreen

These evergreen shrubs are perfect for hedges and as edging. All grow in full sun or shade. Need extra summer care: watering, feeding, and spraying. Boxwood will grow soft and billowing if not clipped.

B. microphylla (littleleaf box). Hardy to -5 F.; grows to 5 feet. Evergreen leaves about 1 inch long. Good garden shrub.

B. sempervirens (common box). Hardy to -5 F.; grows to 20 feet. Dark lustrous leaves.

CAMELLIA

Evergreen

These evergreen shrubs bear handsome flowers from January to May. There are over 3,000 named kinds of camellias, varying in color, size, and form. The *japonica* hybrids are perhaps the most popular, with flowers from pure white to dark red, with many shades in between. *Sasanqua* hybrids are desirable too; these bear smaller, generally single flowers that bloom before *japonica.*

Both kinds of camellias need a well-drained rich soil and coolness at the roots. Never plant camellias with the trunk base beneath the soil line. Keep camellias moist but never overly wet; fertilize them with a commercial acid plant food. Prune immediately after they bloom or in fall. Watch for aphids, scale, and mites; apply appropriate remedies if needed. Scorched or yellowed areas on the leaves are due to sunscald; yellow leaves with green veins indicate that the soil needs more iron. (Iron chelate is available at nurseries.) If flower buds drop, do not panic; it is probably caused by overwatering, or often buds dropping is a natural tendency of camellias.

C. japonica (common camellia). Hardy to 5 F.; grows to 45 feet; evergreen foliage and large white to red flowers.

'Adolph Audusson'—Semidouble dark-red to rose flowers.

'Alba Simplex'—Single white.

'Brian'—Large pink flowers.

'Buddha' (Reticulata)—Ruffled rose-pink flowers.

'Drama Girl'—Huge semidouble deep salmon to rose-pink flowers.

'Guest of Honor'—Fine double pink.

'Inspiration'—Semidouble pink, veined.

'Lady Clare'—Semidouble carmine-rose flowers.

'Magnoliae'—Semidouble shell-pink flowers.

'Mary Williams'—Semidouble deep pink.

'Mrs. Tingely'—Small pink flowers; floriferous.

'Yours Truly'—Pale-pink beauty.

C. sasanqua (sasanqua camellia). Hardy to 5 F.; grows to 20 feet. Varies in habit from upright and dense to vinelike and spreading. Dark-green, shiny leaves; white flowers produced in early autumn.

C. williamsii. Hardy to 10 F; grows to 10 feet. Pink flowers; floriferous. Many varieties.

CATALPA

Deciduous

These are common midwestern trees that can withstand hot summers and dry soil; the pyramidal habit is handsome and pretty white flowers are borne in June. Generally an easily grown tree, the small catalpa deserves more attention for home landscaping. Several improved varieties of *C. bignonioides* are available and these are smaller trees; very attractive.

C. bignonioides (southern catalpa). Hardy to -10 F.; grows to 45 feet. A showy tree with large leaves and long beanlike pods in fall.

C. speciosa (common catalpa). Hardy to -10 F.; grows to 90 feet. Large, not as attractive as above species.

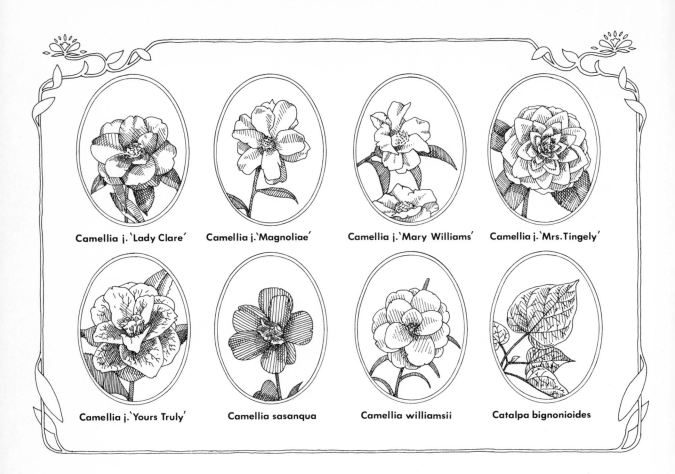

Camellia j. 'Lady Clare' Camellia j. 'Magnoliae' Camellia j. 'Mary Williams' Camellia j. 'Mrs. Tingely'

Camellia j. 'Yours Truly' Camellia sasanqua Camellia williamsii Catalpa bignonioides

CEDRUS Cedar

Evergreen

Good, big evergreen trees that need lots of space; their sculptural growth is desirable in the landscape. Some species are stiff in appearance; but others are more graceful, having pendent branches. Cedars need a somewhat rich soil and are relatively resistant to insects and disease.

C. atlantica 'Glauca' (blue Atlas cedar). Silvery blue needles.

C. deodara (deodar cedar). Hardy to 5 F.; narrow pyramidal growth to 150 feet, with pendulous branches. Dense evergreen needles.

C. libani (cedar of Lebanon). Hardy to -5 F.; narrow pyramidal growth to 120 feet, with stiff horizontal branches.

CERCIS Redbud

Deciduous

Redbuds are small deciduous trees with lovely heart-shaped leaves and clusters of small magenta-pink blossoms in spring. The flowers are long-lasting, and foliage turns bright yellow in fall. The redbuds will grow in full sun or light shade and are not particular about soil conditions.

C. canadensis (Eastern redbud). Hardy to -10 F.; flat-topped tree to 36 feet. Small purplish-pink blooms and yellow leaves in fall.

C. chinensis (Chinese redbud). Hardy to -5 F.; often shrublike, to 40 feet. Dense, pealike, rosy-purple flowers. Yellow autumn color.

C. siliquastrum (Judas tree). Hardy to -5 F.; flat-topped tree to 30 feet. Profuse bright purplish rose flowers.

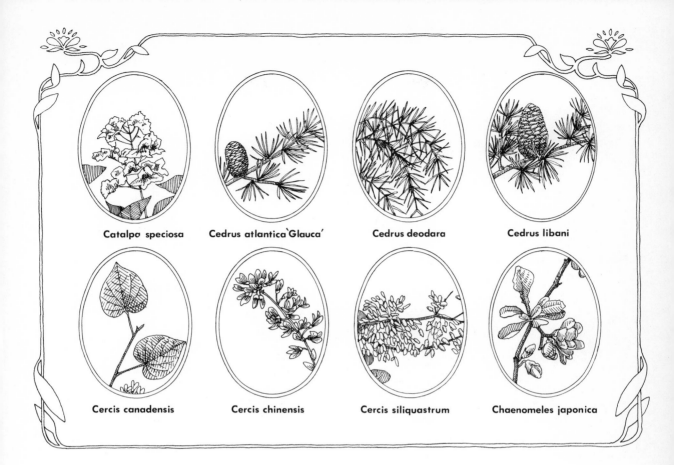

Catalpo speciosa — Cedrus atlantica 'Glauca' — Cedrus deodara — Cedrus libani

Cercis canadensis — Cercis chinensis — Cercis siliquastrum — Chaenomeles japonica

CHAENOMELES   Flowering quince
Deciduous

With bright-colored flowers that appear before the leaves, the flowering quince furnishes brilliant color in the garden for early spring. The plants have been widely hybridized; there are many stunning varieties in a wide range of flower color: white, and shades of pink, red, and orange. Some have single flowers; others have semidouble or double blooms. The fruits are green and turn yellow at maturity. Several varieties are thorny. The majority of quinces grow to about 6 feet, so they are ideal for small gardens.

C. japonica (Japanese quince). Hardy to -10 F.; grows to 3 feet. Red flowers in early May. Deciduous.

C. lagenaria (flowering quince). Hardy to -10 F.; grows to 6 feet. Dark-green, glossy leaves, and red, pink, or white flowers.

'Crimson Beauty'—Single red flowers.
'Nivalis'—Single white flowers.
'Yaegaki—Pink flowers.

CHAMAECYPARIS   False cypress
Evergreen

These are favorite evergreens, with many color forms and varieties. The Japanese species withstand dryer atmosphere than do others in the group. Generally dense and pyramidal in shape, false cypresses are relatively free of insects and disease. They are popular additions to the garden picture and need little care.

C. lawsoniana (Lawson false cypress). Hardy to -5 F.; slender tree to 120 feet. Usually has blue-green foliage and shredding bark.

'Allumii' (scarab Lawson cypress)—Steel-blue foliage; grows to 30 feet.

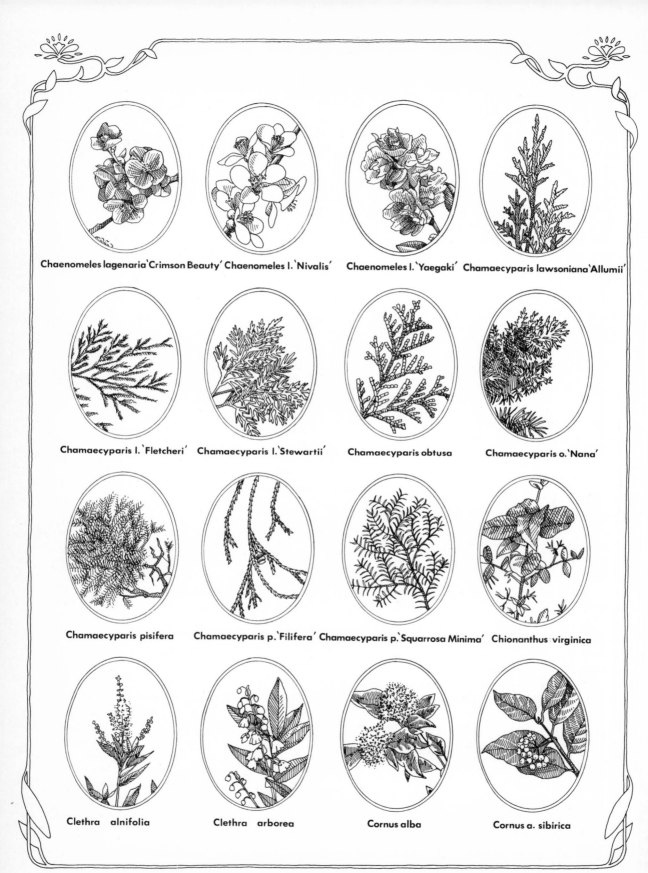

Chaenomeles lagenaria'Crimson Beauty' Chaenomeles l. 'Nivalis' Chaenomeles l. 'Yaegaki' Chamaecyparis lawsoniana'Allumii'

Chamaecyparis l. 'Fletcheri' Chamaecyparis l. 'Stewartii' Chamaecyparis obtusa Chamaecyparis o. 'Nana'

Chamaecyparis pisifera Chamaecyparis p. 'Filifera' Chamaecyparis p. 'Squarrosa Minima' Chionanthus virginica

Clethra alnifolia Clethra arborea Cornus alba Cornus a. sibirica

'Fletcheri'—to 20 feet; blue-gray color that turns purplish or brown in the winter.

'Stewartii'—Grows to 30 feet; golden-yellow foliage, usually turning green.

C. obtusa (hinoki false cypress). Hardy to -10 F.; broad pyramid to 120 feet. Glossy green, dense, scalelike leaves.

'Nana' (dwarf hinoki cypress)—Small form (to 3 feet).

C. pisifera (sawara false cypress). Hardy to -20 F.; pyramidal to 150 feet, with horizontal branching habit. Open foliage.

'Filifera' (thread cypress)—To 8 feet; dark-green foliage.

'Squarrosa Minima'—Dwarf; several forms under this name. Gray-green to dark-green foliage, depending on the form.

CHIONANTHUS VIRGINICA   Fringe tree
Deciduous

This is a splendid ornamental tree with pretty white flowers in June, dark-blue fruit in fall, when foliage turns a lovely golden yellow to complement the berries. It thrives in full sun and even moisture and is a worthwhile addition to any garden. Showy and attractive; hardy to -10 F.

CLETHRA
Deciduous/Evergreen

A group of handsome shrubs and small trees. Clethras are well-known for their showy flowers and lovely growth habits. Plants require some care to thrive. A somewhat acid soil and good light but not necessarily full sun. The dense habit and handsome flowers make Clethra a good addition for gardens.

C. alnifolia (summer sweet). Hardy to 20 F.; grows to 15 feet. Blooms in late summer and leafs out in May. Stellar shrub.

C. arborea (lily-of-the-valley tree). Hardy to 20 F.; grows to 20 feet. A small tree, upright and densely clothed with bronzy-green leaves. Flowers resemble lily of the valley. Pretty.

CORNUS   Dogwood
Deciduous

Dogwood trees and shrubs are just about the best garden plants you can find; they grow rapidly, have splendid color in bloom, and their colorful autumn foliage is equally attractive. There is a dogwood for almost any part of the United States. Some are wide and spreading with horizontal branches; others are narrow and upright. There are many varieties of *C. florida* offered; but not all are good ones, so make choices carefully.

C. alba (Tatarian dogwood). Hardy to -35 F.; upright growth to 9 feet. Branches densely clothed with leaves; red twigs in winter.

C. a. sibirica (Siberian dogwood). Outstanding species.

C. florida (flowering dogwood). Hardy to -10 F.; horizontal branching habit; to 40 feet. Scarlet autumn color.

'Rubra'—Pink or rose flower bracts.

C. kousa (Japanese dogwood). Hardy to -5 F.; horizontal branching habit; to 21 feet. Scarlet autumn color.

C. k. chinensis. Similar to above.

C. mas (cornelian cherry). Hardy to -10 F.; round and dense shrublike tree; to 24 feet. Red autumn color.

C. nuttallii (Pacific dogwood). Hardy to 5 F.; pyramidal, with dense foliage. Grows to 75 feet; large white flowers, spectacular in bloom. Scarlet and yellow in the autumn.

C. stolonifera (red-twig dogwood). Oval deep-green leaves and small white flowers; grows to 15 feet.

COTONEASTER
Deciduous/Semi-evergreen

These shrubs grow under untoward conditions (but do not tolerate full shade) and still produce good growth. The bright-red berries are handsome, and the white or pink flowers are a charming asset to the garden. Many species have interesting growth habits, making them good landscape subjects. Cotoneasters are deciduous,

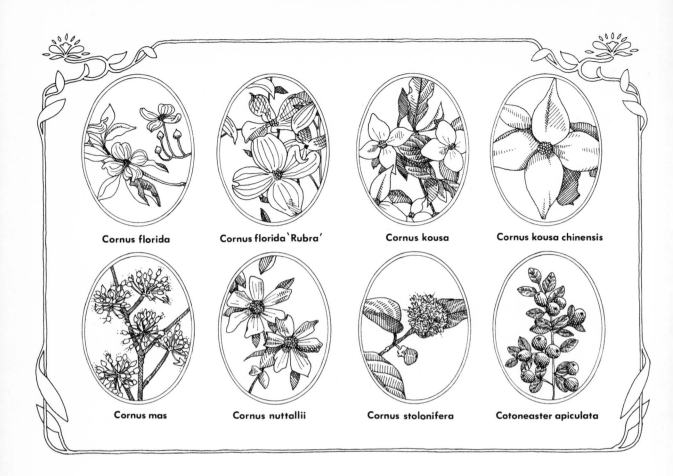

Cornus florida   Cornus florida 'Rubra'   Cornus kousa   Cornus kousa chinensis

Cornus mas   Cornus nuttallii   Cornus stolonifera   Cotoneaster apiculata

semideciduous, or evergreen. Many are native to the cool regions of China. In dry, hot weather cotoneasters are susceptible to red spider or lace-bug attacks that must be kept under control or they will kill the shrubs.

A. apiculata (cranberry cotoneaster). Hardy to -10 F.; grows to 3 feet. Bright-green leaves, pink-white flowers, and red fruit. Deciduous.

C. dammeri (bearberry cotoneaster). Hardy to -5 F.; prostrate trailing habit (to 1 foot). Oval bright-green leaves, white flowers, and red fruit. Beautiful evergreen cascading plant.

C. dielsiana. Hardy to -5 F.; grows to 6 feet. Graceful arching branches, pink flowers, red fruit. Deciduous.

C. divaricata (spreading cotoneaster). Hardy to -5 F.; stiff branches. Grows to 6 feet, with dark-green leaves and pink flowers followed by red fruit. Good hedge or screen. Deciduous.

C. franchetti. Hardy to -5 F.; grows to 10 feet. Pink flowers, orange-red fruit. Semi-evergreen.

C. horizontalis (rock-spray cotoneaster). Hardy to -10 F.; low-growing to 3 feet, but spreading with stiff branches. Small, glossy, bright-green leaves, pink flowers, and red fruit. Good bank cover or espalier subject. Deciduous.

C. microphylla (small-leaved cotoneaster). Hardy to -5 F.; somewhat of a trailer, to 3 feet tall. Small green leaves and white flowers followed by large scarlet fruit. Good ground cover. Evergreen.

C. multiflora (large flowering cotoneaster). Hardy to -5 F.; grows to 8 feet. Very wide-spreading. White flowers, light-red to pink fruit. Deciduous.

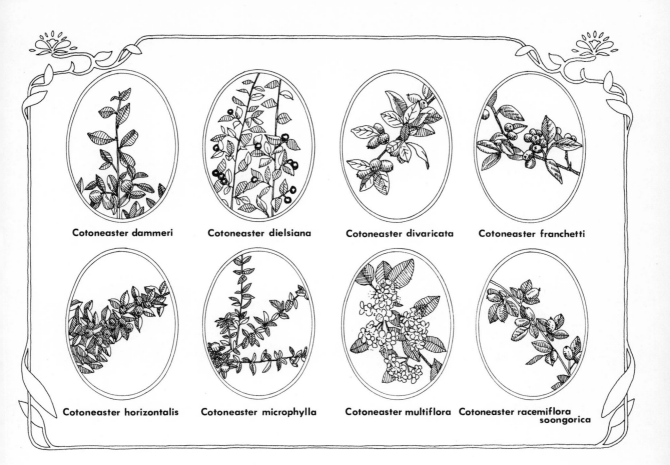

Cotoneaster dammeri

Cotoneaster dielsiana

Cotoneaster divaricata

Cotoneaster franchetti

Cotoneaster horizontalis

Cotoneaster microphylla

Cotoneaster multiflora

Cotoneaster racemiflora soongorica

C. racemiflora soongorica. Hardy to -20 F.; grows to 8 feet. Rounded gray-green leaves, white flowers, pink fruit. Best and hardiest cotoneaster. Deciduous.

C. salicifolia floccosa (hardy willow-leaf cotoneaster). Hardy to -5 F.; grows to 15 feet. Narrow pointed leaves, white flowers, red fruit. Semi-evergreen.

CRATAEGUS   Hawthorn

Deciduous

A widely distributed group of deciduous trees, hawthorns are dense, twiggy, dependable, and loaded with white flowers in May. Slow-growing, hawthorns are desirable because they are picturesquely shaped and have beautiful bright-red fruit in the fall. Hawthorns will grow in poor soil; some keep fruit all winter.

C. monogyna (single-seed hawthorn). Hardy to -10 F.; round-headed with pendulous branches, to 30 feet. Red color in autumn.

C. oxyacantha (English hawthorn). Hardy to -10 F.; round-headed to 15 feet. Densely branching.
   'Paul's Scarlet'—Popular; double red to rose flowers.

C. prunifolia. Hardy to -10 F.; grows to 20 feet. Brilliant dark-green leaves. Rich crimson autumn color.

DEUTZIA

Deciduous

Most species of Deutzia are from parts of China. These are dense-growing shrubs, from 3 to 8 feet. Deutzias' spring flowers make them very desirable. Prune the plants annually in spring to keep

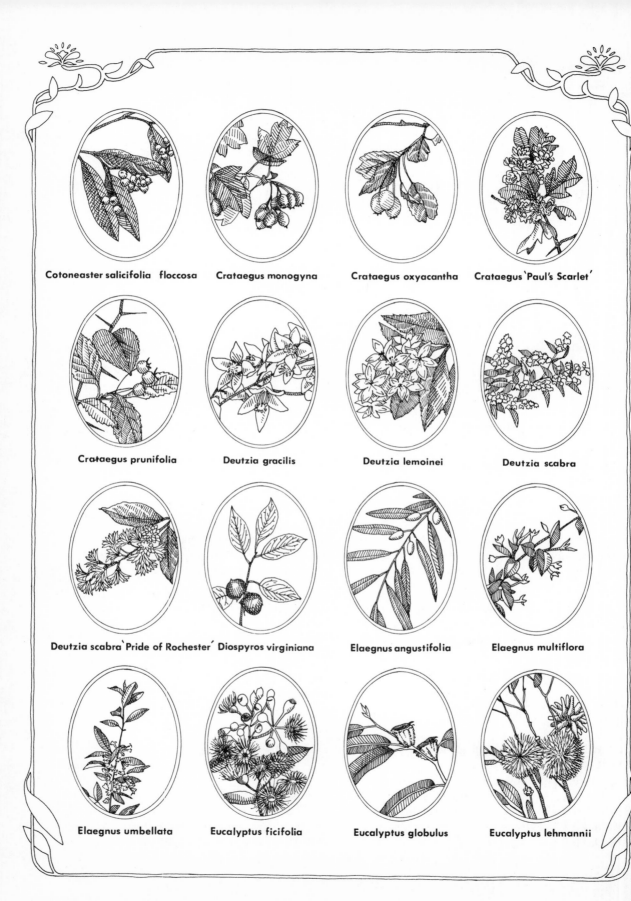

Cotoneaster salicifolia floccosa   Crataegus monogyna   Crataegus oxyacantha   Crataegus 'Paul's Scarlet'

Crataegus prunifolia   Deutzia gracilis   Deutzia lemoinei   Deutzia scabra

Deutzia scabra 'Pride of Rochester'   Diospyros virginiana   Elaegnus angustifolia   Elaegnus multiflora

Elaegnus umbellata   Eucalyptus ficifolia   Eucalyptus globulus   Eucalyptus lehmannii

them handsome. Select species for bloom time: some flower in May, others later. Deutzias grow in any soil and prefer full sun but will withstand light shade. Many kinds are very floriferous. Deutzias are usually free from insect or disease problems.

D. gracilis (slender deutzia). Hardy to -10 F.; slender graceful shrub to 3 feet. Bright-green leaves and snow-white flowers.

L. lemoinei (lemoine deutzia). Hybrid; hardy to -10 F.; compact grower to 7 feet. Toothed leaves and clusters of white flowers.

D. scabra. Hardy to -10 F.; tall species to 10 feet. Dull-green leaves, with clusters of white flowers. Several varieties.
  'Pride of Rochester'—Large clusters of double rose-purple flowers.

DIOSPYROS VIRGINIANA Persimmon
Deciduous

A round-headed tree, nicely shaped with dense foliage and lovely autumn color. Generally slow-growing to about 30 feet, the persimmon tree makes a nice garden subject and the orange fruit is handsome and well-known. The tree is rarely bothered by insects or disease and all in all is a strong robust plant that requires little attention. Hardy to -20 F.

ELAEAGNUS
Evergreen / Deciduous

These deciduous and evergreen trees and shrubs are perfect as screens. All Elaeagnus species are dense, full, firm, and tough and need little upkeep. The evergreens have dotted leaves; the deciduous plants have silvery gray leaves.

E. angustifolia (Russian olive). Hardy to -35 F.; grows to 20 feet. Outstanding gray-green foliage. Yellow berries. Deciduous.

E. multiflora (cherry elaeagnus) Hardy to -10 F.; grows to 9 feet. Red fruits the size of cherries. Deciduous.

E. umbellata (autumn elaeagnus) Hardy to -20 F.; grows to 20 feet. Leaves silvery, fragrant flowers. Tree/shrub, deciduous.

EUCALYPTUS Gum tree
Evergreen

These evergreen trees and shrubs do especially well in California and Arizona. Some types are ideal for landscaping. Many gums have flowers as striking as those of the roses and rhododendrons. Still other gums have leaves so attractive and fragrant that the leaves are often used indoors in a vase. All gums are absolutely free of insect problems. Many gums grow 10 to 15 feet a year; these fast-growing plants can survive for 100 years.

E. ficifolia (scarlet flowering gum). Hardy to 30 F.; grows to 30 feet. Succulent leaves, flowers white or pink.

E. globulus (blue gum). Hardy to 30 F.; grows to 200 feet. Immense tree, attractive.

E. lehmannii. Hardy to 30 F.; grows to 30 feet. Leaves oval, flowers in dense heads. Nice small tree.

E. leucoxylon (white ironbark). Hardy to 30 F.; grows to 60 feet. Grayish-green leaves, small flowers.

E. preissiana. Hardy to 30 F.; grows to 10 feet. Nice shrublike tree; yellow flowers.

EUONYMUS
Deciduous / Evergreen

Although the flowers of this group are small and insignificant, the autumn color is spectacular. Plants grow vigorously in any good garden soil, but they are susceptible to scale and so must be sprayed regularly. Some plants in this group are vines; others are shrubs. Most Euonymus shrubs are excellent landscape subjects.

E. alatus (winged euonymus). Hardy to -20 F.; horizontal and branching habit. Grows to 9 feet,

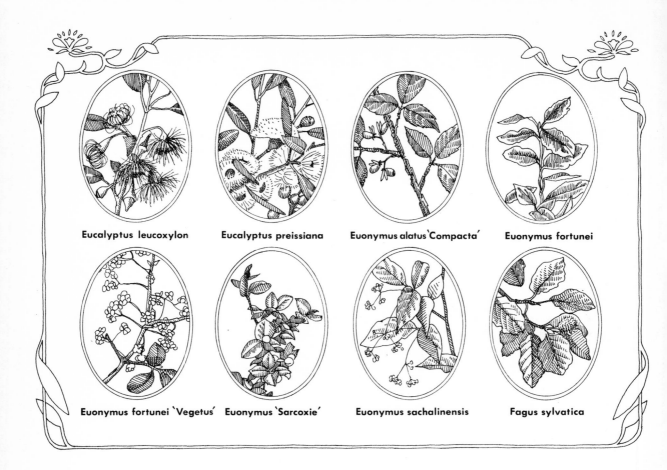

Eucalyptus leucoxylon   Eucalyptus preissiana   Euonymus alatus 'Compacta'   Euonymus fortunei

Euonymus fortunei 'Vegetus'   Euonymus 'Sarcoxie'   Euonymus sachalinensis   Fagus sylvatica

with dark-green leaves that turn scarlet in fall. Deciduous.

'Compacta'—Excellent dwarf plant, to 4 feet. Perfect for hedges.

E. fortunei. Hardy to -5 F.; vine or shrub to 4 feet. Dark-green leaves. Good one. Evergreen.

'Sarcoxie'—Upright to 4 feet.

'Vegetus' (big-leaf wintercreeper).

E. sachalinensis. Hardy to -20 F.; grows to 7 feet. Bright-red pendent fruits.

FAGUS   Beech

Deciduous

These elegant trees are beautiful all year, but especially in fall when they blaze with golden color. Usually, the beeches are large trees with stout trunks and smooth bark. When you plant beeches, remember that very little can be grown underneath them because of the shade their size provides.

F. sylvatica (European beech). Hardy to -10 F.; pyramidal to 90 feet. Glossy, dense, dark-green foliage; bronze autumn color.

F. s. heterophylla (fern-leaved beech). Attractive foliage.

F. s. purpurea (purple beech). Pale-red spring color; beautiful purple color later.

F. s. 'Tricolor' (tricolor beech) Green leaves marked with white or pink.

FORSYTHIA

Deciduous

Forsythias are popular in many regions because their bright flowers are harbingers of spring when all else is bleak. In the north, blooms ap-

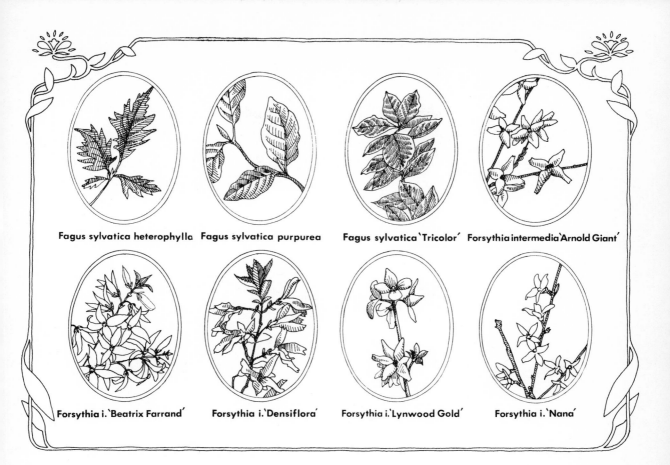

Fagus sylvatica heterophylla | Fagus sylvatica purpurea | Fagus sylvatica 'Tricolor' | Forsythia intermedia 'Arnold Giant'

Forsythia i. 'Beatrix Farrand' | Forsythia i. 'Densiflora' | Forsythia i. 'Lynwood Gold' | Forsythia i. 'Nana'

pear on leafless stems in March or April, and then the plants are outstanding. The flowers are forsythias' chief assets, but many of the plants have a graceful habit of growth. Plants grow rapidly and need space; intelligent pruning is necessary to keep them looking their best.

Forsythias bloom on previous years' wood, so prune them after they flower, *never before.* There are several types of forsythias: dwarf and compact, or upright and spreading. These shrubs survive almost any kind of soil and are practically trouble-free.

F. intermedia (border forsythia). Hardy to -5 F.; grows to 9 feet. Long, arching branches. Pale- to deep-yellow flowers.

'Arnold Giant'—Large yellow flowers.
'Beatrix Farrand'—Vivid yellow flowers.
'Densiflora'—Upright growth; pale-yellow flowers.
'Lynwood Gold'—Upright growth; golden-yellow flowers.

'Nana'—Small but pretty.
'Spectabilis'—Yellow flowers; most floriferous.
'Spring Glory'—Pale-yellow flowers.

F. suspensa fortunei (weeping forsythia). Hardy to -10 F.; grows to 10 feet with vinelike branches. Golden-yellow flowers.

FOTHERGILLA

Deciduous

A group of attractive shrubs most notable for their lovely fall color. Plants also have pretty white midsummer flowers; nice growth habit. Fothergillas need a somewhat shady location and a rich loamy soil. Not spectacular but certainly worthwhile if space is available.

F. gardenii (dwarf fothergilla). Hardy to -20 F.; grows to about 3 feet. A low rounded shrub; red color in autumn.

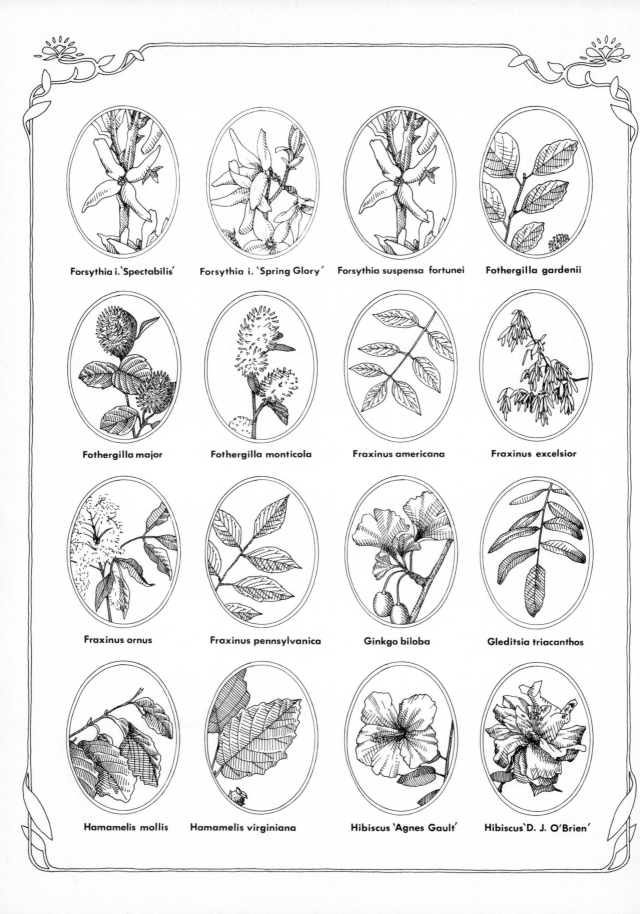

Forsythia i. `Spectabilis` Forsythia i. `Spring Glory` Forsythia suspensa fortunei Fothergilla gardenii

Fothergilla major Fothergilla monticola Fraxinus americana Fraxinus excelsior

Fraxinus ornus Fraxinus pennsylvanica Ginkgo biloba Gleditsia triacanthos

Hamamelis mollis Hamamelis virginiana Hibiscus `Agnes Gault` Hibiscus `D. J. O'Brien`

F. major (large fothergilla). Hardy to -20 F.; grows to 10 feet. Brilliant orange-red color in fall.

F. monticola (Alabama fothergilla). Hardy to -20 F.; grows to 5 feet. Large flower clusters; fall color a handsome crimson.

FRAXINUS   Ash
Deciduous

The deciduous ash, a rapid-growing tree, has beautiful brilliant-yellow to purple fall color. Some grow to 100 feet and need lots of space. Trees grow without much attention in any reasonably good soil.

F. americana (white ash). Hardy to -20 F.; straight trunk, oval-shaped crown. Grows to 120 feet, with dense foliage.

F. excelsior (European ash). Hardy to -20 F.; grows to 120 feet. Round-headed, with open branches.

F. ornus (flowering ash). Hardy to -5 F.; broad, rounded crown. Grows to 60 feet; lavender and yellow foliage in fall.

F. pennsylvanica (green ash). Hardy to -35 F.; dense round-headed tree to 60 feet. Yellow autumn color.

GINKGO BILOBA   Ginkgo
Deciduous

This popular tree has a branching habit and ornamental fan-shaped leaves. The flowers are insignificant and the tree is generally grown because it succeeds in most soils in most regions and is attractive. While the ginkgo can grow to enormous heights, generally in gardens it matures at 35 to 40 feet. Graceful and attractive in any season, the ginkgo is hardy to -10 F.

GLEDITSIA TRICANTHOS   Sweet locust
Deciduous

This is a fast-growing tree with spreading upright branches; foliage turns golden in early fall. Trunks and branches are thorny and pods make a mess but Gleditsia grows well in almost any soil and in most areas. A good lawn tree; good all-around tree. Many varieties including thornless types. Resistant to most insects and hardy to -10 F.

HAMAMELIS   Witch hazel
Deciduous

These very pretty popular shrubs have yellow fall foliage and fragrant yellow flowers. Most species have a neat rounded form and can be trained to height by pruning; some bloom in very early spring, making them very desirable in gardens. Plants are best used in groups rather than singly, and witch hazels will grow in a loamy soil that is somewhat on the acid side.

H. mollis (Chinese witch hazel). Hardy to -5 F.; grows to 30 feet. Very fragrant yellow flowers.

H. virginiana (common witch hazel). Hardy to -10 F.; grows to 10 feet. Sometimes blooms as early as February with small fragrant yellow flowers.

HIBISCUS   Chinese hibiscus
Evergreen/Deciduous

A group of showy flowering shrubs that are old-time favorites. Plants have large flowers and usually dense growth habit. Hibiscus plants like a well-drained soil and need plenty of feeding; sun makes the flowers. Some varieties are hardy, others tender. All make fine additions to the garden and are best used as ornamental accents.

H. mutabilis. Four- to 6-inch flowers that are pink and then change to red. Deciduous.

H. rosa-sinensis (Chinese hibiscus). Fast-growing to 15 feet; handsome large pink flowers. Best in temperate-all-year climates. Evergreen.
 'Agnes Gault'—Big single pink flowers.
 'D. J. O'Brien'—Very large ruffled orange flowers.

H. syriacus (rose-of-Sharon). Deciduous to 10 feet. Can be trained to a handsome shape. Flowers single or double, usually lavender. Deciduous.
 'Blue Bird'—Blue form; stellar.
 'Woodbridge'—Single magenta flowers.

Hibiscus mutabilis **Hibiscus rosa-sinensis** **Hibiscus syriacus** **Hibiscus syriacus 'Blue Bird'**

Hibiscus 'Woodbridge' **Hydrangea macrophylla 'Hamburg'** **Hydrangea m.'Heinrich Seidel'** **Hydrangea m.'Maresii'**

HYDRANGEA

Deciduous

The showy hydrangeas make excellent ornamentals in the garden because they have large bold green leaves and fantastic clusters of white or blue or pink flowers. The plants prefer a sandy, loamy soil and must have good drainage. In bright sun they will be at their best; in shade they will grow but not be as colorful.

H. macrophylla 'Hamburg'. Hardy to -5 F.; grows to 10 feet. Bright-green leaves, blue or pink flowers.

'Heinrich Seidel'—Large purple or purple-red florets.

'Mariesii'—Rosy-pink flowers.

'Nikko Blue'—Clusters of hundreds of blue florets.

H. paniculata 'Grandiflora' (peegee hydrangea). Hardy to -10 F.; grows to 25 feet. White flowers.

H. quercifolia (oak-leaved hydrangea). Hardy to -5 F.; grows to 6 feet. White flowers that turn purple.

ILEX Holly

Evergreen

The hollies are evergreen or deciduous and are very popular because they are amenable plants. European and American hollies have hundreds of varieties. The bright-red or black berries are highly desirable for landscape color. Hollies (with few exceptions) have separate sexes, so both must be present in the area to ensure the fertilization of flowers. (Chinese holly can produce fruit without the pollen of other hollies.) Most plants are easily grown in a good garden soil, but they do need good drainage; hollies are relatively free of pest and diseases.

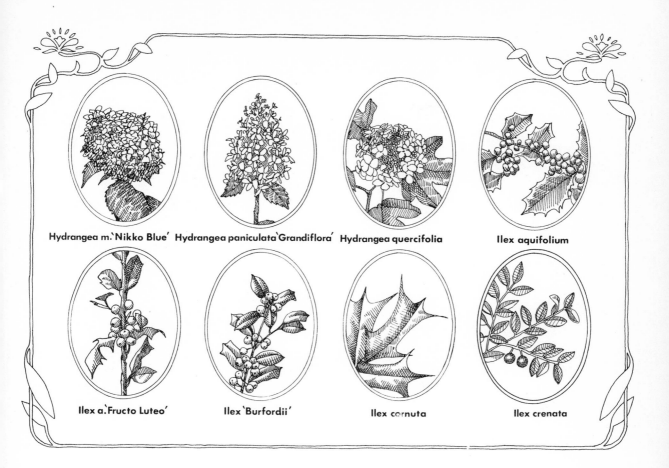

Hydrangea m.'Nikko Blue' Hydrangea paniculata'Grandiflora' Hydrangea quercifolia Ilex aquifolium

Ilex a.'Fructo Luteo' Ilex 'Burfordii' Ilex cornuta Ilex crenata

I. aquifolium (English holly). Hardy to -5 F.; grows to 15 feet. Variable in leaf, shape, and color. Many varieties.

'Fructo Luteo'—Nice yellow foliage.

I. cornuta (Chinese holly). Hardy to 5 F.; dense or open growth to 9 feet. Glossy, leathery leaves; bright-red berries. Evergreen.

'Burfordii'—Spineless leaves.

I. crenata (Japanese holly). Hardy to -5 F.; dense and erect, sometimes to 20 feet. Finely toothed leaves and black berries. Evergreen.

I. glabra (inkberry). Hardy to -20 F.; grows to 9 feet. Black berries. Evergreen.

I. opaca (American holly). Hardy to -35 F.; grows to 50 feet. Spiny leaves, bright-red berries. Most sought after as Christmas decoration.

I. pernyi. Hardy to -5 F.; grows to 30 feet. Glossy leaves, very large red berries.

I. serrata (Japanese winterberry). Hardy to -20 F.; grows to 7 feet. Saw-toothed leaves; red berries.

I. verticillata (winterberry). Hardy to -35 F.; grows to 10 feet. Bright red berries.

JASMINUM   Jasmine

Evergreen/Deciduous

Mostly climbing or sprawling plants, jasmines are well-known for their fragrance and have varied uses in the garden. Most species thrive in regular garden soil and will tolerate shady places but prefer some sun. Jasmine can be used to cover trellises, fences, walls and offers a great deal of lovely color.

J. azoricum. Hardy to 5 F.; a climber to 15 feet. Broad green leaves, white flowers. Evergreen.

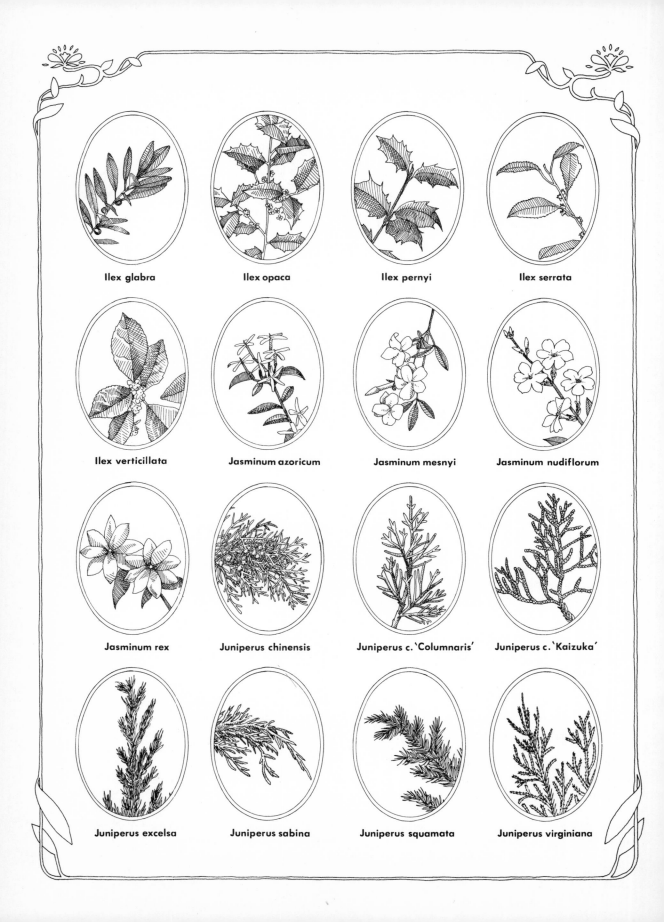

Ilex glabra

Ilex opaca

Ilex pernyi

Ilex serrata

Ilex verticillata

Jasminum azoricum

Jasminum mesnyi

Jasminum nudiflorum

Jasminum rex

Juniperus chinensis

Juniperus c. `Columnaris´

Juniperus c. `Kaizuka´

Juniperus excelsa

Juniperus sabina

Juniperus squamata

Juniperus virginiana

J. mesnyi (primrose jasmine). Hardy to 5 F.; grows to 10 feet. Lovely yellow flowers; a very showy evergreen.

J. nudiflorum (winter jasmine). Hardy to 5 F.; grows to 15 feet. Clambering type with fine yellow flowers. Deciduous; not scented.

J. rex. Hardy to 10 F.; grows to 15 feet. Dazzling large white flowers. Deciduous.

JUNIPERUS Juniper

Evergreen

These evergreen trees and shrubs are valued for their colorful berries in fall and winter. Both male and female plants have to be grown near each other to ensure fruiting. The junipers are tall and dense in habit and prefer a somewhat alkaline soil.

J. chinensis (Chinese juniper). Hardy to -10 F.; pyramidal habit. This tree grows to 60 feet; scalelike leaves.
  'Columnaris'—Columnar, silvery-green foliage.
  'Kaizuka'—Pyramidal, blue-green foliage.

J. excelsa (Greek juniper). Hardy to 10 F.; pyramidal habit. Grows to 60 feet; dense, scalelike leaves.

J. sabina. Hardy to -10 F.; needlelike foliage. Grows to 10 feet.

J. squamata. Hardy to -20 F.; grows to 36 feet. Oval-shaped leaves.

J. virginiana (eastern red cedar). Hardy to -35 F.; dense pyramid tree to 90 feet. Foliage varies, but usually scalelike.
  'Canaertii—Conical shape. Dark-green foliage.
  'Glauca' (silver red cedar)—Silvery blue, to 20 feet.

KALMIA Laurel

Evergreen

These shrubs are related to rhododendrons and bear beautiful flowers. Plants prefer an acid soil but will grow in partial shade and thrive. As garden subjects they are one of our more ornamental plants and make handsome background for flowers as well as being lovely flowering plants themselves. Usually insect-free and of easy culture.

K. latifolia (mountain laurel). Hardy to -35 F.; grows to 10 feet. Lovely long leaves, rose flowers marked with purple.

K. polifolia (bog kalmia). Hardy to -35 F.; grows to 2 feet. Leaves whitish, rose-purple flowers.

KERRIA

Deciduous

A thick-growing shrub that will need some pruning as time goes on. The bright-yellow May flowers are handsome and twigs stay green all winter. Plants grow to about 6 feet and will grow in part shade. Good robust shrubs for the garden.

K. japonica. Hardy to -35 F.; grows to 6 feet or more. Green toothed leaves and lovely yellow flowers.
  'Picta'—Leaves edged white.
  'Pleniflora'—Double flowers.

KOELREUTERIA PANICULATA Golden-rain tree

Deciduous

A very beautiful tree that grows to about 30 feet with yellow flower clusters in May. Plants, if they must, can tolerate drought, wind, cold, or heat and can grow in almost any soil. Some pruning will be necessary to keep the goldenrain tree attractive. A very valuable garden plant. Hardy to -10 F.

LIGUSTRUM Privet

Evergreen/Deciduous

Privets are popular hedge plants. The leaves may be evergreen (in the south) or deciduous. Vigorous and fast-growing, with small white flowers

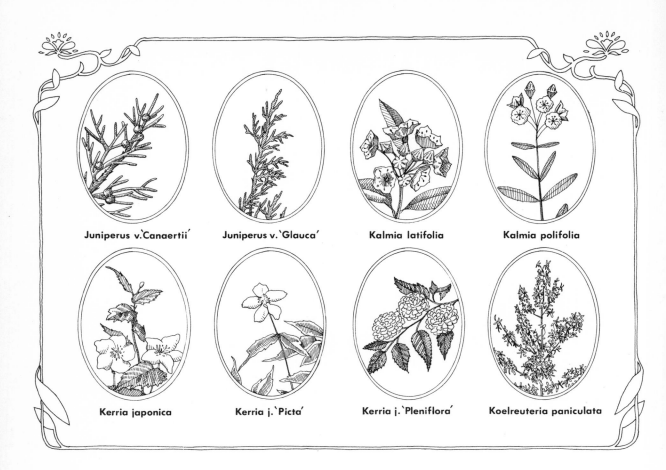

Juniperus v. 'Canaertii'

Juniperus v. 'Glauca'

Kalmia latifolia

Kalmia polifolia

Kerria japonica

Kerria j. 'Picta'

Kerria j. 'Pleniflora'

Koelreuteria paniculata

followed by blue or black berries, privets also make good specimen plants against a fence or a wall. Most of the privets are remarkably free of any problem, and they grow in almost any kind of soil under all kinds of conditions. There are many privets, one hardly distinguishable from the other until they are mature, so ask your nurseryman about them before making purchases.

L. ibolium (ibolium privet). Hardy to -10 F.; grows to 12 feet. Vigorous, with white flowers, black berries.

L. japonicum (Japanese privet). Hardy to 5 F.; dense grower to 18 feet. Clusters of small white flowers.
 'Lusterleaf' *(texanum)*—Very large leaves.

L. vicaryi (golden privet). Hybrid; hardy to -10 F.; grows to 12 feet. Handsome golden-yellow foliage. Blue-black berries.

L. vulgare (common privet). Hardy to -10 F.; grows to 15 feet. Clusters of white flowers, black berries.

LIQUIDAMBAR STYRACIFLUA Sweet gum

Deciduous

This is a very desirable tree because it has lovely form and foliage, is of easy culture, and provides a fine autumn show. The flowers are inconspicuous; tree responds well in ordinary garden soil. Grows to 100 feet; hardy to -10 F.

LIRIODENDRON TULIPIFERA Tulip tree
Deciduous

This tree has tulip-shaped flowers in late spring; they are greenish yellow, orange at base, and most attractive. The tulip tree needs space to

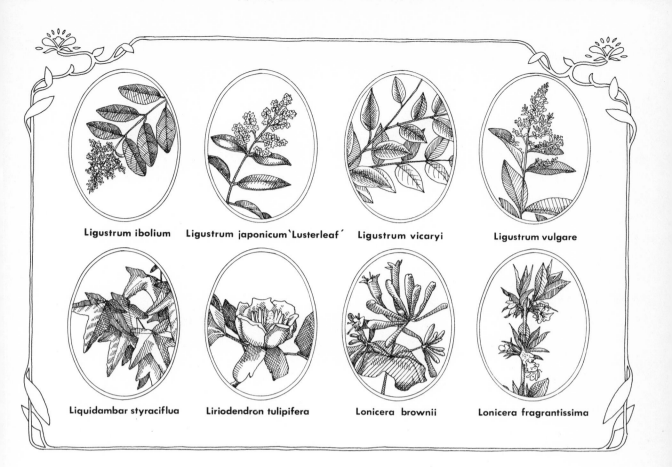

Ligustrum ibolium   Ligustrum japonicum 'Lusterleaf'   Ligustrum vicaryi   Ligustrum vulgare

Liquidambar styraciflua   Liriodendron tulipifera   Lonicera brownii   Lonicera fragrantissima

grow and mature specimens reach 150 feet. Little bothered by insects but needing a good rich soil that is well drained, the tulip tree is a stellar garden subject. Hardy to -20 F.

LONICERA   Honeysuckle
Evergreen/Deciduous

Honeysuckles are vigorous shrubs or vines. They are popular but have no autumn color; some turn brown in winter. Most honeysuckles are trailing or scandent; only a few are upright growers. The plants grow in full sun, although some tolerate light shade. All need little care and have no special problems.

L. brownii (scarlet trumpet honeysuckle). Hardy to 10 F.; grows to 4 feet. Glowing red flowers. Deciduous.

L. fragrantissima (winter honeysuckle). Hardy to -5 F.; grows to 6 feet. Stiff, leathery leaves and fragrant white flowers. Deciduous, but evergreen in mild climates.

L. henryi. Hardy to -35 F.; vine with dark-green leaves and yellow to purple flowers, followed by black fruit. Good bank cover. Evergreen or semi-evergreen.

L. hildebrandtiana (giant Burmese honeysuckle). Hardy to 30 F. Fast-growing vine. White fragrant flowers. Evergreen.

L. maackii (Amur honeysuckle). Hardy to -35 F.; grows to 15 feet. White fragrant flowers and dark-red berries. Good fall color. Deciduous.

L. syringantha (lilac honeysuckle). Hardy to -10 F.; grows to 9 feet. Fragrant rosy-lilac flowers, red to orange berries. Deciduous.

Lonicera hildebrandtiana

Lonicera hildebrandiana

Lonicera maackii

Lonicera syringantha

Lonicera tatarica

Lonicera t. `Sibirica´

Magnolia denudata

Magnolia grandiflora

Magnolia liliflora

Magnolia l. `Nigra´

Magnolia sieboldii

Magnolia soulangeana

Magnolia s. `Lennei´

Magnolia stellata

Magnolia veitchii

Magnolia virginiana

L. tatarica (Tatarian honeysuckle). Hardy to -20 F.; twiggy branches, to 9 feet. Oval blue-green leaves and pink to white flowers. Deciduous.

'Sibirica'—Deep pink blooms.

MAGNOLIA

Evergreen/Deciduous

A popular group because they have splendid flowers; many magnolias bear bloom in early spring before the leaves appear. In a wide range of colors—white, pink, red, reddish purple—the flowers are spectacular. Many magnolias are wide-spreading trees and tall (to 90 feet); others are shrubs. Some are deciduous; others are evergreen. Many have early flowers, and some bloom in summer. All like a good well-drained soil and lots of water in summer. Any pruning should be done immediately after flowers appear. There are magnolias for almost every garden; as flowering trees or shrubs, they are tough to beat.

M. denudata (yulan magnolia). Hardy to -5 F.; round habit. Grows to 45 feet. White, tulip-shaped, fragrant flowers. Deciduous.

M. grandiflora (southern magnolia). Hardy to 5 F.; usually dense pyramidal form. Grows to 90 feet. Pure white fragrant flowers. Evergreen.

M liliflora (lily magnolia). Hardy to -35 F.; grows to 12 feet. This shrub has purple flowers that bloom throughout summer. Deciduous.

'Nigra'—Purple-red flowers.

M. sieboldii. Hardy to -5 F.; grows to 10 feet. Long bloom. Deciduous.

M. soulangana (saucer magnolia). Hybrid; hardy to -5 F.; white to pink or purplish red flowers. Grows to 25 feet. Variable in size and form. Deciduous.

'Lennei'—Very large purple flowers.

M. stellata (star magnolia). Hardy to -5 F.; grows to 20 feet. Very early white flowers. Deciduous.

M. veitchii (Veitch magnolia). Hybrid; hardy to 5 F.; open habit. Grows to 40 feet; pink flowers. Deciduous.

M. virginiana (glauca) (sweet bay). Hardy to -5 F.; globular shape. Grows to 60 feet. Creamy-white flowers. Evergreen.

MAHONIA   Grape holly

Evergreen

Related to barberry, these are handsome shrubs, attractive all year and easy to grow. Leaves have spiny teeth on the edges and flowers are yellow followed by blue-black or red berries. Good for foundation plantings or for screens, mahonias are very resistant to insects and disease. The plants respond well in almost any soil and in sun or shade.

M. aquifolium (grape holly). Hardy to -10 F.; grows to 5 feet. Spiny-edged leaves and clusters of yellow flowers.

M. lomarifolia. Hardy to -10 F.; grows to 10 feet. Leaves crinkled, barbed; handsome yellow flowers followed by blue berries.

MALUS   Crab apple

Deciduous

Good, ornamental, deciduous flowering trees in vivid color in May. Some varieties have single blooms, but others have semidouble or double flowers in colors ranging from pure white to purple-red. Many of the trees have fragrant flowers. The fruit of some crab apples holds color well into winter, making the trees of two-season value. Most crab apples are small, to about 30 feet; although a few reach 50 feet. Several have pendent branches, but shapes usually run the gamut from columnar to round-headed. Crab apples need sun and when young require some additional feeding. A regular schedule of spraying is necessary because these trees have the same problems—fire blight, scale, and borers—as the common apple.

M. arnoldiana (Arnold crab apple). Hardy to -10 F.; broad and spreading. Grows to 20 feet. Fragrant pink flowers.

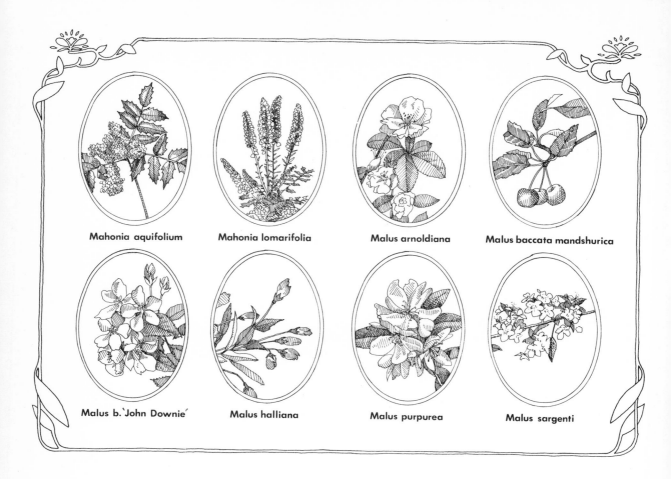

Mahonia aquifolium

Mahonia lomarifolia

Malus arnoldiana

Malus baccata mandshurica

Malus b. 'John Downie'

Malus halliana

Malus purpurea

Malus sargenti

M. baccata mandshurica. Hardy to -35 F.; bushy and dense to 50 feet. Dark-green foliage; fragrant white flowers.

'John Downie'—White flowers; fine fruiting type.

M. halliana. Hardy to -5 F.; dense. Grows to 15 feet. Rose flowers.

M. purpurea. Hardy to -10 F.; dense, Grows to 25 feet. Beautiful deep-rose flowers.

M. sargentii (Sargent crab apple). Hardy to -10 F.; rounded and low-branching. Grows to 8 feet, with pure white fragrant flowers.

M. spectabilis. Hardy to -10 F.; open growth. Grows to 24 feet. Double pink flowers.

MYRICA PENSYLVANICA Bayberry
Deciduous/Evergreen

A handsome shrub with long, narrow, glossy green leaves; grows to 9 feet. Bayberry's dense growth and compact shape makes it a desirable addition to the garden. Further, the plant takes poor soil and still grows well and responds in shade or sun. Hardy to -50 F.

OSMANTHUS Sweet olive
Evergreen

This group of shrubs and trees has attractive leathery foliage and small but sweetly scented flowers. Plants have many uses in the garden as foundation plantings or background for flowers and most do well in a shady place. Several types are broad and dense and are easily pruned to a specific shape.

O. fragrans (sweet olive). Hardy to -5 F.; grows to 20 feet. Lovely foliage, shape.

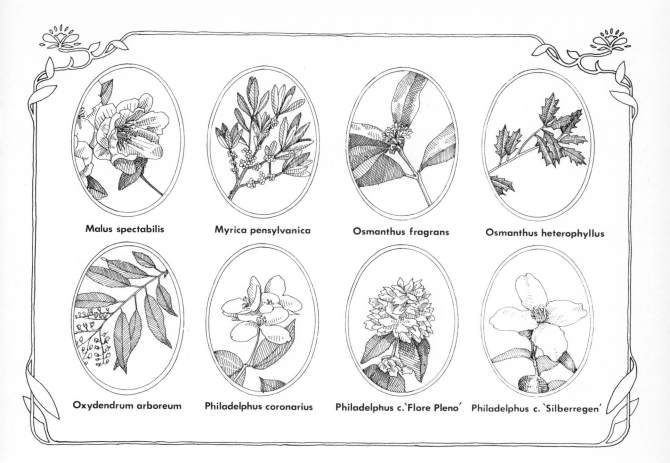

Malus spectabilis   Myrica pensylvanica   Osmanthus fragrans   Osmanthus heterophyllus

Oxydendrum arboreum   Philadelphus coronarius   Philadelphus c. 'Flore Pleno'   Philadelphus c. 'Silberregen'

O. heterophyllus (holly-leaf osmanthus). Hardy to -5 F.; grows to 12 feet. Lovely dark-green accent.

OXYDENDRUM ARBOREUM   Sourwood
Deciduous

A deciduous small tree with narrow leaves that turn scarlet in autumn. Bell-shaped flowers in clusters appear at tip ends in late summer. A attractive tree that likes plenty of water and good drainage as well as an acid soil. A good all-year-round tree. Hardy to -10 F.

PHILADELPHUS   Mock orange
Deciduous

Grown for their white flowers and heady fragrance, mock oranges are vigorous and bloom when young. There are low growers and tall ones,

and most can take heavy pruning. The plants grow in almost any kind of soil. There is great variation in shape; many are sculptural and very handsome. They make excellent screens. All in all, mock orange is a very valuable group of shrubs.

P. coronarius (sweet mock orange). Hardy to -10 F.; robust, to 9 feet. Oval leaves and very fragrant white flowers.
  'Flore Pleno'—Double-flower form of *P. coronarius.*
  'Silberregen'—Upright, narrow grower. Fragrant flowers.

P. lemoinei. Hybrid; hardy to -5 F. Grows to 8 feet, with single or double white flowers.
  'Belle Etoile'—Single flowers.

P. virginalis. Hybrid; hardy to -5 F. Grows to 9 feet, with single or double white flowers.
  'Glacier'—Double blooms.

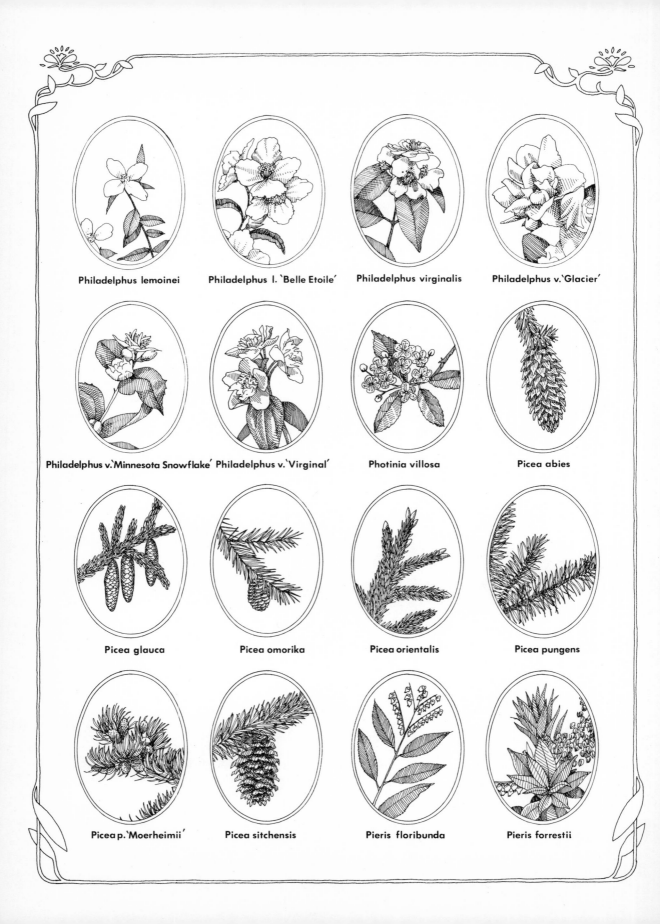

Philadelphus lemoinei

Philadelphus l. `Belle Etoile´

Philadelphus virginalis

Philadelphus v.`Glacier´

Philadelphus v.`Minnesota Snowflake´  Philadelphus v.`Virginal´

Photinia villosa

Picea abies

Picea glauca

Picea omorika

Picea orientalis

Picea pungens

Picea p.`Moerheimii´

Picea sitchensis

Pieris floribunda

Pieris forrestii

'Minnesota Snowflake'—Double fragrant flowers.

'Virginal'—Fast grower. More suited for cut flowers.

PHOTINIA VILLOSA Photinia

Deciduous

Sometimes classed as a shrub, other times as a small tree, Photinia grows to about 15 feet and has lovely pale-gold foliage which turns scarlet in autumn. Bright-red fruits follow to decorate the tree through fall and early winter. A handsome addition to the garden. Hardy to -20 F.

PICEA Spruce

Evergreen

Young spruce trees make a pretty picture in the landscape, but mature ones generally lose their lower branches and become unsightly. Because most spruces grow to about 100 feet, they are not for the small garden. Still, there are some good evergreens in the group.

P. abies (Norway spruce). Hardy to -35 F.; pyramidal growth to 150 feet. Dark-green needles.

P. glauca (white spruce). Hardy to -35 F.; pyramidal growth to 90 feet. Bluish green needles.

P. omorika (Serbian spruce). Hardy to -10 F.; grows to 90 feet. Densely pyramidal. Bluish green needles.

P. orientalis (Oriental spruce). Hardy to -10 F.; densely pyramidal growth to 150 feet. Glossy dark-green, evergreen needles that are the smallest of all the spruces.

P. pungens (Colorado spruce). Hardy to -35 F.; stiff pyramidal branches. Grows to 100 feet.

'Moerheimii'—Very blue foliage.

P. sitchensis (Sitka spruce). Hardy to -5 F.; tall pyramidal tree to 140 feet, with wide-spreading branches. Bright-green and silvery needles.

PIERIS

Evergreen

These handsome shrubs have excellent form and foliage all year, always look good. Plants are related to rhododendrons and require an acid soil and excellent drainage. Protection from wind will assure maximum beauty. Choose a place for Pieris that is somewhat shady. Very useful garden plants.

P. floribunda. Hardy to -10 F.; grows to 6 feet. Dull gray-green leaves with blossoms in clusters.

P. forrestii (Chinese pieris). Hardy to -10 F.; grows to 8 feet. Denser than *P. floribunda.*

P. japonica (Japanese andromeda). Hardy to -20 F.; grows to 7 feet. Creamy-white fragrant flowers in drooping clusters.

'Chandleri'—Colorful foliage turning from pink to green.

P. phillyreifolia. Hardy to 10 F.; grows to 15 feet. Vinelike with white vase-shaped flowers in early spring.

PINUS Pine

Evergreen

These are good evergreens; some are better than others for ornamental use. Needles vary in length on each tree, but they are usually from 2 to 12 inches long. Some pines are dwarfs in stature and very picturesque; others are open and shrubby in habit; and still others are rounded. Many pines look graceful in the landscape, but a few are quite stiff and not desirable, so make selection carefully.

P. cembra (Swiss stone pine). Hardy to -35 F.; slow-growing, dense pyramid to 60 feet. Not often seen, but good.

P. contorta (beach pine). Hardy to 10 F.; round-top, dense-headed tree to 30 feet. Dense, dark-green needles.

P. densiflora (Japanese red pine). Hardy to -10 F.; horizontal branching tree to 100 feet. Bright, bluish green needles.

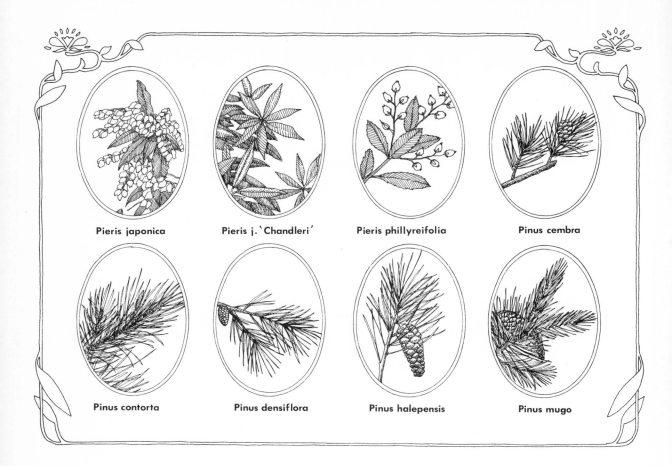

Pieris japonica   Pieris j. 'Chandleri'   Pieris phillyreifolia   Pinus cembra

Pinus contorta   Pinus densiflora   Pinus halepensis   Pinus mugo

P. halepensis (Aleppo pine). Hardy to 20 F.; open, rounded-top tree to 60 feet. Light-green needles.

P. mugo (Swiss mountain pine). Hardy to 10 F.; pyramidal growth to 15 feet. Dark-green, stout needles.

P. nigra (Austrian pine). Hardy to -10 F.; dense, stout pyramid to 90 feet. Very dark-green needles.

P. parviflora (Japanese white pine). Hardy to -5 F.; dense pyramid to 90 feet. Wide-spreading branches, with bluish green to gray needles.

P. peuce (Macedonian pine). Hardy to -10 F.; dense pyramidal growth to 60 feet. Evergreen needles.

P. pinea (Italian stone pine). Hardy to 20 F.; broad and flat-topped to 80 feet. Gray-green, stiff needles.

P. resinosa (red pine). Hardy to -35 F.; spreading tree to 75 feet. Dark-green needles.

P. strobus (eastern white pine). Hardy to -20 F.; rounded or pyramidal growth to 150 feet. Blue-green, soft needles.

P. sylvestris (Scotch pine). Hardy to -35 F.; pyramidal when young, round-topped when mature. Grows to 75 feet. Bluish green, stiff needles.

P. thunbergiana (thunbergii) (Japanese black pine). Hardy to -5 F.; dense spreading habit. Grows to 90 feet. Dark-green, stiff needles.

PITTOSPORUM

Evergreen

A group of attractive shrubs (some trees) known for their ornamental foliage and form. Good all-around plants, pittosporums grow well in full sun to half-shade; and while they do withstand drought if necessary, plants prefer good moisture. Some have fragrant flowers, and plants are

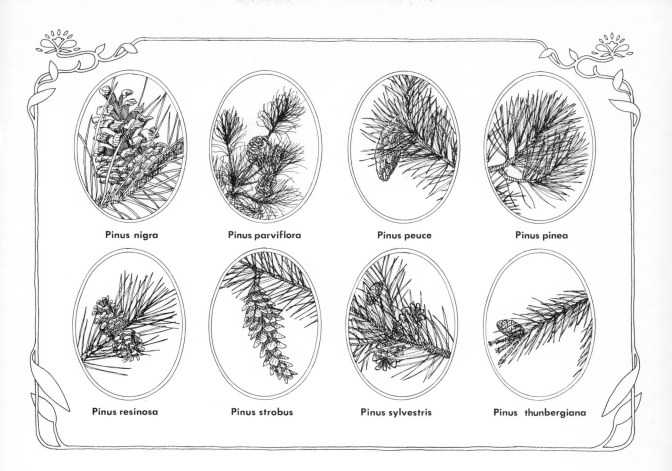

Pinus nigra   Pinus parviflora   Pinus peuce   Pinus pinea

Pinus resinosa   Pinus strobus   Pinus sylvestris   Pinus thunbergiana

good for hedges if clipped or left natural as background material.

P. crassifolium. Hardy to 30 F.; grows to 8 feet. Gray-green leaves, dense.
   'Variegatum'—Variegated leaf type.

P. tobira. Hardy to 30 F.; grows to 15 feet. Leaves are shiny green; nice branching habit.

P. undulatum. Hardy to 30 F.; grows to 30 feet. Leaves dark green and wavy edges. Dome shaped growth.

PLATANUS   Plane tree/Sycamore
Deciduous

Handsome trees with maplelike leaves, fast-growing. While some do reach considerable heights, most used in gardens do not exceed 50 feet. In winter, sycamores have a nice sculptural effect in the landscape and generally are not fussy about growing conditions. Most species, though, have their problems with insects and disease, but these can be controlled with proper spraying.

P. acerifolia (London plane tree). Hardy to -10F.; grows to 100 feet. Maplelike leaves and nice spreading habit.

P. hispanica. Hardy to -20 F.; grows to 100 feet. Branching, handsome, long-lived tree.

P. orientalis (Oriental plane tree). Hardy to -5 F.; grows to 80 feet. Maple leaves, broad round head. Nice shade tree.

POPULUS   Poplar
Deciduous

Poplars have long been favorite trees because they grow fast, so fast that roots can cause havoc with sidewalks and sewer lines. Some are excel-

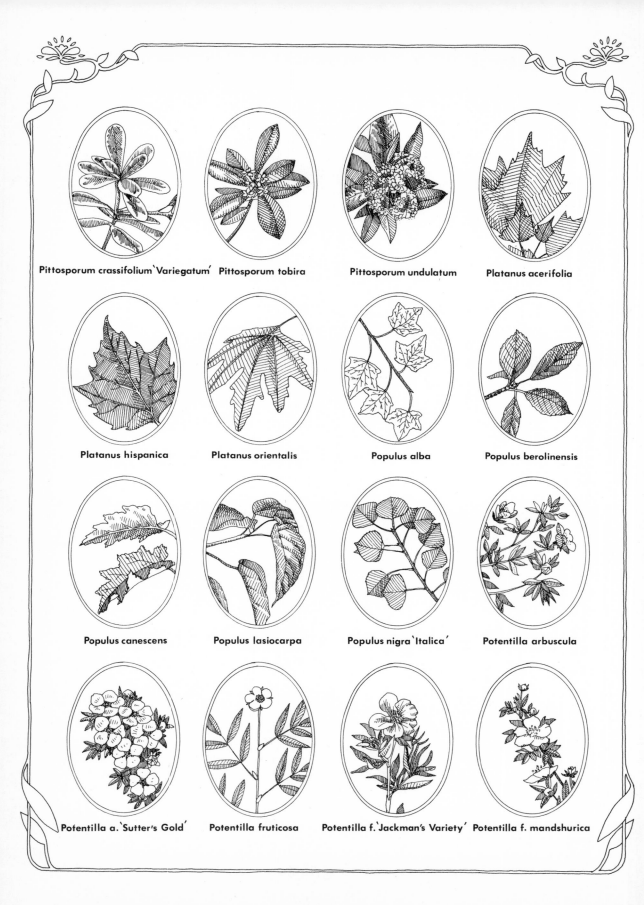

Pittosporum crassifolium `Variegatum` Pittosporum tobira Pittosporum undulatum Platanus acerifolia

Platanus hispanica Platanus orientalis Populus alba Populus berolinensis

Populus canescens Populus lasiocarpa Populus nigra `Italica` Potentilla arbuscula

Potentilla a. `Sutter's Gold` Potentilla fruticosa Potentilla f. `Jackman's Variety` Potentilla f. mandshurica

lent, however, for their ornamental value and because they need little maintenance. Most can tolerate drought if necessary as well as hot summers. A good garden tree where fast "fillers" are needed.

P. alba (white poplar). Hardy to -35 F.; grows to 90 feet. Leaves grayish green; good fall color.

P. berolinensis (Berlin poplar). Hardy to -50 F.; grows to 150 feet. Glossy coarse leaves; highly invasive root system. Use only where there is plenty of space.

P. canescens (gray poplar). Hardy to -20 F.; grows to 90 feet. Nice habit, small leaves.

P. lasiocarpa (Chinese poplar). Hardy to -5 F.; grows to 60 feet. Large bright-green leaves; round-headed habit. Very pretty.

P. nigra 'Italica' (Lombardy poplar). Hardy to -35 F.; grows to 80 feet. Dense habit; lovely columnar shape. Short-lived.

POTENTILLA   Cinquefoil

Deciduous/Evergreen

Handsome shrubs that are becoming more popular in gardens recently. Most plants are varieties of P. *fruticosa* with flowers in several colors—white to pale yellow to orange. Most potentillas are low-growing, bloom a long time, and will withstand poor soil conditions if necessary. All need a good sunny location.

P. arbuscula (bush cinquefoil). Hardy to -35 F.; grows to 4 feet. One-inch yellow or white flowers.
   'Sutter's Gold'—Beautiful yellow.

P. fruticosa (cinquefoil). Hardy to -50 F.; grows to 4 feet. Popular species with many varieties.
   'Jackman's Variety'

P. f. mandshurica. Hardy to -35 F.; grows to 2 feet. A good dwarf form with white flowers.

P. tridentata. Hardy to -20 F.; grows to 3 feet. Yellow flowers in summer.

PRUNUS   Plum

Deciduous/Evergreen

There are many ornamental species (spring flowers) and fruit trees among the deciduous and evergreen plums. Most plums are hardy. Because plums are susceptible to borers, scale, and cankerworm, you should spray plants once a year. The beautiful flowers range from ¼ to 2 ½ inches. The evergreen shrubs are ideal for shade, hedges, and screens.

P. alleghaniensis. Hardy to -10 F.; grows to 15 feet. White flowers turn pink. Narrow, sharply toothed leaves.

P. americana. Hardy to -10 F.; grows to 20 feet. Long leaves, white flowers. Good red plum fruits.

P. angustifolia. Hardy to -5 F.; grows to 12 feet. Shining red twigs, white flowers.

P. besseyi (Western sand cherry). Hardy to -20 F.; grows to 7 feet. Very sweet black fruit.

P. cistena (purpleleaf sand cherry). Hardy to -35 F.; grows to 7 feet. Blackish purple cherries, colorful reddish flowers.

P. dulcis. Hardy to -20 F.; grows to 20 feet. A favorite flowering spring tree.

P. glandulosa (dwarf flowering cherry). Hardy to -35 F.; grows to 7 feet. Showy pink or white flowers. Red cherries.

P. laurocerasus (cherry laurel). Hardy to -10 F.; grows to 30 feet. Creamy-white flowers in summer; grows easily.

P. maritima (beach plum). Hardy to -20 F.; grows to 10 feet. Oval leaves, white flowers, and red berries.

P. nigra. Hardy to -10 F.; grows to 40 feet. Stiff habit; white flowers.

P. subhirtella (rosebud cherry). Hardy to -5 F.; grows to 30 feet. One of the earliest cherries to bloom and one of the most floriferous. Single light-pink flowers.

P. susquehanae (sand cherry). Hardy to -20 F.; grows to 4 feet. Short oval leaves, white flowers. Likes moisture.

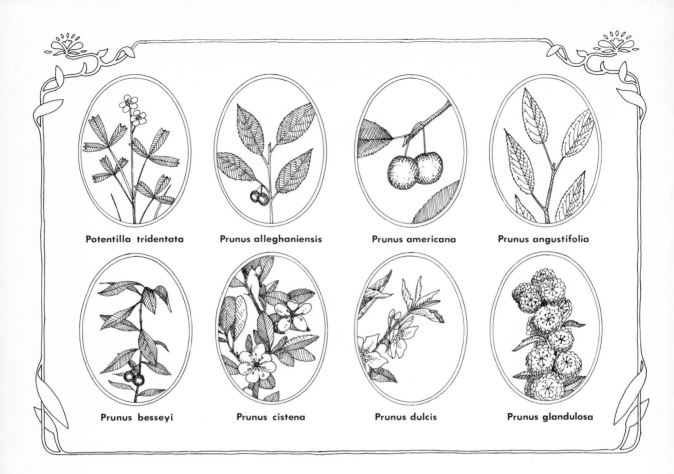

Potentilla tridentata · **Prunus alleghaniensis** · **Prunus americana** · **Prunus angustifolia**

Prunus besseyi · **Prunus cistena** · **Prunus dulcis** · **Prunus glandulosa**

P. tomentosa (Nanking cherry). Hardy to -35 F.; grows to 9 feet. White flowers, tasty scarlet cherries.

P. triloba (flowering almond). Hardy to -10 F.; small, to 12 feet. Red fruit, pink-white flowers.

P. virginiana (chokecherry). Hardy to -5 F.; grows to 12 feet. Smooth, shining green leaves, white flowers. Dark-red harsh-tasting fruit.

P. angustifolia. Hardy to -10 F.; grows to 12 feet. Prostrate branches; orange berries.

P. atalantioides. Hardy to -5 F.; grows to 15 feet. Lustrous green leaves, small bright-red berries.
  'Aurea'—Somewhat taller; more robust.

P. coccinea 'Lulandi'. Hardy to -20 F.; grows to 10 feet. Bright red-orange berries.

P. rogersiana 'Flava'. Hardy to 5 F.; grows to 10 feet. Bright-green leaves; orange-red berries.

PYRACANTHA Fire thorn

Evergreen

Large group of decorative shrubs grown widely for their bright fruits and evergreen foliage. Fast-growing, Pyracantha has a variety of landscape uses and is of easy culture. All species have glossy green leaves; most have thorns. Plants do best in full sun; can be trained to almost any shape. Dozens of uses in the garden.

QUERCUS Oak

Evergreen/Deciduous

These sturdy, long-lived trees are valued for their autumn color; the majority of oaks reach large size. The wood is strong and does not split easily. Only the North American species have autumn color; European ones do not. The oaks are fine shade trees for large properties, but they can

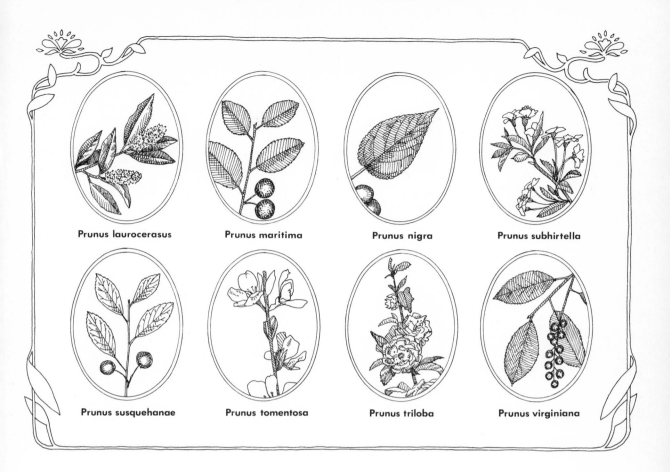

Prunus laurocerasus

Prunus maritima

Prunus nigra

Prunus subhirtella

Prunus susquehanae

Prunus tomentosa

Prunus triloba

Prunus virginiana

have their problems—borers, oak gall, various leaf diseases—and must have routine spraying.

Q. alba (white oak). Hardy to -10 F.; broad, open-crowned tree to 90 feet. Bright-green leaves, turning purple in fall. Deciduous.

Q. cerris (turkey oak). Hardy to -5 F.; broad pyramidal growth to 100 feet. Dark-green leaves. Deciduous.

Q. coccinea (scarlet oak). Hardy to -10 F.; open-branching habit that can reach 75 feet. Leaves turn brilliant red in autumn. Deciduous.

Q. frainetto (Hungarian oak). Hardy to 10 F.; grows to 130 feet. Dull-green leaves. Deciduous.

Q. ilex (holly oak). Hardy to 20 F.; round-headed habit. Grows to 60 feet. Dark-green foliage that is yellow underneath. Evergreen.

Q. laurifolia (laurel oak). Hardy to 5 F.; dense, round-topped oak. Grows to 60 feet. Dark-green leaves. Semi-evergreen.

Q. palustris (pin oak). Hardy to -20 F.; pyramidal in shape, with drooping branches. Grows to 75 feet. Red leaves in autumn. Deciduous.

Q. robur (English oak). Hardy to -5 F.; broad-headed tree, with open habit. Grows to 150 feet. No autumn color. Deciduous.

Q. virginiana (live oak). Hardy to 5 F.; grows to 60 feet. Wide-spreading tree; leaves small and narrow. Evergreen.

RHODODENDRON Rhododendron/Azalea
Evergreen/Deciduous

A group of many ornamental woody plants—rhododendrons with broad evergreen leaves, and azaleas with small leaves—rhododendrons are evergreen, semi-evergreen, or deciduous. The flowers of both types of plants are well-known; and when in bloom, plants are a striking display. Both kinds of plants thrive in an acid soil and

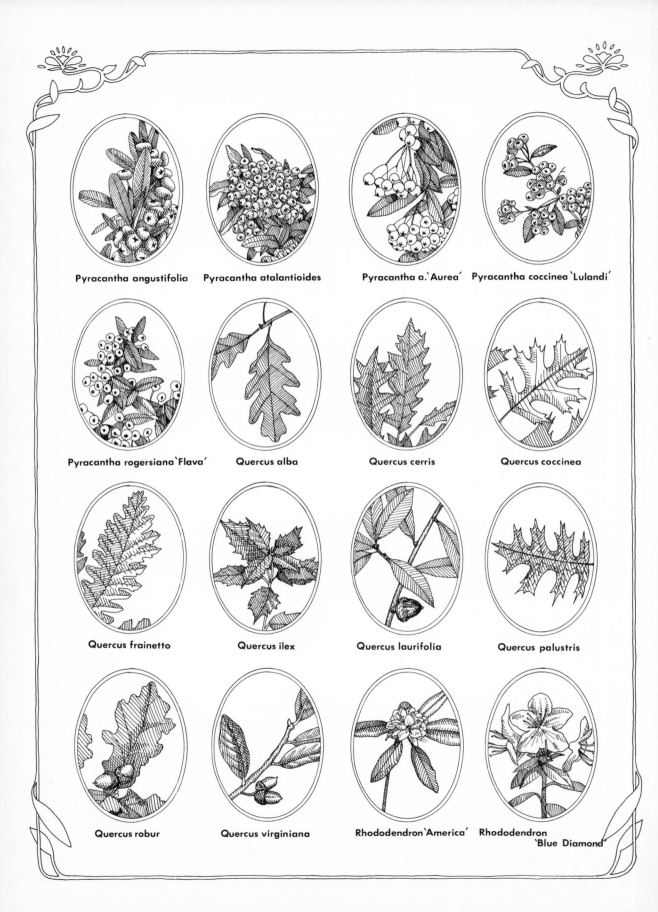

Pyracantha angustifolia

Pyracantha atalantioides

Pyracantha a. 'Aurea'

Pyracantha coccinea 'Lulandi'

Pyracantha rogersiana 'Flava'

Quercus alba

Quercus cerris

Quercus coccinea

Quercus frainetto

Quercus ilex

Quercus laurifolia

Quercus palustris

Quercus robur

Quercus virginiana

Rhododendron 'America'

Rhododendron 'Blue Diamond'

need plenty of water. The rhododendrons dislike hot summers and drying winds and need a partially shaded place with only a little sun. On the other hand, the azaleas can take more sun; the deciduous types need cooler winters than the evergreen azaleas.

Plant rhododendrons in early spring while they are blooming; plant deciduous azaleas when they are dormant unless they are in cans. Plant the evergreen azaleas any time of the year, except in late spring and summer, when buds for the following year are developing.

Rhododendrons and azaleas are shallow-rooted, so dry conditions injure them. Keep the soil moist, especially in early summer, when new growth is forming. Use an acid-type fertilizer as specified on the container. Always remove decayed blooms from rhododendrons so that seed does not develop.

There are low-growing, spreading, and tall rhododendrons; species and hybrids by the hundreds; so make selections carefully. Azaleas, too, are offered in many varieties: some for mild climates, others for areas with severe winters, and still others for in-between areas. Check with your local nurseryman.

R. 'America'—Fine red flowers; floriferous.

R. 'Blue Diamond'—Dark purple-blue blooms.

R. 'Britannia'—Bright crimson-red flowers.

R. 'Cadis'—Fragrant large light-pink flowers.

R. calophytum Hardy to 20 F.; grows to 15 feet. Flowers in large clusters; white or pale pink with crimson blotch.

R. 'Cecile'—Deep-salmon flowers with yellow tinge.

R. 'Christmas Cheer'—Dazzling pink flowers.

R. 'Crest'—Beautiful primrose-yellow blooms.

R. 'Elizabeth'—Large bright rose-pink flowers.

R. 'Fedora'—Small bright-pink flowers.

R. 'Kings Pink Glow'—Large pink blooms.

R. 'Knapp Hill Hybrid'—Orange or yellow-orange flowers.

R. laetevirens. Hardy to -20 F.; grows to 4 feet. Small pink flowers. Evergreen.

R. luteum. Hardy to -10 F.; grows to 12 feet. Yellow fragrant flowers. Deciduous.

R. mucronulatum (Korean rhododendron). Hardy to -15 F.; grows to 5 feet. Purple flowers; deciduous.

R. 'Nancy Waterer'—Golden-yellow flowers; deciduous.

R. obtusum. Hardy to -5 F.; grows to 3 feet. Orange to red flowers. Semi-evergreen.

R. 'Pink Pearl'—A very fine pink form.

R. roseum elegans (rose-shell rhododendron). Hardy to -20 F.; grows to 9 feet. Fragrant pink flowers.

R. schlippenbachii (royal azalea). Hardy to -20 F.; grows to 4 feet. Large rose-pink flowers. Splendid. Deciduous.

R. strigillosum. Hardy to -10 F.; grows to 20 feet. brilliant scarlet flowers. Evergreen.

R. 'Susan'—Lavender-blue flowers.

R. vaseyi (pink-shell azalea). Hardy to -10 F.; grows to 9 feet. Rose-pink flowers. Deciduous.

R. wardii. Hardy to -10 F.; grows to 10 feet. Splendid yellow-flowered species.

R. yedoense. Hardy to -5 F.; grows to 5 feet. Purple flowers.

ROBINIA Locust

Deciduous

A group of trees or shrubs that has attractive foliage and white or pink flowers in early summer. Fast-growing robinias will tolerate heat and almost any soil. Good small plants for the garden.

R. hispida (rose acacia). Hardy to -10 F.; grows to 7 feet. Oval leaves and lovely rose flowers.

R. nana. Hardy to -10 F.; grows to 10 feet. Small-leaved shrub.

R. pseudoacacia (black locust). Hardy to -10 F.; grows to 70 feet. Fast-growing tree with thorny branchlets; white fragrant flowers.

R. viscosa. Hardy to -10 F.; grows to 40 feet. A tree with fine pink flowers in May and June.

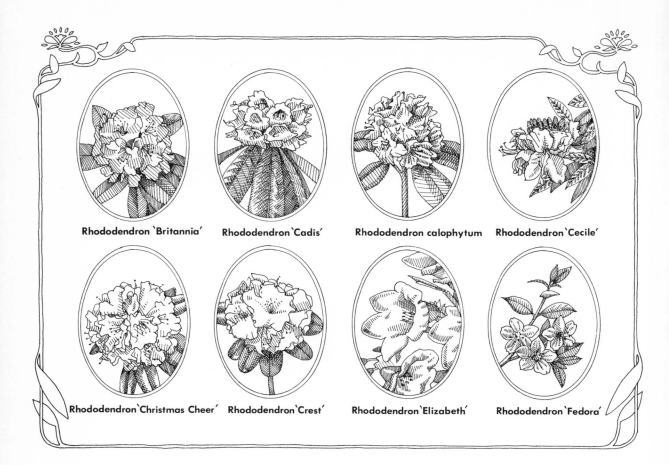

Rhododendron 'Britannia' Rhododendron 'Cadis' Rhododendron calophytum Rhododendron 'Cecile'

Rhododendron 'Christmas Cheer' Rhododendron 'Crest' Rhododendron 'Elizabeth' Rhododendron 'Fedora'

ROSA Rose

Deciduous/Evergreen

Without doubt roses are the most popular garden flower, and their value is well-known. Besides the traditional "old roses," there are thousands of hybrids—teas, floribundas, grandifloras—and ample information on them; all require a definite program of maintenance to keep them at their best. The native or wild roses are easier to grow and do not have as many problems as the hybrids. Many wild species can be grown as hardy shrubs for almost all-year color. They have single or double flowers in a range of colors, pure white to pale yellow to pink and the reddest purple. Roses vary greatly in size, will grow in a poor soil if necessary, and do not need a great deal of attention. The hybrids certainly have their place in the garden, but the wild or shrub roses have immense interest, too, and should be grown more.

R. bracteata 'Mermaid'. Hardy to 10 F.; grows to 40 feet. Fine single yellow flowers, 5 inches across.

R. centifolia 'Muscosa' (moss rose). Hardy to -10 F.; grows to 6 feet. Prickly stems. Intensely fragrant pink, white, or red flowers.

R. 'Charlotte Armstrong'—Blood-red flowers.
R. 'Elizabeth of Glamis'—Deep-salmon flowers. Favorite.

R. foetida. Hardy to -35 F.; grows to 10 feet. Dark-green smooth leaves and single yellow flowers.

B. gallica (French rose). Hardy to -10 F.; grows to 4 feet. Smooth green leaves, red or purple flowers. Deciduous.

R. Golden Rambler'—Blooms in early summer and spring with fragrant yellow flowers.

R. 'Golden Slippers'—Red-yellow flowers; vigorous.

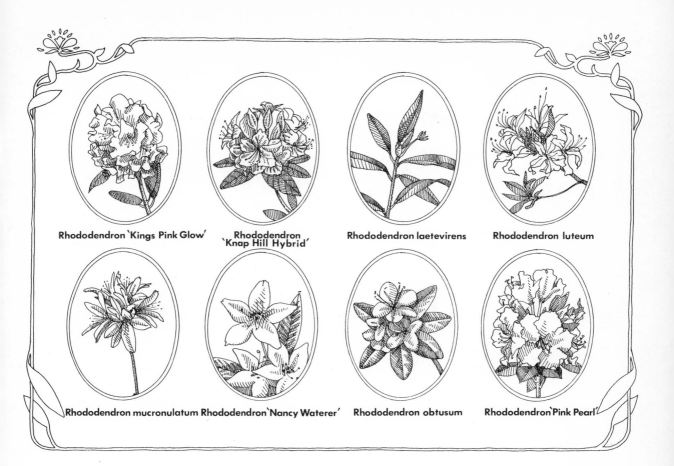

Rhododendron 'Kings Pink Glow'   Rhododendron 'Knap Hill Hybrid'   Rhododendron laetevirens   Rhododendron luteum

Rhododendron mucronulatum   Rhododendron 'Nancy Waterer'   Rhododendron obtusum   Rhododendron 'Pink Pearl'

R. hugonis (Father Hugo's rose). Hardy to -35 F.; grows to 8 feet. Deep-green leaves; bright-yellow flowers. Deciduous.

R. moyesii (Moyes rose). Hardy to -5 F.; grows to 9 feet. Single blood-red flowers.

R. multiflora (Japanese rose). Hardy to -35 F.; grows to 10 feet. Clustered flowers are small, white. Deciduous.

R. 'New Dawn'—One of the best climbers; pink flowers.

R. 'Royal Highness'—Large light-pink fragrant flowers.

R. rugosa (rugosa rose). Hardy to -35 F.; vigorous grower to 6 feet. Glossy green leaves, single or double flowers in a wide range of colors.

R. spinosissima (Scotch rose). Hardy to -10 F.; grows to 3 feet. Single pink, white, or yellow flowers.

R. 'Sutter's Gold'—Beautiful golden-yellow flowers.

SALIX Willow

Deciduous

The deciduous willows like water and moist conditions. Although the weeping willow is certainly graceful and lovely, remember that in many regions willows are troubled with insects and disease and have weak wood that cracks easily.

S. babylonica (Babylon weeping willow). Hardy to -5 F.; long, pendulous branches. Grows to 30 feet. Fine-textured foliage; best of the willows.

S. bebbiana. Hardy to 5 F.; grows to 40 feet. Oval leaves.

S. caprea (goat willow). Hardy to -10 F.; small tree, to 27 feet. Dark-green, broad branches.

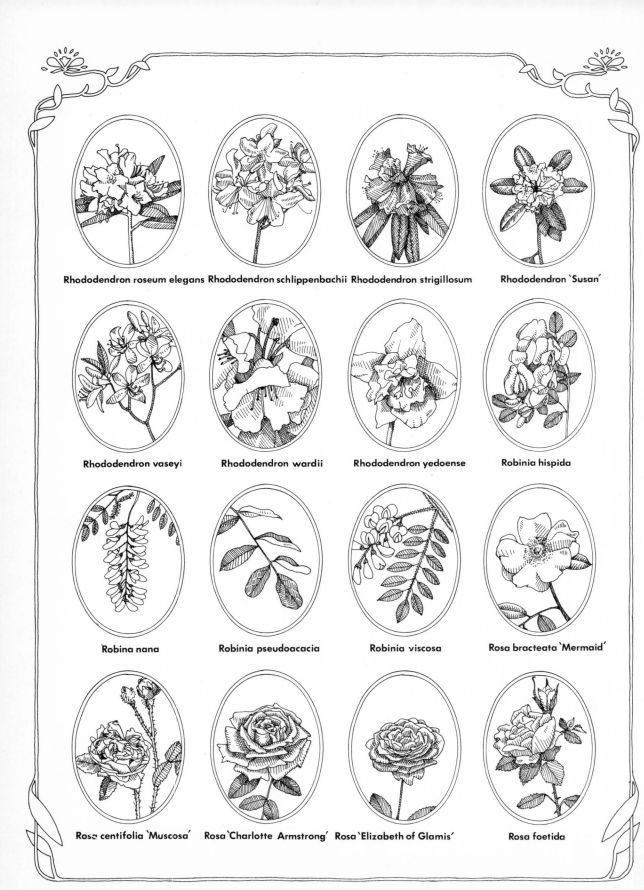

Rhododendron roseum elegans Rhododendron schlippenbachii Rhododendron strigillosum Rhododendron 'Susan'

Rhododendron vaseyi Rhododendron wardii Rhododendron yedoense Robinia hispida

Robina nana Robinia pseudoacacia Robinia viscosa Rosa bracteata 'Mermaid'

Rosa centifolia 'Muscosa' Rosa 'Charlotte Armstrong' Rosa 'Elizabeth of Glamis' Rosa foetida

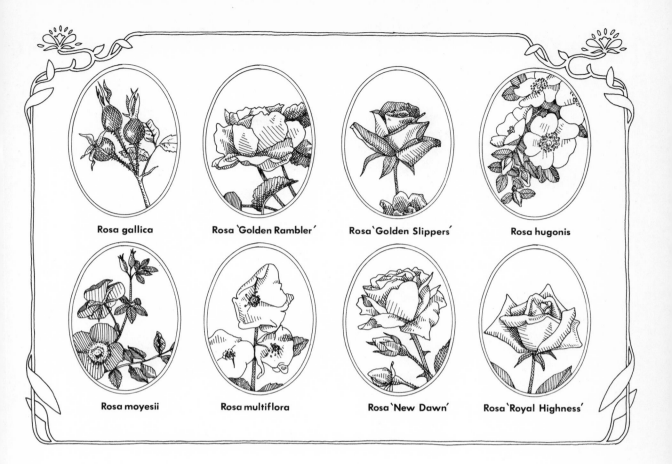

Rosa gallica   Rosa 'Golden Rambler'   Rosa 'Golden Slippers'   Rosa hugonis

Rosa moyesii   Rosa multiflora   Rosa 'New Dawn'   Rosa 'Royal Highness'

S. chrysoloma. Hardy to -10 F.; grows to 70 feet. Golden-yellow foliage; handsome.

S. discolor (pussy willow). Hardy to -20 F.; grows to 20 feet. Bright-green leaves.

S. fragilis. Hardy to -35 F.; grows to 60 feet. Long leaves, toothed and bright green. Brittle twigs.

S. lucida. Hardy to -35 F.; grows to 20 feet. Oval shiny leaves, finely toothed.

S. matsudana 'Tortuosa' (corkscrew willow). Hardy to -20 F.; upright pyramidal growth to 50 feet. Bright green, narrow leaves.

SAMBUCUS   Elderberry

Deciduous

These fast-growing shrubs (some trees) are not overly popular in gardens because they are large and grow rampant unless pruned. Still, they do make good hedges and grow in almost any soil with little care other than pruning. The fruit of the American elder is popular for preserves and wine. The red elder is pretty in fruit too. Improved varieties of each type are offered with larger flowers, and for quick cover elderberries do have their uses.

S. canadensis (American elder). Hardy to -35 F.; grows to 12 feet. Blue to black berries and white flowers.

S. racemosa (red elder). Hardy to -20 F.; grows to 12 feet. Yellow fruit and pretty golden foliage.

SOPHORA

Deciduous/Evergreen

Graceful shrubs, sophoras grow in almost any soil that drains well and still are handsome. Plants bear sweet-pea-shaped flowers followed by pods, and some plants are evergreen, others deciduous. Flowers are violet blue or yellow and generally

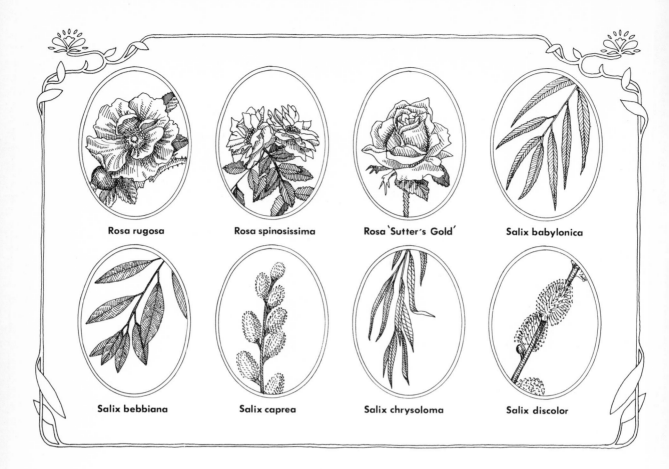

Rosa rugosa Rosa spinosissima Rosa 'Sutter's Gold' Salix babylonica

Salix bebbiana Salix caprea Salix chrysoloma Salix discolor

fragrant. Foliage is in the shape of leaflets and is quite pretty. In general plants are slow-growing; make good garden background.

S. microphylla. Hardy to -20 F.; grows to 40 feet. Small leaflets, yellow flowers. Evergreen.

S. secundiflora (Texas mountain laurel). Hardy to -5 F.; grows to 20 feet. Upright treelike grower with violet flowers in early spring. Evergreen.

S. tetraptera. Hardy to 10 F.; grows to 40 feet. Plants grow into narrow trees, yellow flowers in spring. Usually drops leaves.

SORBUS   European mountain ash

Deciduous

Trees of moderate to rapid growth with a spreading habit; foliage dull green, gray green beneath, and turns yellow in fall. Flowers are borne in late spring, followed by orange berries.

Plants can take sun or part shade. Good ornamental trees for a colorful spot of interest. Sorbus does, however, have one serious drawback; it is attacked by borers, especially in eastern gardens.

S. americana (American mountain ash). Hardy to -10 F.; grows to 30 feet. Small leaflets, tiny flowers.

S. aucuparia (European mountain ash). Hardy to -35 F.; grows to 40 feet. Small white flowers in May; bright red berries in fall. Good tree.

S. cashmariana (Kashmir mountain ash). Hardy to -10 F.; grows to 40 feet. A beautiful tree with lovely pink flowers and red fruit.

S. cuspidata. Hardy to -10 F.; grows to 20 feet. Creamy-white flower clusters.

S. intermedia. Hardy to -10 F.; grows to 30 feet. Foliage grayish green. Nice small tree.

Salix fragilis

Salix lucida

Salix matsudana 'Tortuosa'

Sambucus canadensis

Sambucus racemosa

Sophora microphylla

Sophora secundiflora

Sophora tetraptera

Sorbus americana

Sorbus aucuparia

Sorbus cashmariana

Sorbus cuspidata

Sorbus intermedia

Sorbus vilmorinii

Spiraea billiardii

Spiraea bumalda 'Anthony Waterer'

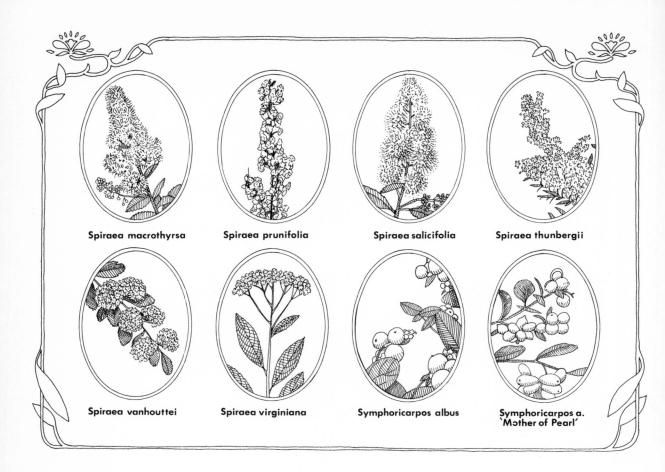

Spiraea macrothyrsa

Spiraea prunifolia

Spiraea salicifolia

Spiraea thunbergii

Spiraea vanhouttei

Spiraea virginiana

Symphoricarpos albus

Symphoricarpos a. 'Mother of Pearl'

S. vilmorinii (mountain ash). Hardy to -5 F.; grows to 20 feet. Small white flowers in spring; red berries that mature to white. Good for small garden.

SPIRAEA Spirea

Deciduous

Deciduous spireas, with their red or white flowers, are versatile plants that add a high note of outdoor color. There are two groups: spring-blooming and summer-blooming. Some spireas have a lovely branching habit and are small; others reach 15 feet. Most are vigorous, not particular about soil conditions or demanding about light. Spireas grow in sun or light shade; in general, they need little pruning and are not bothered by insects. Summer bloom comes at a time when few other woody plants are in color, making spireas especially worthwhile.

S. billiardii (billiard spirea). Hybrid; hardy to -10 F. Arching branches, to 6 feet, and tiny bright-rose flowers.

S. bumalda 'Anthony Waterer'. Hardy to -5 F.; grows to 2 feet. Narrow, oval leaves and bright red blooms.

S. macrothyrsa. Hardy to -20 F.; grows to 6 feet. Horizontal branching plant with pink flowers.

S. prunifolia (bridal-wreath spirea). Hardy to -10 F.; grows to 9 feet. Leaves turn orange in fall. Double white flowers.

S. salicifolia. Hardy to -10 F.; grows to 6 feet. Double-toothed, long, dark-green leaves. Pale rose or rose-white flowers.

S. thunbergii (Thunberg spirea). Hardy to -10 F.; grows to 5 feet. Leathery branchlets and single pure-white flowers.

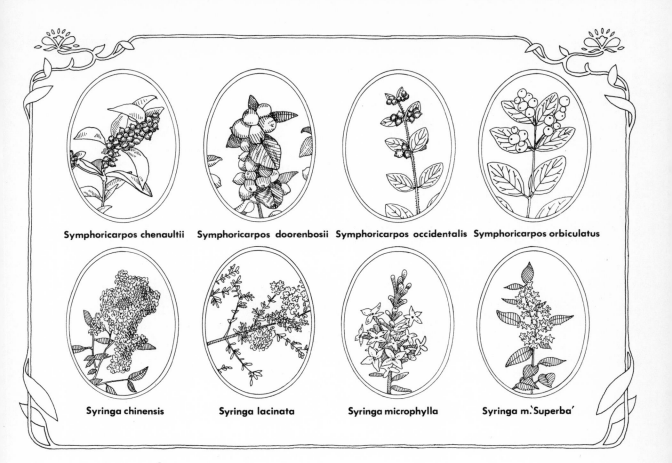

Symphoricarpos chenaultii   **Symphoricarpos doorenbosii**   **Symphoricarpos occidentalis**   **Symphoricarpos orbiculatus**

Syringa chinensis   **Syringa lacinata**   **Syringa microphylla**   **Syringa m.'Superba'**

S. vanhouttei. Hardy to -10 F.; grows to 6 feet. Graceful arching habit and profuse white flower clusters. The most valued spirea.

S. virginiana. Hardy to 10 F.; grows to 5 feet. A slender-branching shrub.

SYMPHORICARPOS   Snowberry

Deciduous

A group of ornamental shrubs with handsome growth habit and pink-tinged or white flowers in clusters. The berrylike fruits are attractive and splendid color for fall. Most plants are low-growing and tough so they can withstand neglect if necessary. Most have a pretty arching habit and make fine garden accents especially valued where horizontal mass is needed.

S. albus (snowberry). Hardy to -5 F.; grows to 6 feet. Pink flowers in May or June and white

berries in the fall. Very handsome.
   'Mother of Pearl'—pale pink.

S. chenaultii (coralberry). Hardy to -10 F.; grows to 3 feet. Red fruits in fall make this an effective shrub.

S. doorenbosii. Hardy to -10 F.; grows to 10 feet. Dark-green leaves; large red berries.

S. occidentalis. Hardy to -35 F.; grows to 5 feet. Oval grayish green leaves, pink flowers.

S. orbiculatus (Indian currant). Hardy to -50 F.; grows to 6 feet. Inconspicuous flowers and lovely red berries in fall. Plant spreads rapidly.

SYRINGA   Lilac

Deciduous

All homeowners have a spot in their hearts and in their gardens for fragrant lilacs. There are at least 250 named varieties offered today. Basically, lilacs are vigorous upright shrubs valuable not only for their flowers but also for use as screens and hedges. They are easily grown in almost any kind of soil, but they have a slight preference for a lime-type soil. Some lilacs do have insect trouble, but there are many new types that are resistant to pest and disease. Lilacs grow vigorously from the base, and pruning is important to keep them healthy. Flowers become less numerous and smaller if suckers take away plant strength. Lilacs can stand severe pruning in early spring and still have a good growing season. However, for best results, prune lilacs this way: take out one-third of the old stems of mature plants one year, another third the next year, and the remaining third year; then the plants will always appear handsome.

S. chinensis (Chinese lilac). Hybrid; hardy to -5 F.; grows to 15 feet. Fine-textured foliage and fragrant rose-purple flowers.

S. lacinata (cut-leaf lilac). Hardy to -5 F.; open growth to 6 feet. Rich green foliage and fragrant pale lilac flowers.

S. microphylla (littleleaf lilac). Hardy to -5 F.; grows to 6 feet. Pale lilac flowers.
    'Superba'—Single pale-pink flowers.

S. oblata dilatata (Korean early lilac). Hardy to -20 F.; grows to 12 feet. Nice autumn color. Pink flowers; earliest lilac to bloom.

S. reflexa alba. Hardy to -20 F.; grows to 12 feet. Upright grower; pale-pink flowers.

S. velutina (Korean lilac). Hardy to -20 F.; grows to 20 feet. Pinkish or bluish lavender flowers.

S. vulgaris (common lilac). Hardy to -10 F.; bulky shrub to 20 feet. Fragrant lilac flowers. Many varieties.
    'Clarke's Giant'—Large flower form.

TAXUS   Yew

Evergreen

These are dark-green evergreen trees and shrubs that thrive in almost any type of soil, making them a good choice where soil is poor. The plants are tough and can take neglect. Many yews make excellent hedges and screens and plants bear bright-red fruits in fall. Most yews are slow-growing and in general good sturdy trees.

T. baccata (English yew). Hardy to -5 F.; grows to 60 feet. Branching habit; dark-green needles.
    'Fastigiata Aureomarginata' (golden Irish yew)—Upright growth; golden-yellow needles.

T. b. stricta (Irish yew). Hardy to -5 F.; grows to 60 feet. Very upright in habit.

T. cuspidata (Japanese yew). Hardy to -10 F. grows to 50 feet. Dark-green needles.
    T. c. capitata. Hardy to -10 F.; grows to 20 feet. Fine red berries in fall.

T. media 'Hicksii'. Hardy to -10 F.; grows to 40 feet. Columnar or pyramidal in habit.

THUJA   Arborvitae

Evergreen

Generally with flat leaves, arborvitaes are quite shrubby and somewhat pyramidal in shape. None tolerate dry conditions; they prefer moisture at the roots and in the air. A few arborvitaes are unsatisfactory because their leaves turn brown in winter. Still, these are attractive trees and well worth their space in the garden. Generally, plants are slow-growing.

T. occidentalis 'Douglasi Pyramidalis'. Hardy to -35 F.; columnar growth to 60 feet. Bright-green to yellow-green needles.
    T. o. fastigiata. More narrow and columnar than *T. occidentalis.*

T. plicata (giant arborvitae). Hardy to -5 F.; narrow form to 180 feet. Scalelike foliage that does not turn brown in winter.

T. standishii (Japanese arborvitae). Hardy to -10 F.; grows to 40 feet. Very spreading habit. Handsome.

TILIA   Linden

Deciduous

Lindens make stellar trees and probably the best for shade. They have handsome heart-shaped

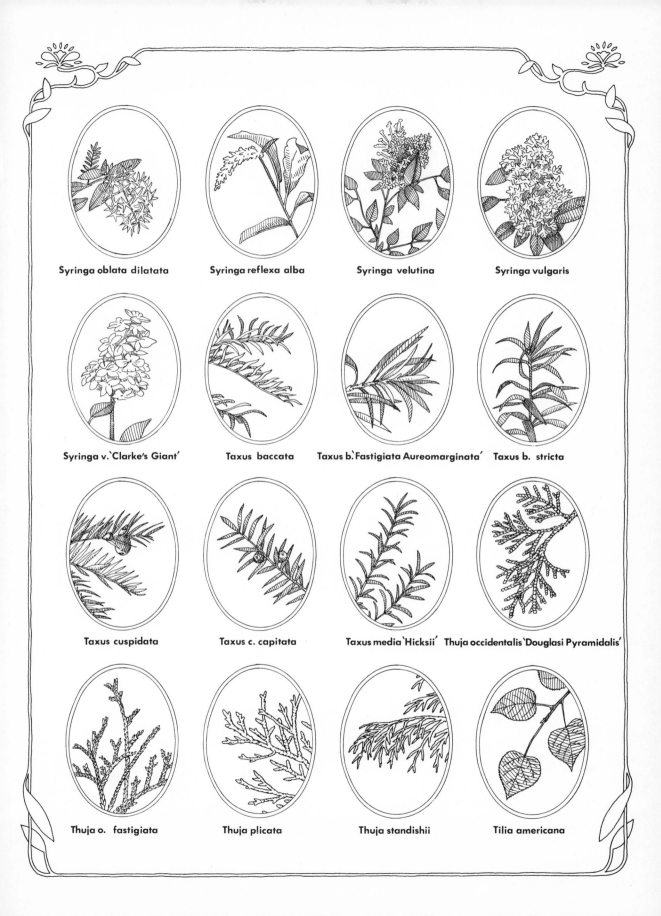

Syringa oblata dilatata

Syringa reflexa alba

Syringa velutina

Syringa vulgaris

Syringa v. 'Clarke's Giant'

Taxus baccata

Taxus b. 'Fastigiata Aureomarginata'

Taxus b. stricta

Taxus cuspidata

Taxus c. capitata

Taxus media 'Hicksii'

Thuja occidentalis 'Douglasi Pyramidalis'

Thuja o. fastigiata

Thuja plicata

Thuja standishii

Tilia americana

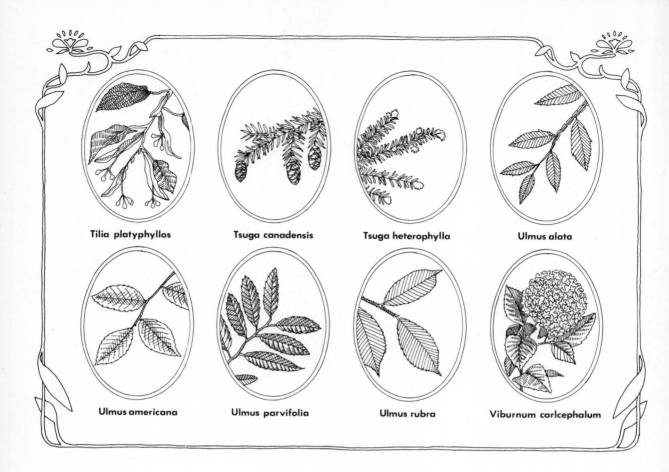

Tilia platyphyllos

Tsuga canadensis

Tsuga heterophylla

Ulmus alata

Ulmus americana

Ulmus parvifolia

Ulmus rubra

Viburnum carlcephalum

leaves and lovely sweet-scented pendulous flowers in early summer. Most species are easy to grow and respond well even with minimum attention. As a group the lindens have much to offer and require very little care.

T. americana (American linden). Hardy to -35 F.; grows to 60 feet. Dark dull-green leaves.

T. platyphyllos (big-leaf linden). Hardy to -20 F.; grows to 120 feet. Small, yellowish flowers, Nice round habit.

TSUGA Hemlock

Evergreen

Narrow-leaved evergreens, the hemlocks make beautiful trees but they do require copious watering. All hemlocks withstand shade but they will grow better with some sun. The Japanese hemlock is possibly the best in the group. Trees

bear small cones but not every year; there is a wide variety of hemlocks to choose from.

T. canadensis (Canadian hemlock). Hardy to -20 F.; grows to 90 feet. Dark-green needles; slender horizontal branches.

T. heterophylla (western hemlock). Hardy to -5 F.; grows to 125 feet. Fine-textured dark-green to yellowish green foliage. Short drooping branches.

ULMUS Elm

Deciduous

A very popular group of shade trees easy to grow in any soil but unfortunately plagued by insects and disease. Still, they are so widely grown they must be included. Some are vast-growing, others of moderate growth. Elms may be columnar in growth, vase-shaped, or of weeping habit. New

Preceding page: A fine perennial display of Monarda, phlox, Achillea, delphiniums, and lilies. (Photo by Guy Burgess)

Above: A tapestry of color—delphiniums, Achillea, Shasta daisies, and Veronica—grows in this perennial garden which is good for cutting too. (Photo by Guy Burgess)

Opposite: This hillside ornamental garden is draped with lavender, alyssum, spring phlox, and snow-in-summer. (Photo by Guy Burgess)

Above: Azaleas, tulips and ranunculuses combine handsomely to create this fine ornamental flower garden. Design by Parsons. (Photo by Max Eckert)

Opposite: A formal garden beautifully maintained is always a pleasure to see. This scene relies on the greens of trees and shrubs for its beauty. Design by Bechtol. (Photo by Max Eckert)

Lupine (Russel hybrids), daisies, and phlox promise a long period of bloom.
(Photo by Guy Burgess)

Raised beds of brilliant primulas, geraniums, daffodils, and cyclamens border a free-form pool. (Photo by Max Eckert)

Against a massive tree and shrub background, iris provide a stellar display.
(Photo by Guy Burgess)

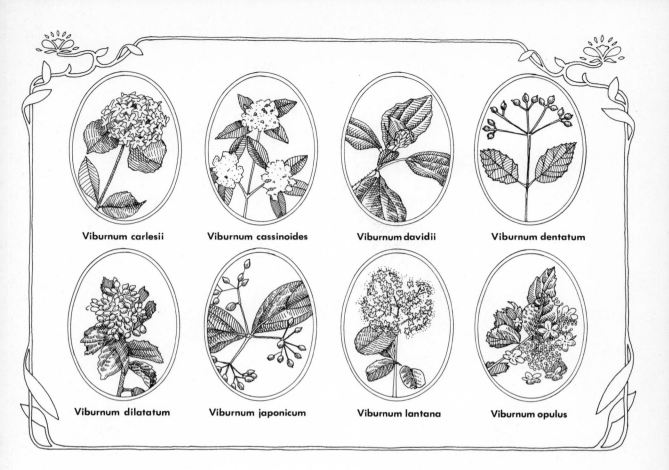

Viburnum carlesii   Viburnum cassinoides   Viburnum davidii   Viburnum dentatum

Viburnum dilatatum   Viburnum japonicum   Viburnum lantana   Viburnum opulus

varieties are appearing that are more resistant to disease than former types.

U. alata. Hardy to -10 F.; grows to 50 feet. Small leaves and flowers on pendent stalks.

U. americana (American elm). Hardy to -10 F.; grows to 120 feet. Long leaves and flowers on pendent stalks.

U. parvifolia (Chinese elm). Hardy to -20 F.; grows to 50 feet. Small-leaved, open-headed, attractive tree.

U. rubra. Hardy to -20 F.; grows to 40 feet. Small open-headed tree with large leaves.

VIBURNUM

Deciduous/Evergreen

For every season of the year there is a viburnum for the garden. Many are valued for their spring flowers, and others for their beautiful, glossy, green foliage in summer. Almost all viburnums grow without much care and are tolerant of practically any soil; many grow in light shade. Several have vivid autumn color, and a few hold berries all through winter. The leaves are deciduous or evergreen. Viburnums are rarely attacked by insects. They are dependable shrubs that offer much satisfaction for little effort.

V. carlcephalum (fragrant snowball). Hardy to -5 F.; grows to 9 feet. Dull, grayish green leaves and fragrant white flowers. Deciduous.

V. carlesii (Korean spice viburnum). Hardy to -10 F.; grows to 5 feet. Sweetly fragrant pink blooms. Deciduous.

V. cassinoides. Hardy to -35 F.; grows to 6 feet. Creamy-white clustered flowers. Vivid red autumn color.

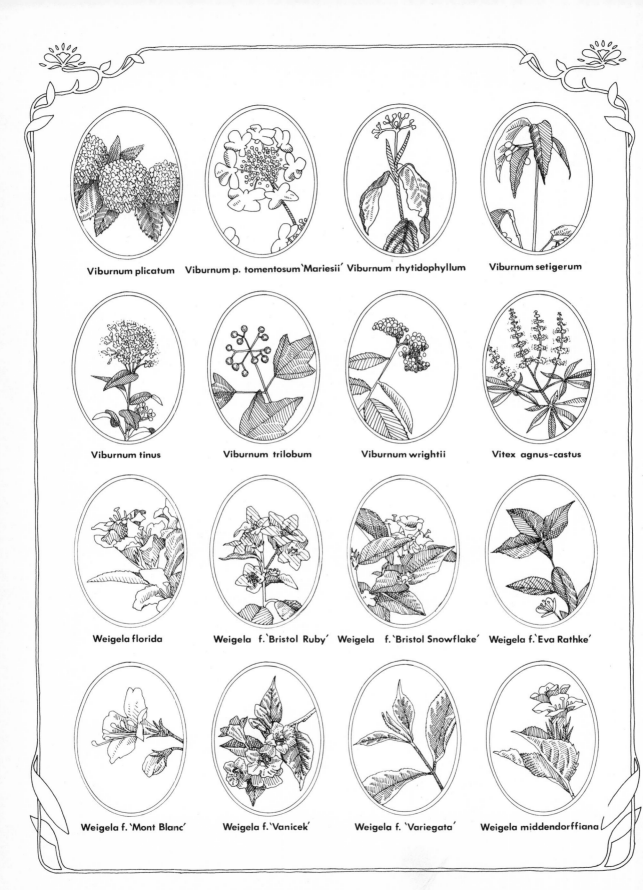

Viburnum plicatum   Viburnum p. tomentosum 'Mariesii'   Viburnum rhytidophyllum   Viburnum setigerum

Viburnum tinus   Viburnum trilobum   Viburnum wrightii   Vitex agnus-castus

Weigela florida   Weigela f. 'Bristol Ruby'   Weigela f. 'Bristol Snowflake'   Weigela f. 'Eva Rathke'

Weigela f. 'Mont Blanc'   Weigela f. 'Vanicek'   Weigela f. 'Variegata'   Weigela middendorffiana

V. davidii (David viburnum). Hardy to 5 F.; grows to 3 feet. Dark-green veined leaves and white flowers. Evergreen.

V. dentatum (arrowwood). Hardy to -35 F.; grows to 15 feet. Creamy-white flowers and glossy-red autumn color. Deciduous.

V. dilatatum (linden viburnum). Hardy to -5 F.; grows to 9 feet. Gray-green leaves and creamy-white flowers. Deciduous.

V. japonicum (Japanese viburnum). Hardy to 5 F.; grows to 6 feet. Glossy dark-green leaves and fragrant white flowers. Evergreen.

V. lantana (wayfaring tree). Hardy to -20 F.; grows to 15 feet. Oval leaves that turn red in autumn; tiny white flowers. Deciduous.

V. opulus (European cranberry bush). Hardy to -20 F.; grows to 12 feet. Maple-shaped leaves that turn red in fall; clusters of white flowers. Deciduous.

V. plicatum (Japanese snowball). Hardy to -10 F.; grows to 9 feet. Dark-green leaves and snowball clusters of white flowers. Deciduous.

V. p. tomentosum 'Mariesii'—Large handsome form.

V. rhytidophyllum (leather-leaf viburnum). Hardy to -5 F.; grows to 9 feet. Yellowish white flowers. Semi-evergreen.

V. setigerum. Hardy to -10 F.; grows to 12 feet. Dark-green leaves, white flowers. Deciduous.

V. tinus. Hardy to 5 F.; grows to 20 feet. Dense mass of leaves, white to pink flowers. Evergreen.

V. trilobum (American cranberry bush). Hardy to -35 F.; grows to 12 feet. Similiar to *V. opulus,* but not as susceptible to aphid damage. Deciduous.

V. wrightii. Hardy to -5 F.; grows to 9 feet. Bright-green leaves and small white flowers. Deciduous.

VITEX AGNUS-CASTUS   Chaste tree
Deciduous

A very pretty small tree growing to about 10 feet. Foliage is gray and the lilac flowers fragrant; they appear in August. Dies back to the ground in some regions but recovers in a short time. A nice accent in the garden; not often grown but worth the space. Hardy to 5 F.

WEIGELA
Deciduous

A group of beautiful shrubs with brilliantly colored flowers; most are vigorous growers. Some start blooming in May, with flowers until June. Plants require plenty of water and good sun; excellent drainage is essential too. Weigelas make handsome background plantings in the garden for foliage and flower, and some types are valued for their distinctive leaves of bronze.

W. florida (old-fashioned weigela) Hardy to -10 F.; grows to 6 feet. Pink to red flowers. Many varieties.
   'Bristol Ruby'—Ruby-red flowers.
   'Bristol Snowflake'—Dazzling white flowers.
   'Eva Rathke'—Bright- to deep-crimson flowers.
   'Mont Blanc'—The best white flowering form.
   'Vanicek'—Lovely red flowers.
   'Variegata'—A fancy-leaved multicolored form.

W. middendorffiana. Hardy to -10 F.; grows to 4 feet. Dense and broad shrubs. Dark-green leaves, yellow flowers.

common-name/botanical-name CROSS-REFERENCE CHART

TREES AND SHRUBS

Alabama fothergilla	*(Fothergilla monticola)*
Aleppo pine	*(Pinus halepensis)*
Allegheny serviceberry	*(Amelanchier laevis)*
American cranberry bush	*(Viburnum trilobum)*
American elder	*(Sambucus canadensis)*
American elm	*(Ulmus americana)*
American holly	*(Ilex opaca)*
American linden	*(Tilia americana)*
American mountain ash	*(Sorbus americana)*
Amur honeysuckle	*(Lonicera maackii)*
Arnold crab apple	*(Malus arnoldiana)*
Arrowwood	*(Viburnum dentatum)*
Austrian pine	*(Pinus nigra)*
Autumn elaeagnus	*(Elaeagnus umbellata)*
Babylon weeping willow	*(Salix babylonica)*
Bailey acacia	*(Acacia baileyana)*
Bayberry	*(Myrica pensylvanica)*
Beach pine	*(Pinus contorta)*
Beach plum	*(Prunus maritima)*
Bearberry cotoneaster	*(Cotoneaster dammeri)*
Berlin poplar	*(Populus berolinensis)*
Big-leaf linden	*(Tilia platyphyllos)*
Billiard spirea	*(Spiraea billiardii)*
Black locust	*(Robinia pseudoacacia)*
Blue atlas cedar	*(Cedrus atlantica 'Glauca')*
Blue gum	*(Eucalyptus globulus)*
Blue leaf wattle	*(Acacia cyanophylla)*
Bog kalmia	*(Kalmia polifolia)*

Border forsythia	*(Forsythia intermedia)*	Common catalpa	*(Catalpa speciosa)*
Bridal-wreath spirea	*(Spiraea prunifolia)*	Common lilac	*(Syringa vulgaris)*
Bush cinquefoil	*(Potentilla arbuscula)*	Common privet	*(Ligustrum vulgare)*
		Common witch hazel	*(Hamamelis virginiana)*
Canadian hemlock	*(Tsuga canadensis)*	Coralberry	*(Symphoricarpos chenaultii)*
Canoe birch	*(Betula papyrifera)*	Corkscrew willow	*(Salix matsudana 'Tortuosa')*
Cedar of Lebanon	*(Cedrus libani)*		
Chaste tree	*(Vitex agnus-castus)*	Cornelian cherry	*(Cornus mas)*
Cherry elaeagnus	*(Elaeagnus multiflora)*	Cranberry cotoneaster	*(Cotoneaster apiculata)*
Cherry laurel	*(Prunus laurocerasus)*	Cut-leaf lilac	*(Syringa lacinata)*
Chinese elm	*(Ulmus parvifolia)*		
Chinese hibiscus	*(Hibiscus rosa-sinensis)*	David viburnum	*(Viburnum davidii)*
Chinese holly	*(Ilex cornuta)*	Deodar cedar	*(Cedrus deodara)*
Chinese juniper	*(Juniperus chinensis)*	Dwarf flowering cherry	*(Prunus glandulosa)*
Chinese lilac	*(Syringa chinensis)*	Dwarf fothergilla	*(Fothergilla gardenii)*
Chinese pieris	*(Pieris forrestii)*	Dwarf hinoki cypress	*(Chamaecyparis obtusa 'Nana')*
Chinese poplar	*(Populus lasiocarpa)*		
Chinese redbud	*(Cercis chinensis)*	Eastern redbud	*(Cercis canadensis)*
Chinese witch hazel	*(Hamamelis mollis)*	Eastern red cedar	*(Juniperus virginiana)*
Chokecherry	*(Prunus virginiana)*	Eastern white pine	*(Pinus strobus)*
Cinquefoil	*(Potentilla fruticosa)*	English hawthorn	*(Crataegus oxyacantha)*
Coastal juneberry	*(Amelanchier obovalis)*	English holly	*(Ilex aquifolium)*
Colorado spruce	*(Picea pungens)*	English oak	*(Quercus robur)*
Common box	*(Buxus sempervirens)*	English yew	*(Taxus baccata)*
Common camellia	*(Camellia japonica)*	European alder	*(Alnus glutonusa)*

European ash	*(Fraxinus excelsior)*
European beech	*(Fagus sylvatica)*
European cranberry bush	*(Viburnum opulus)*
European mountain ash	*(Sorbus aucuparia)*
European silver fir	*(Abies alba)*
European white birch	*(Betula pendula) (verrucosa)*
Father Hugo's rose	*(Rosa hugonis)*
Fern-leaf maple	*(Acer japonicum 'Aconitifolium')*
Fern-leaved beech	*(Fagus sylvatica heterophylla)*
Fire thorn	(Pyracantha)
Flowering almond	*(Prunus triloba)*
Flowering ash	*(Fraxinus ornus)*
Flowering dogwood	*(Cornus florida)*
Flowering quince	*(Chaenomeles lagenaria)*
Fragrant snowball	*(Viburnum carlcephalum)*
French rose	*(Rosa gallica)*
Fringe tree	*(Chionanthus virginica)*
Full-moon maple	*(Acer japonicum)*
Giant arborvitae	*(Thuja plicata)*
Giant Burmese honeysuckle	*(Lonicera hildebrandtiana)*
Ginkgo	*(Ginkgo biloba)*

Goat willow	*(Salix caprea)*
Golden Irish yew	*(Taxus baccata* 'Fastigiata Aureomarginata')*
Golden privet	*(Ligustrum vicaryi)*
Goldenrain tree	*(Koelreuteria paniculata)*
Grape holly	*(Mahonia aquifolium)*
Gray poplar	*(Populus canescens)*
Greek juniper	*(Juniperus excelsa)*
Green ash	*(Fraxinus pennsylvanica)*
Hardy willow-leaf cotoneaster	*(Cotoneaster salicifolia floccosa)*
Hedge maple	*(Acer campestre)*
Hinoki false cypress	*(Chamaecyparis obtusa)*
Holly-leaf osmanthus	*(Osmanthus heterophyllus)*
Holly oak	*(Quercus ilex)*
Hungarian oak	*(Quercus frainetto)*
Ibolium ligustrum	*(Ligustrum ibolium)*
Indian currant	*(Symphoricarpos orbiculatus)*
Inkberry	*(Ilex glabra)*
Irish yew	*(Taxus baccata stricta)*
Italian stone pine	*(Pinus pinea)*
Japanese andromeda	*(Pieris japonica)*
Japanese arborvitae	*(Thuja standishii)*

Japanese barberry *(Berberis thunbergii)*

Japanese black pine *(Pinus thunbergiana)*

Japanese dogwood *(Cornus kousa)*

Japanese holly *(Ilex crenata)*

Japanese maple *(Acer palmatum)*

Japanese privet *(Ligustrum japonicum)*

Japanese quince *(Chaenomeles japonica)*

Japanese red pine *(Pinus densiflora)*

Japanese rose *(Rosa multiflora)*

Japanese snowball *(Viburnum plicatum)*

Japanese viburnum *(Viburnum japonicum)*

Japanese white pine *(Pinus parviflora)*

Japanese winterberry *(Ilex serrata)*

Japanese yew *(Taxus cuspidata)*

Judas tree *(Cercis siliquastrum)*

Kashmir mountain ash *(Sorbus cashmariana)*

Korean barberry *(Berberis koreana)*

Korean early lilac *(Syringa oblata dilatata)*

Korean lilac *(Syringa velutina)*

Korean rhododendron *(Rhododendron mucronulatum)*

Korean spice viburnum *(Viburnum carlesii)*

Laceleaf Japanese maple *(Acer palmatum* 'Dissectum')

Large flowering cotoneaster *(Cotoneaster multiflora)*

Large fothergilla *(Fothergilla major)*

Laurel oak *(Quercus laurifolia)*

Lawson false cypress *(Chamaecyparis lawsoniana)*

Leather-leaf viburnum *(Viburnum rhytidophyllum)*

Lemoine deutzia *(Deutzia lemoinei)*

Lilac honeysuckle *(Lonicera syringanthar)*

Lily magnolia *(Magnolia liliflora)*

Lily-of-the-valley tree *(Clethra arborea)*

Linden viburnum *(Viburnum dilatatum)*

Littleleaf box *(Buxus microphylla)*

Littleleaf lilac *(Syringa microphylla)*

Live oak *(Quercus virginiana)*

Lombardy poplar *(Populus nigra* 'Italica')

London plane tree *(Platanus acerifolia)*

Macedonian pine *(Pinus peuce)*

Magellan barberry *(Berberis buxifolia)*

Moss rose *(Rosa centifolia* 'Muscosa')

Mountain ash *(Sorbus vilmorinii)*

Mountain laurel *(Kalmia latifolia)*

Moyes rose *(Rosa moyesii)*

Nanking cherry	*(Prunus tomentosa)*	Red-twig dogwood	*(Cornus stolonifera)*
Nordmann fir	*(Abies nordmanniana)*	Rock-spray cotoneaster	*(Cotoneaster horizontalis)*
Norway maple	*(Acer platanoides)*	Rose acacia	*(Robinia hispida)*
Norway spruce	*(Picea abies)*	Rosebud cherry	*(Prunus subhirtella)*
Oak-leaved hydrangea	*(Hydrangea quercifolia)*	Rose-of-Sharon	*(Hibiscus syriacus)*
Old-fashioned weigela	*(Weigela florida)*	Rose-shell rhododenron	*(Rhododendron roseum elegans)*
Orange-eye butterfly bush	*(Buddleia davidii)*	Round-leaf Juneberry	*(Amelanchier sanguinea)*
Oriental plane tree	*(Platanus orientalis)*	Royal azalea	*(Rhododendron schlippenbachii)*
Oriental spruce	*(Picea orientalis)*	Rugosa rose	*(Rosa rugosa)*
Pacific dogwood	*(Cornus nuttallii)*	Running Juneberry	*(Amelanchier spicata)*
Peegee hydrangea	*(Hydrangea paniculata 'Grandiflora')*	Russian olive	*(Elaeagnus angustifolia)*
Persimmon	*(Diospyros virginiana)*	Sand cherry	*(Prunus susquehanae)*
Photinia	*(Photinia villosa)*	Sargent crab apple	*(Malus sargentii)*
Pink-shell azalea	*(Rhododendron vaseyi)*	Sasanqua camellia	*(Camellia sasanqua)*
Pin oak	*(Quercus palustris)*	Sauer magnolia	*(Magnolia soulangana)*
Plum	*(Prunus)*	Sawara false cypress	*(Chamaecyparis pisifera)*
Primrose jasmine	*(Jasminum mesnyi)*	Scarab Lawson cypress	*(Chamaecyparis lawsoniana 'Allumii')*
Purple beech	*(Fagus sylvatica purpurea)*	Scarlet flowering gum	*(Eucalyptus ficifolia)*
Purpleleaf sand cherry	*(Prunus cistena)*	Scarlet oak	*(Quercus coccinea)*
Pussy willow	*(Salix discolor)*	Scarlet trumpet honeysuckle	*(Lonicera brownii)*
Red-elder	*(Sambucus racemosa)*	Scotch pine	*(Pinus sylvestris)*
Red maple	*(Acer rubrum)*	Scotch rose	*(Rosa spinosissima)*
Red pine	*(Pinus resinosa)*		

Serbian spruce	(*Picea omorika*)
Shadblow serviceberry	(*Amelanchier canadensis*)
Siberian dogwood	(*Cornus alba sibirica*)
Silk tree	(*Albizzia julibrissin*)
Silver red cedar	(*Juniperus virginiana* 'Glauca')
Single-seed hawthorn	(*Crataegus monogyna*)
Sitka spruce	(*Picea sitchensis*)
Slender deutzia	(*Deutzia gracilis*)
Small-leaved cotoneaster	(*Cotoneaster microphylla*)
Snowberry	(*Symphoricarpos albus*)
Sourwood	(*Oxydendrum arboreum*)
Southern catalpa	(*Catalpa bignonioides*)
Southern magnolia	(*Magnolia grandiflora*)
Speckled alder	(*Alnus incana*)
Spreading cotoneaster	(*Cotoneaster divaricata*)
Star magnolia	(*Magnolia stellata*)
Sugar maple	(*Acer saccharum*)
Summer sweet	(*Clethra alnifolia*)
Swamp Juneberry	(*Amelanchier intermedia*)
Sweet bay	(*Magnolia virginiana*)
Sweet gum	(*Liquidambar styraciflua*)
Sweet locust	(*Gleditsia triacanthos*)
Sweet mock orange	(*Philadelphus coronarius*)

Sweet olive	(*Osmanthus fragrans*)
Swiss mountain pine	(*Pinus mugo*)
Swiss stone pine	(*Pinus cembra*)
Tatarian dogwood	(*Cornus alba*)
Tatarian honeysuckle	(*Lonicera tatarica*)
Texas mountain laurel	(*Sophora secundiflora*)
Thread cypress	(*Chamaecyparis pisifera* 'Filifera')
Thunberg spirea	(*Spiraea thunbergii*)
Tree-of-heaven	(*Ailanthus altissima*)
Tricolor beech	(*Fagus sylvatica* 'Tricolor')
Tulip tree	(*Liriodendron tulipifera*)
Turkey oak	(*Quercus cerris*)
Veitch Magnolia	(*Magnolia veitchii*)
Warty barberry	(*Berberis verruculosa*)
Wayfaring tree	(*Viburnum lantana*)
Weeping forsythia	(*Forsythia suspensa*)
Western hemlock	(*Tsuga heterophylla*)
Western sand cherry	(*Prunus besseyi*)
White ash	(*Fraxinus americana*)
White fir	(*Abies concolor*)
White ironbark	(*Eucalyptus leucoxylon*)
White oak	(*Quercus alba*)

White poplar   *(Populus alba)*

White spruce   *(Picea glauca)*

Winged euonymus   *(Euonymus alatus)*

Winterberry   *(Ilex verticillata)*

Wintergreen barberry   *(Berberis julianae)*

Winter honeysuckle   *(Lonicera fragrantissima)*

Winter jasmine   *(Jasminum nudiflorum)*

Young's weeping birch   *(Betula pendula "Youngii')*

Yulan magnolia   *(Magnolia denudata)*

7. annuals, perennials, bulbs, and vines

In Chapter 5 we mentioned some basic gardening ideas; here are some comprehensive cultural suggestions about caring for your flowers. Once plants are in the ground, they will more or less fend for themselves if absolutely necessary and will produce somewhat of a harvest of flowers. But for maximum beauty—big flowers, healthy plants—you will have to give plants some help. Watering seems to be the most important part of cultivation, with feeding (already discussed) following at its heels. Mulching and weeding, too, must be considered, and thinning and disbudding plants can be very significant, so these points are covered also.

WATERING

Watering has been previously discussed. Now we will concentrate on *how* to water. To help preserve our natural resources, it is wise to save as much water as possible; what I call intelligent watering is most important. It is hardly sensible (for your plants or your water bill) to have sprinklers going for hours if the water simply rolls off the soil and does not get to plant roots. So follow the four how-to's of watering:

1. Water soil around each plant with a slow-running hose or sprinkler. Like rain, the water will sink into the soil, with very little water being wasted. Position and set the sprinkler—no matter what kind—until you are sure the water hits the exact location. If you are growing flowers on a hill, try the plastic soil-soaker hose around the plants.

2. Most flowers need deep watering—at least 12 to 16 inches of the soil must be wet. How long will this take? It depends on the condition of your soil

and the sprinkler. Generally, under average conditions and water pressure, it takes 3 to 4 hours for water to penetrate a depth of 16 inches.

3. If possible, water early in the morning so foliage dries before evening.

4. Every so often, about twice a season, soak and soak the soil to drive out salts and excess plant-food residue. Do this in early spring before you plant the garden, and in midsummer.

CULTIVATING THE GARDEN

Every minute you spend cultivating your flower-garden plants is well worth the time because of the colorful seasonal display the flowers will provide. You can just let gardens go wild and have flowers, but this is not what you want. Nature needs a helping hand every so often, and you have to be that helping hand.

Disbudding

Disbudding certain annuals and perennials is an easy operation, yet most people simply do not do it or are not aware of how important this small task is. The removal of the first buds of the flowers (do this with your fingers or a pair of scissors) forces many plants to grow into bushier, better plants with more flowers. The plants transfer the energies spent on producing flowers to putting out side branches. These side branches will, of course, all bear flowers. Petunias and chrysanthemums especially grow bigger and better if you disbud them in the early stages.

With annuals, remove the terminal buds. With established perennials, remove the smaller, terminal side buds, *not* the *top ones*.

Cutting Back

Cutting back perennials such as Shasta daisies for a second blooming is somewhat different from disbudding. Instead of buds, remove faded flowers and part of the stem to force a second crop of blooms. The removal of faded flowers is essential, because if you do not get them off they will start to set seed, which saps the plant of strength. If seed starts to disperse, the seedlings will interfere with the growth of the established plants.

Cutting Flowers

Cut flowers are to the soul what vegetables are to the palate. Fresh flowers save you oodles of money, will last days longer than purchased ones, prevent trips to the florist, and, of course, are a delight to look at. Many annuals and perennials last for weeks, such as lilies; petunias last about one week; and even the lowly nasturtiums make a stellar table bouquet that will last for days.

If you cut flowers properly, forget the mumbo jumbo of adding pennies, aspirins, sugar, or what have you to the water. Cut your flowers in late afternoon or early evening. Use a clean sharp knife, and do make an angle cut to allow more tissue to be exposed to the water in the vase.

After you cut the flowers, take them inside and plunge them into a bucket of tepid water until you want to use them. Arrange flowers in clean vases and keep them out of sunlight and direct heat if you want them to last a long time. Remove lower leaves so they do not decay in the water. Every other day snip off about 1 inch of the stem and change the water to keep the flowers as long as possible.

BULBS

For the gardener who wants a wealth of early spring color, plant bulbs. Merely plant bulbs in soil and cover them; that is that—no weeding, no pruning, and generally no battle with the bugs. Most of the dependable bulbs—crocus, narcissus, snowdrops—have to be planted in the fall. Later in the fall, plant tulips, hyacinths, and scillas. Plant the summer-flowering bulbs in spring, the fall-blooming bulbs in the summer, and winter-blooming plants in the late summer. Thus you can have some kind of bulb blooming in the garden almost all year. There is no reason to plant just the popular spring-flowering bulbs (beautiful though they are); also plant callas and cannas, dahlias and gladiolus for summer color.

Mail-order suppliers' and growers' catalogs list all plants with fleshy counterparts under the term bulbs. Actually, this catchall category includes bulbs, corms, tubers, and rhizomes. But no matter how you define bulbs, the makings for the flowers are already in the bulbs, and all you do is plant them.

Many of the most beautiful bulb flowers are winter-hardy—they need cold weather to grow—and can be left in the ground year after year. Other bulbs must be planted and lifted each year. The life cycle of a bulb can be stated as: (1) blooming; (2) foliage growth, which is stored in the bulb; and (3) the resting period.

Planting

First, buy top-quality bulbs only from *reputable,* trustworthy dealers. Plant bulbs in a very organic, moisture-retaining, but rapidly draining soil. Bulbs rarely live in sandy soil, although they can survive but not thrive in clayey soil. Dig round holes, making sure the bottom is concave rather than pointed; pointed holes leave an air pocket below the bulb. Plant the growing side up, that is, the pointed end or the one showing growth. Plant to the recommended depth. For example, a 3-inch depth means that the bulb's top should be 3 inches below ground level. Firm the soil over the bulb; do *not* leave it loose.

Bulbs can live off their own storehouse of food for some time, but they must be attended to when they are in active growth. Water regularly from the time they start growing and after the flowers fade. Then taper off watering *gradually.* Dormant bulbs need only the water natural conditions provide. You can, if you want, fertilize spring-flowering bulbs once a season. Definitely feed summer-blooming bulbs as soon as growth appears and again in the few weeks before they bloom. Use a balanced feeding mix that has little nitrogen.

Spring-flowering Bulbs

Spring-blooming bulbs bear color in late winter or very early spring. These hardy bulbs should be left in the ground all year. (Note: some bulbs may be hardy in one climate but not in another.) Winter aconite and dogtooth violet should be planted at the end of August or in early September, but plant the other spring bulbs in September until the ground freezes.

After spring bulbs bloom, do *not* cut off the leaves or the bulb will not regain the strength it lost from growing and blooming.

Summer-flowering Bulbs

In most of the United States, summer-flowering bulbs must be dug up in fall and stored through the winter. However, you can leave them in the ground if your area's temperatures do not drop below freezing. Some summer-flowering bulbs like tuberous begonias and Agapanthus can be started indoors and transplanted later in the garden. But plant most of these bulbs when temperatures are definitely frost-free.

Dig up summer bulbs and let them dry off in an airy place after the foliage stops growing in the fall. Cut off any foliage that has not dropped off to about 5 inches. Remove all soil from the bulbs. Store bulbs in a dry cool place (50 F.) in boxes of dry sand or peat, on open trays, or in brown paper bags.

VINES

Contemporary architecture often stresses bare expanses of walls and rather sterile lines. Vines can break up this monotonous and sometimes depressing scene, screening walls or fences or blocking out an objectionable view. Vines fit into small spaces, assume many shapes, and look breathtaking if they are the flowering kinds. For pergolas, trellises, and fences, vines are perfect plants and will quickly add color to the scene. However, as many gardeners complain, vines require constant pruning and attention. But this complaint is true only if you select the vines that are rampant growers, the ones which take over an area unless properly trained.

However, there are many vines that stay within bounds with little care. Some of the climbing vines—clematis, bougainvillea, and morning glory—can become with proper care delightful screens of living color in the garden. Vines such as stephanotis, wisteria, and sweet pea have a dainty loveliness about them, a fragile quality that is often necessary to soften harsh garden walls and house lines. And many vines, including bittersweet and pyracantha, have colorful winter berries that are indispensable in the snow landscape.

Many vines climb by means of twining stems that need support; others have tendrils or disks. Some vines have leaflike appendages that act as tendrils, grasping the object on which they grow. Vines like jasmine have long, slender, and arching stems and thus need support. Ivy geranium and trailing lantana are prostrate in growth. Along with growth habit, vines may be open and delicate or heavy with masses of foliage. Several varieties grow rapidly in a few months, but others take years to fill a space. So select vines carefully or you will have to give them constant care.

Plant woody vines in a deep planting hole to a depth of about 3 to 4 feet so the roots will have ample space to grow. Replace the dug-out soil with good topsoil, but do not include manure or fertilizers because they may burn the plants. When the plant is in place, gently tamp the earth around the collar of the plant so air pockets will not form. Water thoroughly and deeply. For the first few weeks give the plant some extra attention, that is, merely watch it to see that it is getting started. Once it is established, give the vine routine care.

Put vines in the ground at the same level at which they were growing in the nursery, and by all means try not to disturb the roots. If you keep the root ball intact, the chances of the vine becoming established with little trouble are excellent. If roots are disturbed, the vine will need more time to adjust to its new condition.

Prune, thin, and shape vines regularly to keep them looking handsome.

Flower Disease and Insect Chart

For specific insects or diseases that affect some plants follow these remedies:

Disease or Insect	Symptoms or Appearance	Control
Aster wilt (disease)	Streaks on stems; plants wilt and die.	Do not grow plants in the same soil every year. Diseased organisms live in same soil for years.
Aster yellows (virus)	Carried to chrysanthemum by leafhoppers and aphids. Stunted growth.	Ladybugs.
Bacterial leaf spot (disease)	Black spots on leaves, stems, and buds.	Bacteria overwinter in soil on dead leaves and crowns of infected plants. Keep area scrupulously clean of debris.
Bacterial wilt (disease)	Sudden wilting and death of plants.	Bacteria of disease persist in soil. Remove all parts from soil and change planting site yearly.
Basal rot (fungus)	Attacks through roots; tip on leaves.	Disease exists in soil. Plant in new areas yearly; destroy infected bulbs.
Beetle	Black or golden. Foliage chewed or with holes.	Destroy debris so pest cannot overwinter.
Black cucumber beetle	Destroys foliage.	Use potion of ground pepper and boiling water.

Disease or Insect	Symptoms or Appearance	Control
Blister beetle	Long-legged, about 1 inch long, black to gray with yellow stripes. Eats foliage and flowers.	Handpick (wear gloves), or dust with lime and flour, or spray with Malathion.
Borer	Worms. Wilted stems that topple.	Use light traps to collect borer moths.
Botrytis blight (fungus)	Small, round, orange-red spots on leaves; destroys foliage.	Select growing site with good air circulation and good drainage.
Botrytis rhizome rot (disease)	Soft, foul-smelling rot in rhizomes.	Plant only healthy rhizomes.
Caterpillars	Chewed foliage.	Stinkbugs eat caterpillar beetles in immature stage. Use ground hot pepper and water, or handpick, or spray with Malathion.
Chrysanthemum stunt (virus)	Small flowers; leaves pale green or reddish.	Disease is carried in planting stock; buy only from reputable dealers.
Color breakdown (virus)	Streaks or blotches in flower color.	Destroy any diseased plants when you see them to eliminate aphids; they spread the virus.
Crown and root rot (disease)	Destroys plant.	Sterilize soil before planting; destroy infected plants.
Cyclamen mite	White, microscopic insect. Distorted leaves; blackened buds.	Mites travel fast from plant to plant. Keep plants well spaced to avoid infestation. Use rotenone if necessary.
Damping off (disease)	Affects plants in seedling stage; stems collapse and rot off at soil surface.	Eliminate excessive moisture; water sparsely.

Disease or Insect	Symptoms or Appearance	Control
Gall midge	Slender, two-winged fly; larva forms a cone-shaped gall. Adults are tiny gnats whose only host is chrysanthemum. Twisted stems and distorted buds.	Use only clean cuttings; destroy infected plants by burning.
Gladiolus thrips	Minute insects. Distort flower buds.	Gladiolus thrips feed on host plants such as iris, lily, calendula, aster, and delphinium. Plant bulbs in early fall.
Gray mold (fungus)	Oval or circular spots on leaves.	Thin out plants; destroy infected plant parts. Afford good air circulation.
Ground mealybug	Smaller than mealybug. Lives off roots in soil.	Use healthy cuttings and plant in different locations. Dry out soil bed for 1 month.
Japanese beetle	Iridescent beetle with metallic green, copper, brown wings. Feeds on foliage and flowers.	Milky spore disease. "Doom" (trade name).
Leafhopper	Small green-yellow, wedge-shaped insects that eat foliage.	Use pyrethrum, quassia, or ladybugs.
Leaf nematode	Very tiny worm. Yellow wedge-shaped spots; leaves dry up and fall.	Remove and burn infected plant; maintain high humus soil.
Nematode	Live worms. Knots or swellings on roots.	Good humus content in soil; fungi are natural enemies of nematodes.
Petal blight (fungus; *Botrytis cinera*)	Deformed flowers.	Allow adequate ventilation in flower bed; dry out growing area.
Powdery mildew (disease)	White powdery spots on foliage.	Dry out soil somewhat; apply fungicide.

Disease or Insect	Symptoms or Appearance	Control
Rust (disease)	Brown pustules on leaves and stems.	Use resistant varieties. Maintain good humus content in soil.
Slug, snail	Eat holes in leaves; work at night.	Use Snarol without metaldehyde; try beer n small bottle caps.
Spider mite	Tiny yellow, green, or reddish spiders. Grayish speckled foliage.	Use strong pressure and spray underside of foliage with water, or spray with Dimite.
Stalk borer	Larvae in stalks; grayish brown larvae with white stripes. Wilted, fallen stalks.	Keep old stalks and weeds out of growing area. Use light traps later in year to control borer moths.
Tarnished plant bug	Tiny, oval, brownish insect; sucks juices from new shoots and buds.	Insect overwinters in weeds and debris, so keep garden clean. Use rotenone.
Violet sawfly	Bluish black larvae with white stripes. Leaves skeletonized.	Apply rotenone.
Wilt and stem rot (disease)	Decayed roots; shriveled brown stems.	Sterilize soil; use resistant strains of plants.

PLANT DICTIONARY—
annuals, perennials, bulbs, and vines

ABRONIA UMBELLATA
Pink-sand verbena

Annual
To ½ foot

Light: Sun
Water: Moderate
Bloom: Spring

Trailing plant with dense rosy-lavender flower clusters. Excellent for walkways and borders or wherever a low mass of color is needed for definition. Also good long-lasting cut flowers.

ABUTILON HYBRIDUM   **Flowering maple**
Annual
To 10 feet

Light: Shade
Water: Heavy
Bloom: Spring/Summer

Arching upright shrub. Good for background plantings or for use as a filler; attractive bell-shaped flowers in pink, white, orange, and red.

ACHILLEA   **Yarrow**

Perennial
To 4 feet

Light: Sun
Water: Moderate
Bloom: Spring/Summer

A large group of excellent garden flowers, some alpine. Flower heads are generally in clusters, with white, yellow, or rosy-red rays. Several species are excellent as cut flowers. Plants can provide brilliant displays of color when arranged in drifts. Excellent drainage required.

A. filipendulina (fern-leaved yarrow). Bright-yellow flowers.

A. millefolium (common yarrow). Flower heads small and white in clusters.

A. ptarmica (sneezewort). Flower heads white and profuse. Best for cut flowers.

A. tomentosa (woolly yarrow). Compact bright-yellow flower heads. Handsome.

Suggested Varieties:
 'Angel's Breath'
 'Coronation Gold'

ACIDANTHERA   **Abyssinian sword lily**
Corm
To 3 feet

Light: Sun
Water: Moderate
Bloom: Summer

These plants are somewhat similar to gladiolus and bear 3-inch flowers, usually scented. Plant

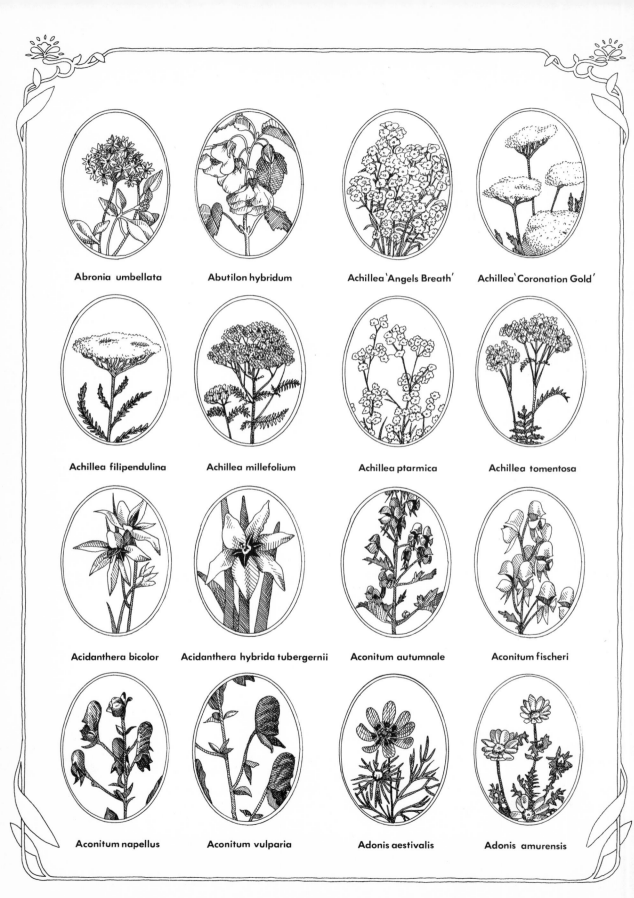

Abronia umbellata

Abutilon hybridum

Achillea 'Angels Breath'

Achillea 'Coronation Gold'

Achillea filipendulina

Achillea millefolium

Achillea ptarmica

Achillea tomentosa

Acidanthera bicolor

Acidanthera hybrida tubergernii

Aconitum autumnale

Aconitum fischeri

Aconitum napellus

Aconitum vulparia

Adonis aestivalis

Adonis amurensis

corms 3 to 4 inches deep in a bright or sunny location. Start the corms in spring. After flowers fade lift corms and store in a cool dry place until the following year, when they can be replanted. Acidantheras make good cut flowers.

A. bicolor. An upright grower with grasslike foliage and loose spikes of fragrant creamy flowers blotched with brown.

A. hybrida tubergernii. A tall grower that produces large creamy-white flowers, highly scented.

ACONITUM   Monkshood

Perennial
To 5 feet

Light: Shade
Water: Heavy
Bloom: Summer/Fall

Simple spikes of blue, lilac, or white flowers in masses make for a showy high border. Good substitute for delphinium in light shade. Flowers and roots are poisonous. Will not grow in wet soil, so good drainage is a must.

A. autumnale (autumn monkshood). Blue, lilac, or white flower spikes.

A. fischeri (azure monkshood). Violet flowers.

A. napellus (English monkshood). Blue, reddish purple, violet, or white spikes. The best-known and most poisonous species.

A. vulparia (wolfsbane). Yellow flowers.

ADONIS

Annual/Perennial
To 1 foot

Light: Sun/Shade
Water: Moderate
Bloom: Spring/Fall

Hardy garden favorites grown for their showy yellow or red flowers. These perennials are especially suited for borders and rock gardens.

A. aestivalis (summer adonis). Crimson flowers in June. Annual.

A. amurensis (Amur adonis). Yellow, white, rose, or bright-red striped flowers in February. Perennial.

A. autumnalis (autumn adonis). Intense red flowers with a black center. Annual.

A. vernalis (spring adonis). Yellow flowers in March. Perennial.

AGAPANTHUS   Lily of the Nile

Bulb
To 5 feet

Light: Sun
Water: Heavy
Bloom: Summer

Effective border plant, with star-shaped leaves and bell-shaped flowers in umbels. Protect in cold winter areas. Useful as container plants; wonderful as either fresh or dry cut flowers. Heavy feeder.

A. africanus (lily of the Nile). Deep-blue flowers, dozens to a cluster.

A. orientalis. Blue or white flowers. Bears more flowers than *A. africanus.*

Suggested Varieties:
 'Dwarf White'
 'Peter Pan'

AGERATUM
HOUSTONIANUM   Flossflower

Annual
To 2 feet

Light: Sun
Water: Moderate
Bloom: Summer

These excellent bedding flowers provide dependable summer and fall color—a lovely blue. Ageratums do fine in loamy garden soil and like

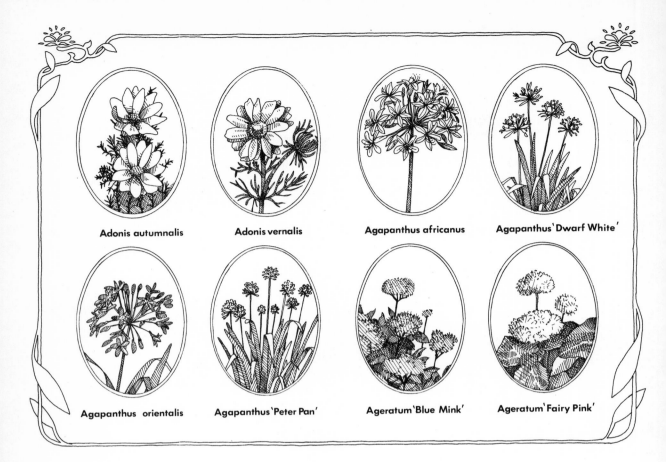

Adonis autumnalis

Adonis vernalis

Agapanthus africanus

Agapanthus 'Dwarf White'

Agapanthus orientalis

Agapanthus 'Peter Pan'

Ageratum 'Blue Mink'

Ageratum 'Fairy Pink'

lots of sun; they are especially suitable for borders or in flower beds and also make excellent cut flowers.

Suggested Varieties:
  'Blue Mink'
  'Fairy Pink'
  'Snow Carpet'

AGROSTEMMA GITHAGO Corn cockle

Annual
To 3 feet

Light: Sun
Water: Moderate
Bloom: Summer

A plant with dainty lilac-pink flowers, the corn cockle is a hardy lovely annual to brighten any garden. It grows in almost any soil and can if necessary tolerate a dry situation or one where there is excessive moisture. The wild-flower quality of the plant makes it suitable for woodland landscapes or natural flower beds.

AKEBIA QUINATA Five-leaf akebia

Vine
To 20 feet

Light: Sun
Water: Moderate
Bloom: Spring

This graceful open vine provides filtered shade or effective tracery against pillars and walls. The dainty-leaved plant is deciduous and requires annual pruning to keep it attractive; flowers are rose-purple. Fast-growing, Akebia offers a lot of green for little effort.

ALLAMANDA CATHARTICA Trumpet vine

Vine
To 10 feet

Light: Sun
Water: Moderate
Bloom: Summer

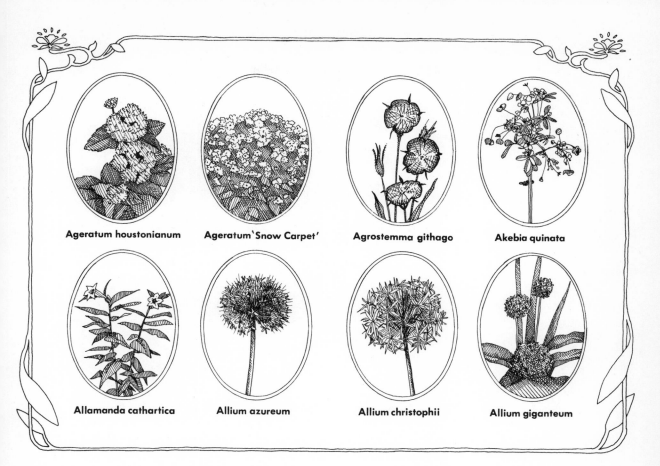

Ageratum houstonianum Ageratum 'Snow Carpet' Agrostemma githago Akebia quinata

Allamanda cathartica Allium azureum Allium christophii Allium giganteum

This is a vigorous evergreen shrubby vine with dark-green oval leaves. It is the flowers that make it a spectacular plant; they are large, golden-yellow. While Allamanda will tolerate almost any soil it must have almost all-day sun to prosper. Only suitable for all-year temperate climates.

ALLIUM   Flowering onion

Bulb
To 5 feet

Light: Sun
Water: Moderate
Bloom: Spring/Summer

Excellent for the sunny border, alliums are overlooked plants that have much beauty. The plants are easy to establish in a deep sandy loam. Plant bulbs in fall about 5 inches deep.

A. azureum. A ball of deep-blue flowers. Very pretty.

A. christophii (star of Persia). Lavender to dark-blue starlike flowers.

A. giganteum (giant onion). Bright lilac flowers in July.

A. moly (lily leek). Yellow starlike flowers in July.

A. neapolitanum (Naples onion). White flowers from March to May.

ALONSOA WARSCEWICZII   Mask-flower

Annual
To 2 feet

Light: Sun
Water: Moderate
Bloom: Summer

Covered with small red flowers, the mask-flower is a colorful spot in gardens. It likes a light sandy soil; will not grow well in hot weather. Good for cool areas where the drama of red color is needed for garden beds.

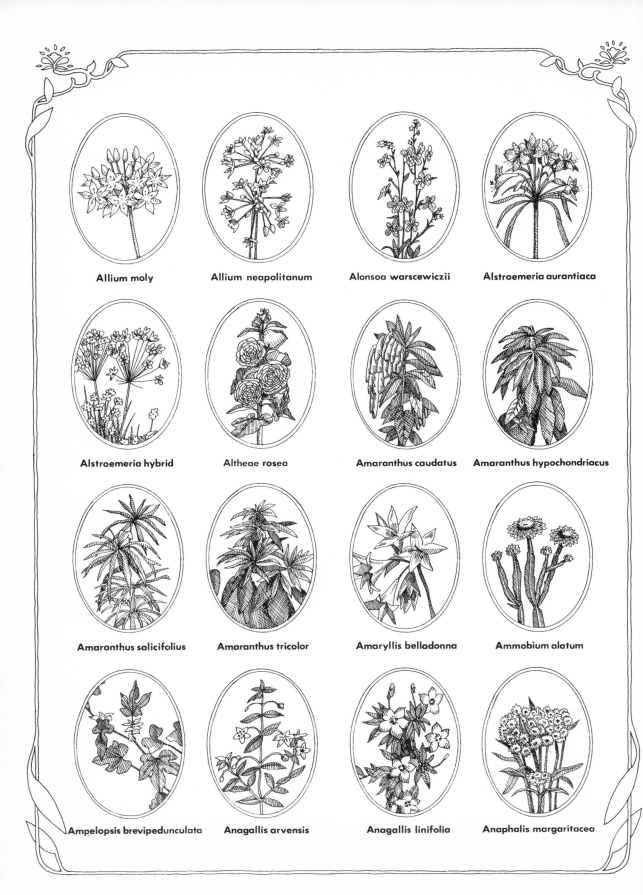

Allium moly

Allium neapolitanum

Alonsoa warscewiczii

Alstroemeria aurantiaca

Alstroemeria hybrid

Altheae rosea

Amaranthus caudatus

Amaranthus hypochondriacus

Amaranthus salicifolius

Amaranthus tricolor

Amaryllis belladonna

Ammobium alatum

Ampelopsis brevipedunculata

Anagallis arvensis

Anagallis linifolia

Anaphalis margaritacea

ALSTROEMERIA Peruvian Lily

Bulb
To 3 feet

Light: Shade
Water: Moderate
Bloom: Summer

These plants have 1½-inch flowers of red, yellow, or purple and lance-shaped leaves. Plant dormant bulbs in early spring or early fall; set them horizontally in holes 6 to 8 inches deep. Plants need good drainage and rich loamy soil. Lift bulbs after they bloom and store in cool dry place for following year. Peruvian lilies are excellent for a mass of color in the garden and also make good cut flowers.

A. aurantiaca (Peruvian lily). Bright-yellow flowers spotted brown.

A. hybrid. Lilac or bright rosy-lilac flowers striped both outside and inside.

ALTHEAE ROSEA Hollyhock

Annual
To 8 feet

Light: Sun
Water: Scant
Bloom: Summer

An erect plant with hairy, toothed, and rough leaves. Rose flowers borne on tall spikes. Hollyhocks grow in almost any soil, are hardy and fine ornamental flowers for the garden.

AMARANTHUS Tassel flower

Annual
To 4 feet

Light: Sun
Water: Moderate
Bloom: Summer

These are long-lasting flowers, and plants are easy to grow in almost any type of soil. Shrublike amaranthus plants have vividly colored tassel-like flowers, and if the plants are well placed in the garden they make a nice display.

A. caudatus (tassel flower). Red drooping flowers. Very colorful.

A. hypochondriacus (prince's-feather). Oblong leaves and deep-crimson flowers on densely packed erect spikes.

A. salicifolius (fountain plant). Multicolored drooping leaves; a rainbow of color.

A. tricolor. Purplish red leaves; bright-red flowers with red bracts.

AMARYLLIS BELLADONNA Belladonna lily

Bulb
To 2 feet

Light: Sun
Water: Moderate
Bloom: Summer/Fall

A large tender bulb. The strap-shaped leaves are produced in winter or early spring. Fragrant rose-red flowers. Draft-resistant and grow in almost any soil. Set bulb with tip just above soil line.

AMMOBIUM ALATUM Winged everlasting

Annual
To 3 feet

Light: Sun
Water: Scant
Bloom: Year-round

Oblong leaves form a rosette. Flower heads are about 1 inch across, silvery white, with many yellow tubular flowers in a loose cluster.

AMPELOPSIS BREVIPEDUNCULATA
Porcelain ampelopsis

Vine
To 40 feet

Light: Sun/Shade
Water: Heavy
Bloom: Fall (berries)

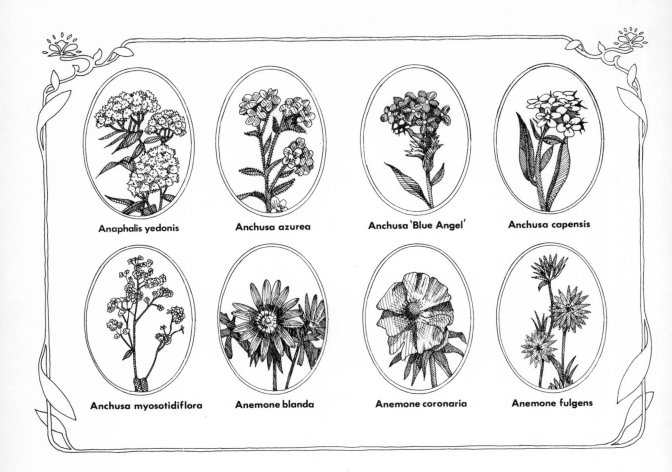

Anaphalis yedonis

Anchusa azurea

Anchusa 'Blue Angel'

Anchusa capensis

Anchusa myosotidiflora

Anemone blanda

Anemone coronaria

Anemone fulgens

This is a vigorous climber with hairy, lobed, and broadly oval leaves that are coarsely toothed. It is a dense vine that grows very fast and makes a cascade of color further enhanced by bright-blue berries in fall. A superb cover for walls and fences, and it grows in almost any kind of soil.

ANAGALLIS   Pimpernel

Annual/ Perennial
To 4 feet

Light: Sun
Water: Moderate
Bloom: Summer/Fall

Very showy flowers in vibrant colors, usually orange; makes spectacular accent in masses in garden. Slow to germinate if you sow seed. Can tolerate most soil conditions.

A. arvensis. Branching plant with oval leaves. Flower color is usually reddish pink but can vary.

A. linifolia. Perennial often grown as annual. Narrow leaves; handsome blue flowers.

ANAPHALIS

Perennial
To 3 feet

Light: Sun
Water: Moderate
Bloom: Summer

Perennials with leafy stems and tubular white flowers, anaphalis plants are excellent for borders. Plants tolerate shade but do better in sun, and soil should be evenly moist. Try these for cut flowers, too.

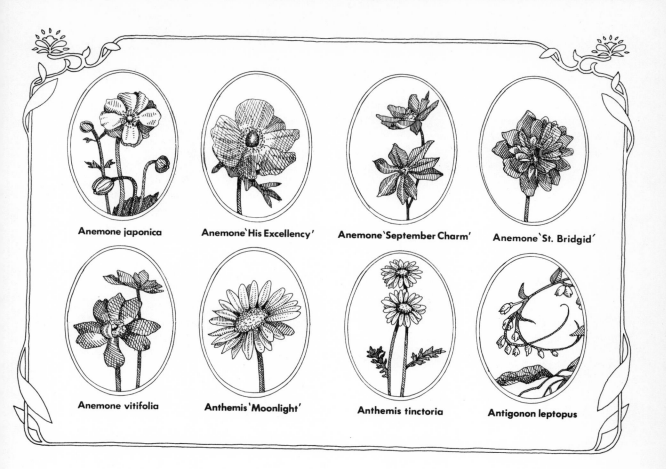

Anemone japonica

Anemone 'His Excellency'

Anemone 'September Charm'

Anemone 'St. Bridgid'

Anemone vitifolia

Anthemis 'Moonlight'

Anthemis tinctoria

Antigonon leptopus

A. margaritacea (pearl everlasting). Leaves green above, white underneath. Flower heads white.

A. yedonis. Clusters of buttonlike flowers, silvery white.

ANCHUSA   Alkanet

Perennial
To 5 feet

Light: Sun
Water: Moderate
Bloom: Summer

Lots of blue flowers in this fine group. Plants spread quickly, making a nice display. Plants need even moisture and a loamy garden soil. Excellent for flower borders or as a foil for other, less tall plants.

A. azurea. Shiny lancelike leaves; large blue to blue-purple flowers.

A. capensis (summer forget-me-not). Lancelike leaves; splendid blue flowers in July.

A. myosotidiflora (Brunnera macrophylla). Heart-shaped leaves and blue flowers with yellow throats.

Suggested Variety:
  'Blue Angel'

ANEMONE

Bulb
To 1 foot

Light: Bright/Shade
Water: Heavy
Bloom: Spring/Fall

A popular group of plants that do well in well-drained and neutral soil. Greek anemones are best for cool climates, while poppy-flowered anemones like mild winter regions. Set tubers 4 to 6 inches apart, 2 inches deep. The handsome flowers are excellent for borders or wherever dramatic color is needed.

A. blanda (Greek anemone). Deeply cut leaves; deep-blue flowers 2 inches across. Many varieties.

A. coronaria (poppy-flowered anemone). Oblong and toothed leaves; large solitary flowers of red, blue, violet, or yellow.

A. fulgens (flame anemone). Vining type with vermilion flowers 2 inches across. Needs good rich soil.

A. japonica (Japanese anemone). Purple, red, rose, or white flowers to 3 inches across.

A. vitifolia (grape leaf anemone). White flowers 2 inches across.

Suggested Varieties:
  'His Excellency'
  'September Charm'
  'St. Brigid'

ANTHEMIS   Chamomile

Perennial
To 2 feet

Light: Sun
Water: Moderate
Bloom: Summer/Fall

These floriferous easy-to-grow plants have daisylike flowers and fernlike foliage. Plants grow well in almost any soil as long as drainage is good. Anthemis plants are resistant to most insects, and even the beginner can succeed with these flowers. Fine cut flower.

A. tinctoria (golden marguerite). Branching plant with toothed leaves; flowers vary in color but are usually yellow.

Suggested Variety:
  'Moonlight'

ANTIGONON LEPTOPUS   Coralvine

Vine
To 40 feet

Light: Sun
Water: Moderate
Bloom: Summer/Fall

A very beautiful deciduous vine that does well in almost any kind of soil. Plants have heart-shaped leaves and rose-pink flowers with a deeper center. Likes high summer heat (but is not hardy in the north). The coralvine dies off somewhat through winter but recovers in early spring, so treat it as a perennial. The plant has a long season of bloom, making it a very worthwhile garden subject.

ANTIRRHINUM MAJUS   Snapdragon

Annual
To 5 feet

Light: Sun
Water: Moderate
Bloom: Spring/Summer/Fall

These popular cut flowers are available in three heights: small to 1 foot, intermediate to 2 feet, and tall to 5 feet. Plants produce many flowers and there is a good choice of color. Snapdragons need a loamy garden soil that drains well. Pinch the stems and tips when plants are about 4 inches tall to produce abundant flowers. Excellent as background in flower beds and as cut flowers.

APHANOSTEPHUS SKIRROBASIS   Lazy daisy

Annual
To 1½ feet

Light: Sun
Water: Moderate/Heavy
Bloom: Summer/Fall

This white daisy has overlapping petals branching from small yellow centers. An excellent annual in areas of dry sandy soil. Plants bloom profusely and make handsome garden accents. Not spectacular, but easy to grow.

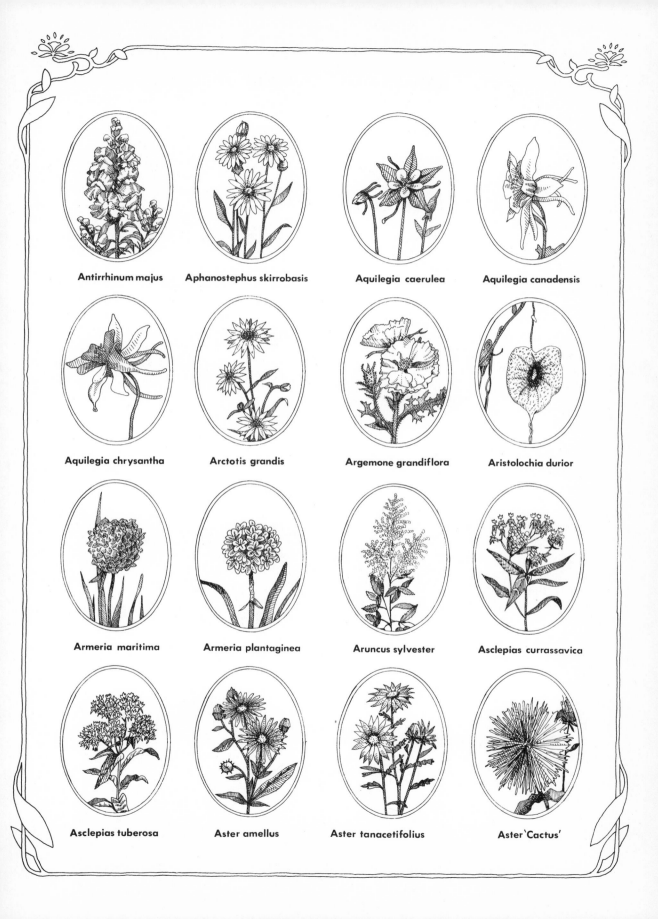

Antirrhinum majus

Aphanostephus skirrobasis

Aquilegia caerulea

Aquilegia canadensis

Aquilegia chrysantha

Arctotis grandis

Argemone grandiflora

Aristolochia durior

Armeria maritima

Armeria plantaginea

Aruncus sylvester

Asclepias currassavica

Asclepias tuberosa

Aster amellus

Aster tanacetifolius

Aster 'Cactus'

AQUILEGIA   Rocky Mountain columbine
Perennial
To 2½ feet

Light: Sun/Bright
Water: Moderate
Bloom: Spring/Summer

Columbines are pretty plants that need a well-drained soil to prosper. Flowering ends rather early in season, and faded plants should be camouflaged with other plants. Some new hybrids offer large flowers in an array of colors. Columbines are good as border plants.

A. caerulea (Rocky Mountain columbine). Large lower leaves. Flowers are 2 to 3 inches across, whitish, tinged light blue and yellow. Many varieties.

A. canadensis (common American columbine). Flowers are yellowish or tinged red on back. Use for border or in rock garden.

A. chrysantha (golden columbine). Spreading flowers are often 2 to 3 inches across, pale yellow tinged pink, with deep-yellow petals.

ARCTOTIS GRANDIS   African daisy
Annual/Perennial
To 2 feet

Light: Sun
Water: Moderate
Bloom: Summer/Fall

From South Africa, these are very colorful sun-loving plants. Excellent for splashes of color in the garden or as ground covers. Long flowering period; pale-violet blooms close in evening.

ARGEMONE GRANDIFLORA   Prickly poppy
Annual
To 3 feet

Light: Sun
Water: Moderate
Bloom: Summer

A seldom grown plant that is worthwhile because of its lovely large showy flowers, satiny white and 4 inches across. Plants need a sandy loam and good drainage to prosper, and they like heat.

ARISTOLOCHIA DURIOR   Dutchman's-pipe
Vine
To 30 feet

Light: Bright/Shade
Water: Heavy
Bloom: Summer

A popular vine with heart-shaped leaves, Dutchman's-pipe covers an area quickly and forms a dense curtain of green. The plant grows well in most soils but needs plenty of water. Will not tolerate high winds, so plant it in protected places. Treat as a perennial.

ARMERIA   Sea pink/thrift
Perennial
To 1½ feet

Light: Sun
Water: Moderate
Bloom: Summer

Nice small plants with pretty flowers; need excellent drainage. Keep on dry side and do not feed. Excellent for borders.

A. maritima. Somewhat hairy leaves and pink, rose-red, lilac, or white flowers. For border or rock garden.

A. plantaginea. Tufted, slightly hairy leaves; pink flowers.

ARUNCUS SYLVESTER   Goatsbeard
Perennial
To 7 feet

Light: Shade
Water: Heavy
Bloom: Summer

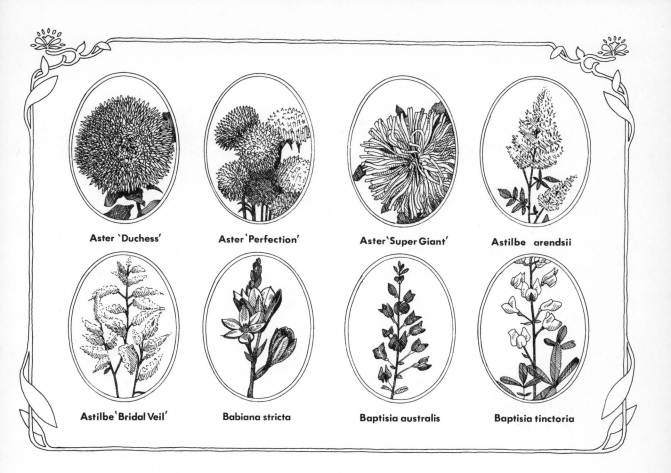

Aster 'Duchess'   Aster 'Perfection'   Aster 'Super Giant'   Astilbe arendsii

Astilbe 'Bridal Veil'   Babiana stricta   Baptisia australis   Baptisia tinctoria

An unusual plant that has flowers that somewhat resemble a goat's beard, Aruncus is desirable because it will grow well in shady locations. While it is certainly not a spectacular perennial, it is amenable to most soils and easy to grow.

ASCLEPIAS Butterfly weed

Perennial
To 5 feet

Light: Sun
Water: Moderate
Bloom: Summer/Fall

The butterfly weeds will withstand drought and that makes them valuable in many areas. Plants have decorative green leaves, and the brightly colored flowers are pretty indeed. Use the plants by themselves as accents rather than intermingled with other flowers.

A. currassavica (bloodflower). Oval narrow leaves; deep purplish-red flowers.

A. tuberosa (butterfly weed). Downy leaves, numerous bright-orange flowers in clusters. Pretty.

ASTER Michaelmas daisy

Perennial
To 5 feet

Light: Sun
Water: Moderate
Bloom: Summer

There are over 600 true species of asters in heights from 6 inches to 6 feet, and in the group are a host of well-known and very fine garden flowers. Whether used in borders or with other plants they serve a definite purpose in the garden and are highly recommended. Plants need a loamy garden soil that is evenly moist; and most species are resistant to insects, another plus.

A. amellus (Italian aster). Rough leaves; solitary purple flowers. Floriferous.

A. tanacetifolius (Tahoka daisy). Hairy foliage; violet-purple flowers.

Suggested Varieties:
  'Cactus'
  'Duchess'
  'Perfection'
  'Super Giant'

ASTILBE ARENDSII Astilbe

Perennial
To 6 feet

Light: Shade
Water: Moderate
Bloom: Summer

The colorful plumes of these garden flowers are well-known and make handsome color accents in the yard. The flowers are rosy-lilac and rise high above other plants, so use them in the background. Astilbes need a loamy soil and plenty of feeding.

Suggested Variety:
  'Bridal Veil'

BABIANA STRICTA Baboonroot

Bulb
To 1 foot

Light: Sun
Water: Moderate
Bloom: Summer/Spring

These small plants have white and blue flowers and are handsome for early spring color. Babianas grow easily and where a mass of color is needed they are fine. Use a well-drained loamy soil for them, and after plants bloom dig up bulbs and store through the winter.

BAPTISIA False indigo

Perennial
To 5 feet

Light: Sun/Shade
Water: Moderate
Bloom: Summer

Indigo will grow in almost any soil and tolerate shade if necessary. The cloverlike leaves and flowers are attractive. An easy plant to grow.

B. australis. Somewhat hairy leaves; flowers blue on stems about 1 foot long.

B. tinctoria (wild indigo). Yellow flowers on tall stalks. Pretty.

BEGONIA

To 2 feet

Light: Sun/Shade
Water: Moderate
Bloom: Summer/Fall

A large group of plants generally classified as bulbs, with the exception of the wax begonia. The begonias mentioned here should be grown in a loamy garden soil that drains readily. Plants will not tolerate excessive moisture at the roots. Grow in shade for the most part with only occasional sun. *B. pendula* and *B. tuberhybrida* are started fresh annually.

B. evansiana. Leaves are green above, red below. Many branching pink flowers. Tuberous rooted.

B. pendula (hanging begonia). A very popular and floriferous begonia in bright colors of orange, yellow, or red. Handsome. Tuberous plant.

B. semperflorens (wax begonia). Popular bedding plants. Small, with halos of white, pink, or red flowers. Fibrous-rooted.

B. tuberhybrida (tuberous begonia). Many, many varieties and forms with large or small flowers in an array of colors. Spectacular in bloom.

BELLIS PERENNIS English daisy

Perennial
To ½ foot

Light: Sun
Water: Heavy
Bloom: Spring

Long, toothed, and slightly hairy leaves, tapering at base. Solitary flower heads are 2 to 5 inches long, 1 inch across. English daisies are delightful

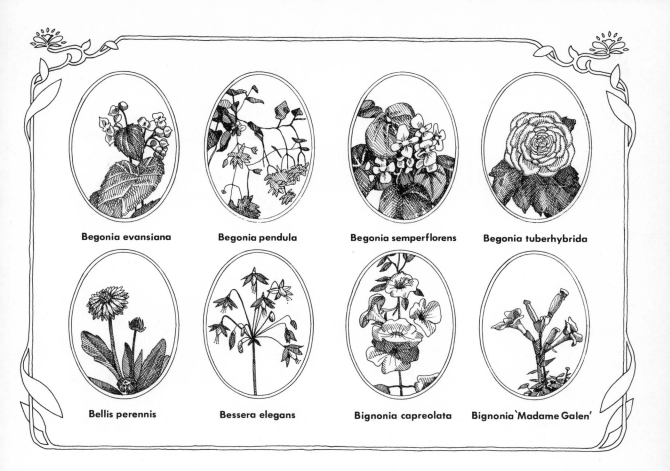

Begonia evansiana **Begonia pendula** **Begonia semperflorens** **Begonia tuberhybrida**

Bellis perennis **Bessera elegans** **Bignonia capreolata** **Bignonia 'Madame Galen'**

small plants that need a somewhat acid soil. Plants need feeding; most bloom profusely.

BESSERA ELEGANS   Coral drops

Bulb
To 3 feet

Light: Sun
Water: Moderate
Bloom: Summer

Scarlet or scarlet-and-white 1-inch long flowers. Plants are attractive in mass; set bulbs 8 inches apart, 4 inches deep. In cold winter regions, dig up and store.

BIGNONIA CAPREOLATA   Trumpet vine

Vine
To 50 feet

Light: Sun
Water: Moderate
Bloom: Summer

Sometimes called Clytostoma, trumpet vines are very handsome with pretty green leaves and large showy orange-red flowers. These plants are heavy feeders and love heat; they grow very quickly. A sandy garden soil suits them; and in any area where you want a colorful cascading plant, this is the one for you. Highly recommended.

Suggested Variety:
  'Madame Galen'

BLETILLA HYACINTHINA
Chinese ground orchid

Bulb
To 1 foot

Light: Shade
Water: Moderate
Bloom: Summer

These plants are not as easy to grow as most people think but because of the orchid tag they

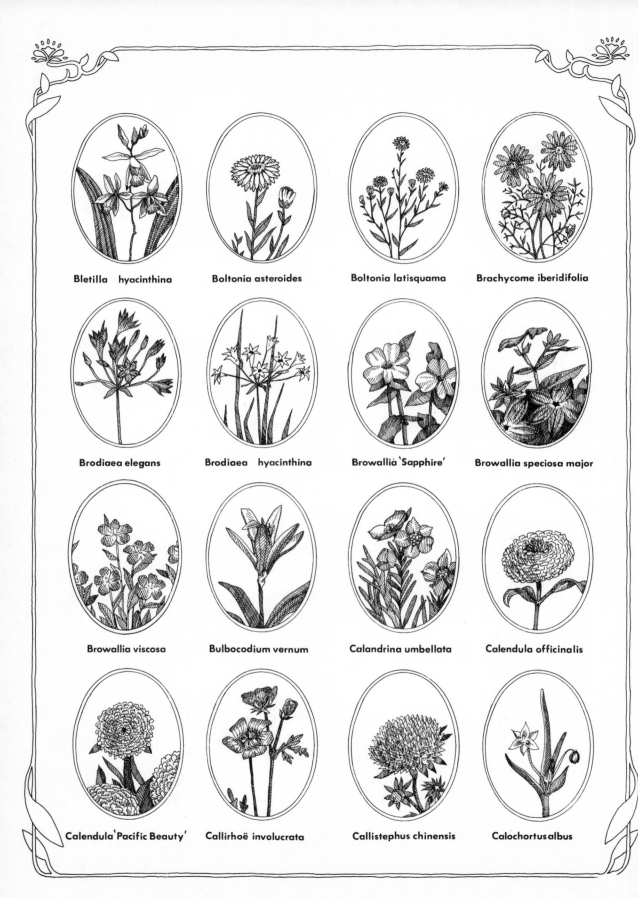

Bletilla hyacinthina

Boltonia asteroides

Boltonia latisquama

Brachycome iberidifolia

Brodiaea elegans

Brodiaea hyacinthina

Browallia 'Sapphire'

Browallia speciosa major

Browallia viscosa

Bulbocodium vernum

Calandrina umbellata

Calendula officinalis

Calendula 'Pacific Beauty'

Callirhoë involucrata

Callistephus chinensis

Calochortus albus

have wide popularity. Bletillas do have lovely amethyst-purple flowers, but plants are fragile and difficult to start and then require a long time to get established. If you want to have some ex-otica in the garden, grow these in an evenly moist, somewhat acid soil.

BOLTONIA

Perennial
To 6 feet

Light: Sun/Shade
Water: Moderate
Bloom: Summer

Rather pretty daisylike flowers with grassy foliage. Plants increase rapidly and grow easily in almost any soil in shade or sun.

B. asteroides. Broad and lancelike leaves; white to lilac or purple flowers form a starlike head.

B. latisquama (violet boltonia). Small-growing; bluish violet flower heads. More showy than *B. asteroides.*

BRACHYCOME IBERIDIFOLIA
Swan River daisy

Annual
To 1 foot

Light: Sun
Water: Moderate
Bloom: Summer/Fall

Large, slightly hairy leaves; blue or white fra-grant flowers about 1 inch across. Nice small plant where masses of color are needed. Plants like rich soil and plenty of sun.

BRODIAEA

Corm
To 3 feet

Light: Sun
Water: Scant
Bloom: Spring

These plants have grassy foliage and small white or purple flowers that are quite pretty. Plant corms 3 to 5 inches apart, 5 inches deep in a sandy garden soil and be sure drainage is excel-lent. Nice plants where you want a mass of early color.

B. elegans (harvest brodiaea). Glossy foliage, pur-ple flowers.

B. hyacinthina. White to purple flowers.

BROWALLIA

Annual
To 2 feet

Light: Sun/Shade
Water: Moderate
Bloom: Summer

Really very pretty plants, browallias are florifer-ous and produce a bounty of fine blue flowers. Plants grow easily in most soils in sun, or if necessary in a shady place. Group them for a dramatic statement in the garden.

B. speciosa major. Flowers dark purple above, lilac beneath.

B. viscosa. Oval leaves, dark-blue flowers with white centers.

Suggested Variety:
  'Sapphire'

BULBOCODIUM VERNUM
Spring meadow saffron

Bulb
To ½ foot

Light: Sun
Water: Moderate
Bloom: Spring

An early-blooming very pretty bulbous plant with graceful funnel-shaped pink flowers. Blooms appear before foliage. Plant the bulbs in early fall 4 inches apart and 3 inches deep; good under trees or in rock gardens.

CALANDRINA UMBELLATA
Rock purslane

Annual
To 3 feet

Light: Sun
Water: Moderate
Bloom: Summer

The crimson magenta flowers of rock purslane are indeed dramatic and plants are excellent for areas with dry soils. Fine for borders or rock gardens, the plants need good heat; do not feed.

CALENDULA   Pot marigold

Annual
To 2 feet

Light: Sun
Water: Heavy
Bloom: Summer

These easy-to-grow plants seem to produce a bountiful crop of flowers over a long season even for the novice gardener. In yellow or orange or shades in between, the flowers are handsome and in masses add a cheerful note to any garden. Marigolds will grow in most any type of soil as long as they have plenty of water and sun.

C. officinalis (pot marigold). Orange flowers, one following another for many weeks.

Suggested Variety:
 'Pacific Beauty'

CALLIRHOË INVOLUCRATA   Poppy
mallow

Perennial
To 3 feet

Light: Sun
Water: Moderate
Bloom: Summer

If you have a sunny place you will delight in having poppy mallows in your garden; they bloom their heads off. The flowers are red-purple and make quite a show. While the kind of soil is not of vital importance, excellent drainage is a prerequisite for a good harvest of bloom.

CALLISTEPHUS CHINENSIS   China aster
Annual
To 2 feet

Light: Sun
Water: Moderate
Bloom: Summer

This is a somewhat difficult plant to grow that requires a rich well-drained loamy soil. It is worth the effort because the flowers are highly colorful—deep violet, flaming red, brilliant yellow—and really make a fine show in masses. The China aster is prone to fungus diseases so take precautions and use a fungicide for it. Blooming season lasts only 3 to 4 weeks.

CALOCHORTUS   Mariposa lily

Bulb
To 2 feet

Light: Sun
Water: Scant
Bloom: Spring/Summer

These plants prefer a somewhat dry and sandy garden soil and produce pretty but small flowers. Plant bulbs 4 to 6 inches apart, 2 inches deep in fall. When foliage dies in summer, allow plants to rest (dig them up and store in a cool dry place). Nice border plants but not spectacular.

C. albus. Delicately fringed snow-white flowers.

C. pulchellus (golden lantern). Golden yellow pendent flowers.

C. venustus (white mariposa). Fine pale-lilac flowers. Color variable.

CALONYCTION
ACULEATUM   Moonflower

Vine
To 20 feet

Light: Sun
Water: Heavy
Bloom: Summer

Moonflowers are large, white, and very handsome, and although blooms last only a day or so

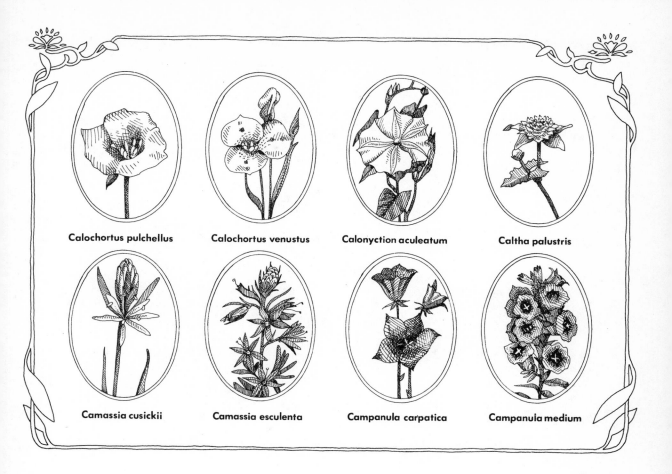

Calochortus pulchellus	Calochortus venustus	Calonyction aculeatum	Caltha palustris
Camassia cusickii	Camassia esculenta	Campanula carpatica	Campanula medium

they are followed by more flowers in quick succession. Plants grow rapidly so make excellent screens where quick cover is needed. Grow moonflowers in a loamy soil.

CALTHA PALUSTRIS   Marsh marigold
Perennial
To 2 feet

Light: Sun
Water: Heavy
Bloom: Spring

If you have a problem spot where water accumulates in the garden, give these beautiful flowers a chance to grow there and see what happens. They will thrive. With lovely heart-shaped leaves and large buttercup-yellow flowers these are ideal plants for that secret garden, and once established in a location to their liking will bloom every spring for many years.

CAMASSIA   Camas
Bulb
To 3 feet

Light: Sun
Water: Heavy
Bloom: Summer

These are nice border plants because they bring blue color to the garden. Plant bulbs in fall in well-drained soil; space them 4 inches apart, 3 inches deep. Leave in ground all year.

C. cusickii. Small pale-blue flowers.

C. esculenta. Very fine light-blue flowers.

CAMPANULA   Bellflower
Perennial/Annual
To 2 feet

Light: Bright/Shade
Water: Moderate
Bloom: Summer

There are so many Campanulas you almost need a score card to keep track of them. Some are annuals, others perennials and a few biennials. Generally, these are easy garden flowers to grow if you give them the right location—a somewhat shady (but not totally dark) area where it is moist and where soil drains readily. Some plants have large flowers, others small ones. Blue is the predominant color although there are white types, too. Campanulas are always handsome in the garden, and here are only a few of these fine plants.

C. carpatica (tussock bellflower). Broadly bell-shaped blue flowers. Handsome.

C. medium (Canterbury bells). Usually violet-blue flowers in abundance.

C. persicifolia (willow bellflower). Large blue flowers; strong grower.

CANNA HYBRIDA Canna

Bulb
To 5 feet

Light: Sun
Water: Heavy
Bloom: Summer/Fall

These popular bulbs have 4- to 5-inch blossoms ranging in color from white through shades of pink and scarlet. Canna need moist soil and can be left in the ground in winter in most areas; in severe winter climates, dig up and store bulbs.

Suggested Variety:
  'Pfitzer'

CARDIOSPERMUM   HALICACABUM
Balloon vine

Annual
To 10 feet

Light: Sun
Water: Heavy
Bloom: Summer

Often classified as a perennial but grown as an annual, the balloon vine is a very fast-growing

decorative screen plant with heart-shaped leaves and small white flowers. The plant grows in most any type of soil as long as it drains readily.

CATANANCHE CAERULEA   Cupid's-dart

Annual/Perennial
To 2 feet

Light: Sun
Water: Moderate
Bloom: Summer

Leaves narrow, somewhat toothed; flower heads blue. The pretty blue flowers are highly prized for dried arrangements. Easily grown. Grow on dry side in a well-drained soil.

CELASTRUS SCANDENS   Climbing bit-
tersweet/American bittersweet

Vine
To 20 feet

Light: Sun
Water: Moderate
Bloom: Fall

This vine has 2- to 4-inch-long, sharply pointed, and finely toothed oval leaves. Small yellow flowers and handsome yellow to orange fruits. Plants need support; highly decorative in their season.

CELOSIA ARGENTEA   Cockscomb

Annual
To 3 feet

Light: Sun
Water: Moderate
Bloom: Summer

Narrow leaves, to 2½ inches long; white flowers in a dense cluster. A handsome plant that can be easily grown in most garden soils. Likes heat.

Suggested Varieties:
  'Fireglow'
  'Flora Dale'
  'Golden Triumph'

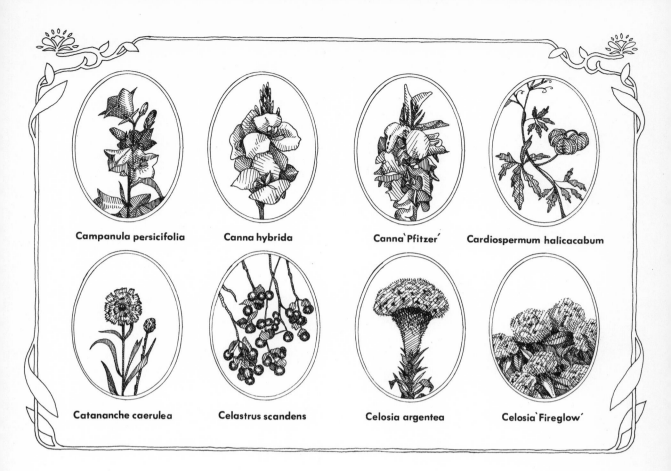

Campanula persicifolia   **Canna hybrida**   **Canna 'Pfitzer'**   **Cardiospermum halicacabum**

Catananche caerulea   **Celastrus scandens**   **Celosia argentea**   **Celosia 'Fireglow'**

CENIA BARBATA   **Pincushion flower**
Annual
To 1 foot

Light: Sun
Water: Moderate
Bloom: Summer

Tufted and silky hairy leaves; bears many yellow flowers. Plants like dry sunny places and grow in almost any soil.

CENTAUREA   **Basket flower**
Annual/Perennial
To 3 feet

Light: Sun
Water: Moderate
Bloom: Summer

A popular group of delightful colorful plants, Centaurea likes sun and a well-drained location. Excellent anywhere in the garden, or use as border plants, dried flowers, or cut flowers. A must for the garden.

C. cyanus (bachelor's button cornflower). This annual has flower heads of all shades, from white to blue to deep rose.

C. dealbata (Persian centaurea). Flower heads rose-purple or pink; deeply fringed. Perennial.

C. macrocephala (golden centaurea). Large yellow flower heads. Perennial.

C. moschata (sweet sultan). Fragrant white, yellow, or purple flowers. Annual.

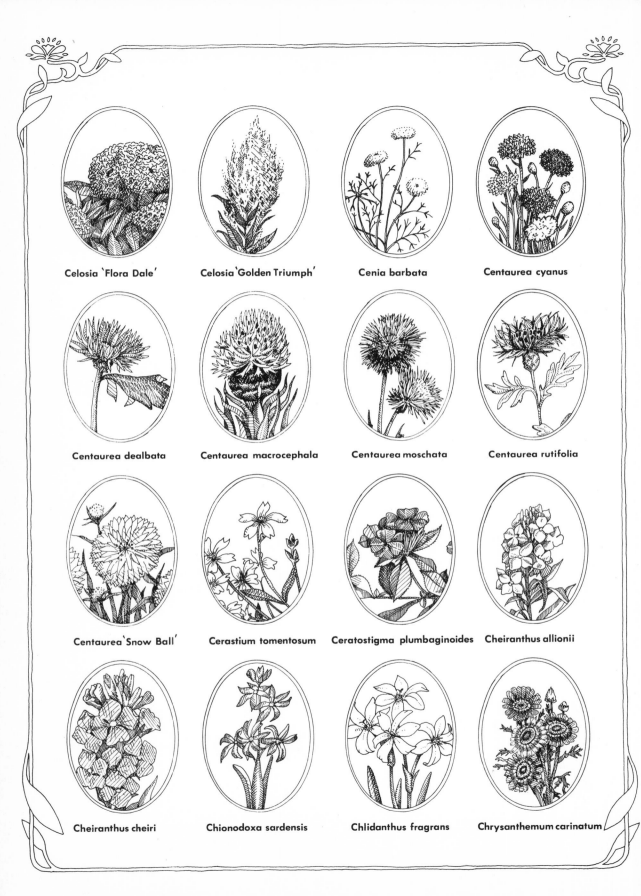

Celosia `Flora Dale`

Celosia `Golden Triumph`

Cenia barbata

Centaurea cyanus

Centaurea dealbata

Centaurea macrocephala

Centaurea moschata

Centaurea rutifolia

Centaurea `Snow Ball`

Cerastium tomentosum

Ceratostigma plumbaginoides

Cheiranthus allionii

Cheiranthus cheiri

Chionodoxa sardensis

Chlidanthus fragrans

Chrysanthemum carinatum

C. rutifolia (dusty miller). Spectacular silvery-white foliage.

Suggested Variety:
'Snow Ball'

CERASTIUM TOMENTOSUM   Snow-in-summer

Perennial
To 1 foot

Light: Sun
Water: Moderate
Bloom: Summer

This plant has many underground creeping stems; snow-in-summer is covered with white and later greenish white hairs (in poor soils, the plant often looks white). The flowers are large and the plant can be used as a ground cover or with other low-growing perennials. Grows in any soil as long as drainage is good.

CERATOSTIGMA PLUMBAGINOIDES   Leadwort

Perennial
To 1 foot

Light: Sun
Water: Moderate
Bloom: Summer/Fall

Oval leaves with brilliant purplish blue flowers. Plants need excellent drainage but otherwise are carefree.

CHEIRANTHUS   Siberian wallflower

Perennial/Annual
To 1 foot

Light: Sun
Water: Moderate
Bloom: Spring/Summer

Wallflowers need a well-drained soil with a pH of 6.0 to 7.0. Pinch off stem tips when plants are 4 inches tall to encourage branching. Excellent for cut flowers.

C. allionii. Erect leaves about 2 to 3 inches long, slightly coarse, and toothed; bright-orange flowers. Best treated as a biennial because it is apt to flower so freely as to kill itself.

C. cheiri (English wallflower). This perennial grows to 2 feet. The fragrant flowers vary greatly in size and color: white, yellow, a brown that is nearly red, and purple.

CHIONODOXA SARDENSIS   Glory-of-the-snow

Bulb
To 1 foot

Light: Sun
Water: Moderate
Bloom: Spring

Blue flowers with white center. Grows best in cool regions; likes well-drained soil. Plant bulbs in fall 3 to 6 inches apart, 3 inches deep. Easily grown.

CHLIDANTHUS FRAGRANS   Delicate lily

Bulb
To 1 foot

Light: Sun
Water: Moderate
Bloom: Summer

Leaves sheathed at base; flower yellow, fragrant, in few flower clusters. These plants need full sun to flourish. Plant bulbs 6 to 8 inches apart, 2 inches deep. In cold climates, dig up and store bulbs.

CHRYSANTHEMUM

Annual/Perennial
To 2 feet

Light: Sun
Water: Moderate
Bloom: Summer/Fall

A large group of popular plants, often used in gardens and rightly so, because they bear handsome flowers in abundance. There are dozens of

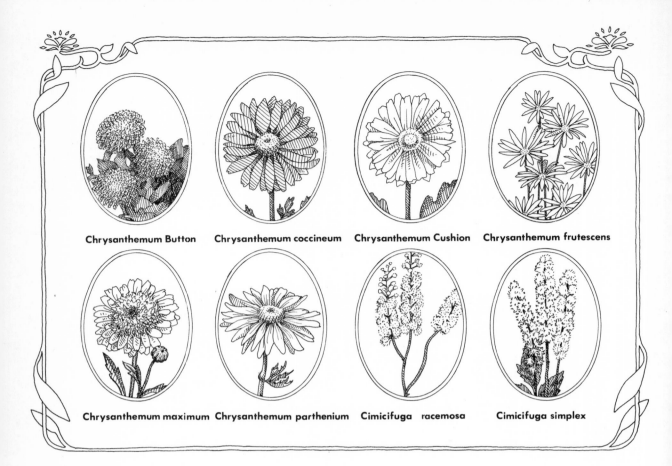

Chrysanthemum Button   **Chrysanthemum coccineum**   **Chrysanthemum Cushion**   **Chrysanthemum frutescens**

Chrysanthemum maximum   **Chrysanthemum parthenium**   **Cimicifuga racemosa**   **Cimicifuga simplex**

flower colors to choose from and many flower forms. The annual types are very easy to grow and the perennials, which include the painted daisy, require somewhat more care; they really need excellent drainage. Most chrysanthemums will tolerate any kind of good garden soil but all of them must have good sunlight.

C. carinatum. Fleshy leaves; 2-inch flowers are white with a yellow area at base and dark-purple splotch. Annual.

C. coccineum (painted daisy). White to red flowers that are sometimes tipped yellow. Perennial.

C. frutescens (marguerite). White or pale-yellow flowers. Perennial.

C. maximum (Shasta daisy). Solitary flowers in a wide range of colors. Perennial.

C. parthenium (feverfew). Small white flowers with yellow centers. Perennial.

Suggested Varieties:
  Button
  Cushion

CIMICIFUGA   Bugbane

Perennial
To 8 feet

Light: Shade
Water: Moderate
Bloom: Summer

These plants are valued because they grow in shade with ease. Plants grow in almost any type of soil and provide nice accents; hardly spec-

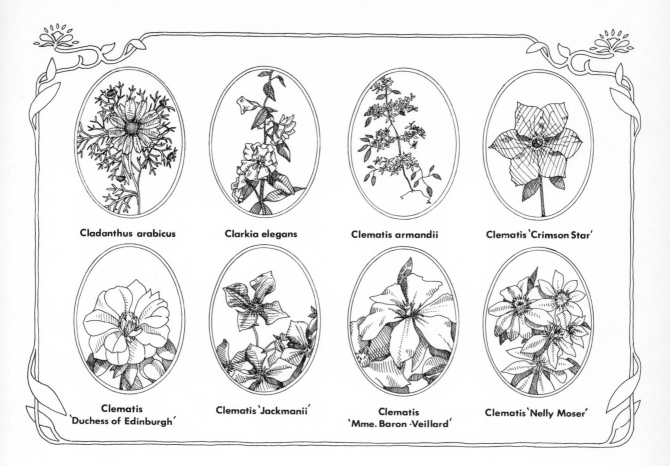

Cladanthus arabicus

Clarkia elegans

Clematis armandii

Clematis 'Crimson Star'

Clematis 'Duchess of Edinburgh'

Clematis 'Jackmanii'

Clematis 'Mme. Baron-Veillard'

Clematis 'Nelly Moser'

tacular but good plants for the beginner. All bugbanes make good cut flowers.

C. racemosa (black snakeroot). A leafy plant with fragrant greenish white flowers.

C. simplex. Greenish yellow or white flowers.

CLADANTHUS ARABICUS   Cladanthus

Annual
To 3 feet

Light: Sun
Water: Moderate
Bloom: Summer

Strong-smelling foliage and lacy leaves; bright-yellow flowers. An overlooked plant that grows easily in most soils and provides good garden color.

CLARKIA ELEGANS   Rocky Mountain
garland

Annual
To 2 feet

Light: Sun
Water: Moderate
Bloom: Summer

Lancelike leaves; purple or rose flowers, with white and double forms in cultivation. Clarkia likes cool summers and dry sandy soil; plants bear profusely. Fine cut flowers.

CLEMATIS   Virgin's bower

Vine
To 20 feet

Light: Sun
Water: Moderate
Bloom: Spring/Summer

These wonderful deciduous vines have handsome large flowers in beautiful colors—rose, blue, white. Clematises need a rich, loose, fast-draining soil with some lime added. Plant deep and provide supports for the vines; feed heavily. The summer-blooming types need pruning in late fall; spring-blooming ones need a light pruning after they flower. A must for the good garden.

C. armandii. Glossy dark-green veined leaves; pure white flowers in clusters.

C. heracleaefolia davidiana. Deep-green leaves and dense clusters of fragrant blue flowers.

Suggested Varieties:
  'Crimson Star'
  'Duchess of Edinburgh'
  'Jackmanii'
  'Mme. Baron-Veillard'
  'Nelly Moser'
  'Ramona'

CLEOME SPINOSA   Spiderflower

Annual
To 4 feet

Light: Sun
Water: Moderate
Bloom: Summer/Fall

These plants grow in almost any soil but prefer hot dry locations to do their best. The leaves are spiny and flowers white or rose, strongly scented. Good background plants.

Suggested Variety:
  'Pink Queen'

CLIVIA MINIATA   Kaffir lily

Bulb
To 3 feet

Light: Sun
Water: Moderate
Bloom: Spring

Dark-green leaves; the many erect flowers (in a cluster) are bright scarlet or orange with a yellow throat. Kaffir lilies grow in almost any soil and

like to be dry between watering. Belgian hybrids are more robust and floriferous.

Suggested Varieties:
  Belgian hybrids

COIX LACRYMA-JOBI   Job's tears

Annual
To 4 feet

Light: Sun
Water: Moderate
Bloom: Summer

This is an ornamental grass grown for its decorative hard-shelled seeds of white, gray, or brown; excellent for dried arrangements. Plants are easy to grow in ordinary garden soil. Something different for the garden lover.

COLCHICUM   Autumn crocus

Bulb
To 1 foot

Light: Sun
Water: Moderate
Bloom: Fall

Always a pleasure in the garden, Colchicum deserves more attention. Plant bulbs 6 to 8 inches apart, 4 inches deep, in August. Leave undisturbed for years.

C. autumnale. Spatula-shaped leaves; pale-rose or white flowers, 1 to 6 on a stem. A variable plant.

C. speciosum (meadow saffron). Oblong 4-inch leaves; rose, purple, or white flowers.

CONSOLIDA AMBIGUA   Larkspur

Annual
To 4 feet

Light: Shade
Water: Moderate
Bloom: Summer

This plant, usually known as *Delphinium ajacis,* has tall spikes of feathery blue or salmon flowers and lacy green foliage.Both tall and dwarf va-

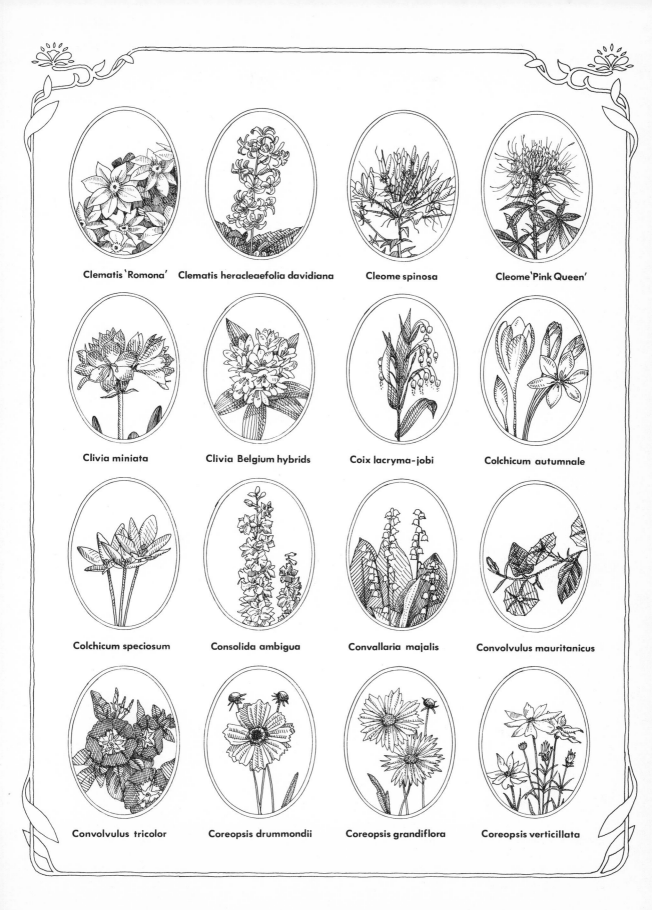

Clematis 'Romona'   Clematis heracleaefolia davidiana   Cleome spinosa   Cleome 'Pink Queen'

Clivia miniata   Clivia Belgium hybrids   Coix lacryma-jobi   Colchicum autumnale

Colchicum speciosum   Consolida ambigua   Convallaria majalis   Convolvulus mauritanicus

Convolvulus tricolor   Coreopsis drummondii   Coreopsis grandiflora   Coreopsis verticillata

rieties available. Excellent for masses of color. Plant likes a fertile, well-drained soil.

CONVALLARIA MAJALIS
Lily of the valley

Bulb
To 1 foot

Light: Shade
Water: Moderate
Bloom: Spring

These plants are highly prized because of their sweet fragrant white flowers. Lily-of-the-valley plants grow best in large masses and once established require little care; they like to be crowded. Select a shady moist place for them that is not too hot; they make nice green accents even if flowers are sparse.

CONVOLVULUS   Morning glory

Perennial
To 20 feet

Light: Sun
Water: Moderate
Bloom: Summer/Fall

These are handsome fast-growing plants that bloom abundantly in hot dry places. Flowers are usually blue and quite handsome. Most species can grow in any soil that is well drained and these plants make lovely summer accents. Some are large trailing types, others are smaller and less pendent.

C. mauritanicus (ground morning glory). Oval leaves; blue flowers with white throats.

C. tricolor (dwarf morning glory). Small pale-blue flowers; semi-upright plant.

COREOPSIS   Tickseed

Annual
To 3 feet

Light: Sun
Water: Heavy
Bloom: Summer/Fall

Usually known as Calliopsis, these plants have a long flowering season. Plants need sun but grow in almost any soil. A colorful show for little effort.

C. drummondii. Bright orange-yellow flowers.

C. grandiflora. To 24 inches. Narrow dark-green leaves; large yellow flowers.

C. verticillata (threadleaf coreopsis). Deep-yellow flowers.

COSMOS

Annual/Perennial
To 5 feet

Light: Sun
Water: Moderate
Bloom: Summer

One of the most valuable background plants for gardens. Graceful and long-lasting, cosmos bloom freely, grow rapidly, and will bloom in dry soil; do not feed. Nothing as nice as these lovely plants; a must for gardens.

C. bipinnatus. Solitary rose or purple flowers with yellow disks.

C. sulphureus (yellow cosmos). Golden-yellow flowers.

Suggested Varieties:
  'Candy Stripe'
  'Crimson Scarlet'
  'Pinky'
  'Sunset'

CREPIS RUBRA   Hawk's-beard

Annual
To 1 foot

Light: Sun
Water: Scant
Bloom: Summer

This plant is considered a weed in some areas but it is worthwhile because it has pretty red flowers. It thrives in even a poor soil and is relatively easy to grow. Good for borders or in rock gardens.

CRINUM

Bulb
To 3 feet

Light: Sun
Water: Heavy (withhold after flowering season)
Bloom: Summer

Beautiful bulbous plants good for pots in garden or patios. Crinums need a well-drained soil and sun most of the day. Bulbs should be lifted in winter in cold climates.

C. asiaticum. Slender, cylindrically shaped white flowers. Largest cultivated species and of special merit.

C. longifolium. Large white or pink flowers.

CROCOSMIA CROCOSMAEFLORA
Montbretia

Bulb
To 3 feet

Light: Sun
Water: Moderate
Bloom: Summer/Fall

Fine garden plants with orange showy flowers on tall stems. Plant bulbs 3 inches apart, 2 inches deep in a well-drained soil. The plants make a nice spot of color in the ornamental bed and are also good as cut flowers. In cold climates lift bulbs after foliage matures and store in a cool dry place.

CROCUS   Scotch crocus

Bulb
To ½ foot

Light: Sun/Shade
Water: Moderate
Bloom: Spring

Crocuses do best in cold-winter regions, where their flowers are one of the first to greet spring. Plant the bulbs 3 to 4 inches apart, 2 inches deep; do not feed. Excellent for rock gardens and woodland garden landscapes.

C. chrysanthus (golden crocus). Bright orange-yellow flowers.

C. sieberii (sieber crocus). Orange-throated flowers.

C. vernus (common crocus). White or lilac flowers.

CROTALARIA RETUSA
Golden-yellow sweet pea

Annual
To 2 feet

Light: Sun
Water: Moderate
Bloom: Summer

This is a showy plant that bears small but pretty sweet-pea-type yellow flowers. Plants will not grow where summers are cool, and they need a loamy garden soil. Good for edgings or as cut flowers.

CUPHEA IGNEA   Cigar plant

Annual
To 2 feet

Light: Bright
Water: Heavy
Bloom: Summer

An overlooked plant rarely grown that blooms profusely; white flowers are blotched with red. Easy to grow in almost any kind of soil, cigar plants are desirable if you have some space for them. Hardly spectacular, but amenable plants.

CYCLAMEN

Bulb
To 1 foot

Light: Bright
Water: Moderate
Bloom: Summer/Fall

Hard to grow for most gardeners, cyclamens need a while to become established, but then they produce good flowers. Use in shade of tree or other shady place in mass for a colorful effect.

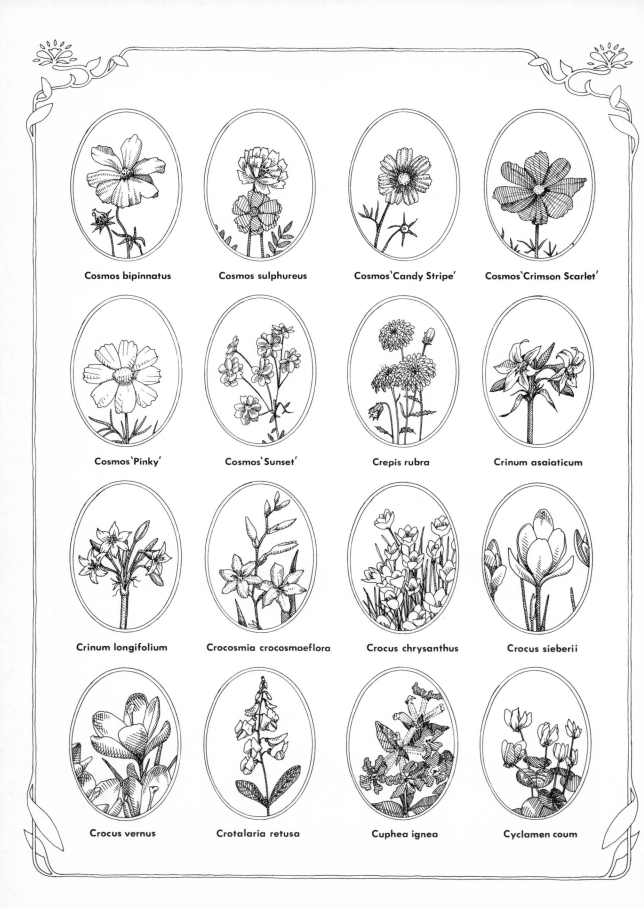

Cosmos bipinnatus

Cosmos sulphureus

Cosmos 'Candy Stripe'

Cosmos 'Crimson Scarlet'

Cosmos 'Pinky'

Cosmos 'Sunset'

Crepis rubra

Crinum asaiaticum

Crinum longifolium

Crocosmia crocosmaeflora

Crocus chrysanthus

Crocus sieberii

Crocus vernus

Crotalaria retusa

Cuphea ignea

Cyclamen coum

C. coum. Purple flowers with deep-carmine spots.

C. neapolitanum (Neapolitan cyclamen). Red or white flowers.

C. persicum (florist's cyclamen). Large white or rose and purple flowers.

CYNOGLOSSUM AMABILE   Chinese forget-me-not

Annual
To 2 feet

Light: Sun
Water: Moderate
Bloom: Summer

These are rather pretty bell-shaped flowers —blue, pink, or white—and plants prosper in almost all conditions. You can grow them in dry or wet soil, in heat or in cold, and they still bear blooms. A good easy annual for beginning gardeners.

DAHLIA

Bulb
To 2 feet

Light: Sun
Water: Heavy
Bloom: Summer

This vast group of very popular plants grows well with minimum care. Dozens of flower colors, forms, and heights. Feed for healthy plants. Keep evenly moist.

Suggested Varieties:
   Cactus
   Collarette
   Miniature
   Pompom
   Semi-Cactus
   Single

DATURA METEL   Trumpet flower

Annual
To 5 feet

Light: Sun
Water: Moderate
Bloom: Summer

Hairy heart-shaped leaves. White flowers 10 inches long, 4 inches across. Spectacular flowers, but its sprawling growth habit can make the plant a nuisance, so use with discretion. Likes heat and sun. Flower parts poisonous.

DELPHINIUM   Larkspur

Perennial/Biennial
To 6 feet

Light: Sun
Water: Heavy
Bloom: Summer/Fall

Delphiniums are the tall blue plants you see in many gardens and they make a dramatic statement. The plants need a well-drained loamy garden soil and plenty of sun. Not easy to grow, delphiniums are worth the challenge because of their beauty. Make fine cut flowers.

D. belladonna. Beautiful blue flowers.

D. elatum (candle larkspur). Blue flowers with a yellow beard.

D. grandiflorum (Chinese larkspur). Large blue or whitish flowers. Very showy.

Suggested Variety:
   Giant Pacific hybrid

DIANTHUS   Pinks

Perennial/Annual
To 4 feet

Light: Sun
Water: Moderate
Bloom: Summer/Fall

A large group of plants that vary in color from white to purplish pink and in habit from small compact plants to tall growers. Plants need a loamy garden soil and even moisture; sun to prosper. Used in groups, Dianthus plants can create a colorful area anywhere in the garden and their long season of bloom makes them very worthwhile. A must for good gardens.

D. barbatus (Sweet William). Flowers are in clusters, almost flat with reddish striped petals that are dotted white and red at base. Perennial.

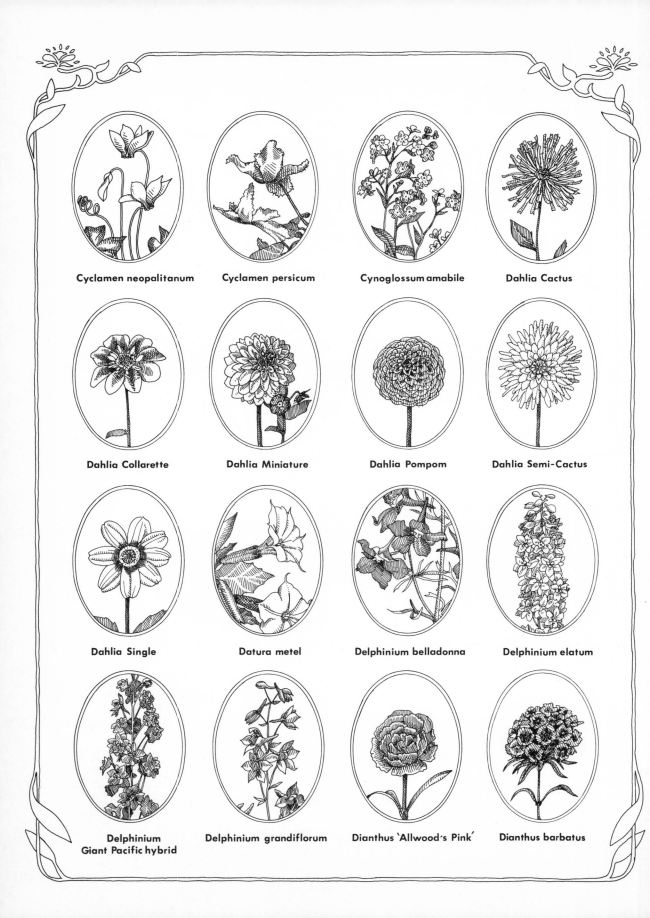

Cyclamen neopalitanum   **Cyclamen persicum**   **Cynoglossum amabile**   **Dahlia Cactus**

Dahlia Collarette   **Dahlia Miniature**   **Dahlia Pompom**   **Dahlia Semi-Cactus**

Dahlia Single   **Datura metel**   **Delphinium belladonna**   **Delphinium elatum**

**Delphinium
Giant Pacific hybrid**   **Delphinium grandiflorum**   **Dianthus 'Allwood's Pink'**   **Dianthus barbatus**

Dianthus caryophyllus   Dianthus chinensis   Dianthus 'Doris'   Dianthus 'Orchid Lace'

Dianthus plumarius   Dianthus 'Robin'   Dianthus 'Zebra'   Diascia barberae

D. caryophyllus (carnation). Red flowers in clusters. Annual.

D. chinensis (China pink). Bright- to dull-red or white flowers. Perennial.

D. plumarius (border pink). Old favorite with lovely pink flowers. Perennial.

Suggested Varieties:
   'Allwoods Pink'
   'Doris'
   'Orchid Lace'
   'Robin'
   'Zebra'

DIASCIA BARBERAE   Twinspur

Annual
To 1½ feet

Light: Sun
Water: Moderate
Bloom: Summer

Oval, bluntly toothed leaves; rosy-pink clustered flowers have a yellow-green-dotted throat. Will grow in any soil if in sunlight. Pinch terminal tips to encourage bushy plants.

DICENTRA   Bleeding heart

Perennial
To 2 feet

Light: Shade
Water: Moderate
Bloom: Summer

Here is a group of plants chiefly grown because they can tolerate a shady place. Bleeding hearts do best in a loamy well-drained soil and are usually very easy to grow once established. While they are not dramatic they have a certain charm and make worthwhile additions to the garden.

D. eximia. Pendent reddish purple flowers.

D. spectabilis (bleeding heart). The most popular species with rosy-red flowers.

DICTAMNUS ALBUS   Gas plant

Perennial
To 3 feet

Light: Sun
Water: Moderate
Bloom: Summer

These pretty garden plants have heart-shaped leaves and white or pale-purple flowers. Plants grow in almost any kind of soil and make fine additions to the garden bed or simply in clumps by themselves. Generally, easy to grow.

DIGITALIS   Foxglove

Perennial/Biennial
To 6 feet

Light: Sun
Water: Moderate
Bloom: Summer

Lovely plants where tall masses of color are needed; need only moist soil—never too dry or wet—and can tolerate shade if necessary. Many new improved varieties available. Nice for wooded landscapes.

D. aurea. A leafy plant; rusty-red clustered flowers.

D. grandiflora (yellow foxglove). Flowers are yellowish, marked with brown.

D. purpurea (common foxglove). Variable color, but flowers are usually purple.

DIMORPHOTHECA HYBRIDS
Cape marigold

Annual/Perennial
To 2½ feet

Light: Sun
Water: Moderate
Bloom: Summer

Fine flowering plants, with brightly colored red or yellow flowers and lobed dull-green leaves. Plants like heat, sun, and a well-drained soil.

Good accent where something different is needed, and usually easy to grow.

DORONICUM CAUCASICUM
Leopard's-bane

Perennial
To 2 feet

Light: Sun
Water: Moderate
Bloom: Spring

Kidney-shaped, deeply toothed leaves. The yellow flowers are about 2 inches across, solitary. Give full sun, and be sure soil drains freely. Not very well known, these perennials deserve more attention.

DOXANTHA UNGUIS-CATI
Trumpet vine

Vine
To 20 feet

Light: Sun/Bright
Water: Heavy
Bloom: Spring

A partly deciduous vine that has glossy-green leaves and yellow trumpet-shaped flowers that are 2 inches long. Climbs high and fast. After it blooms, prune back plant; it will cover almost any surface.

ECHINACEA PURPUREA   Coneflower

Perennial
To 4 feet

Light: Sun
Water: Moderate
Bloom: Summer

Faintly toothed oval leaves. Four-inch reddish purple flowers become gray-green at tips and have an orange center. Plants grow well in most situations and even tolerate some shade and bloom; however, they are touchy about too much moisture at roots. Good color for any garden spot.

Suggested Varieties:
  'Bright Star'
  'White Luster'

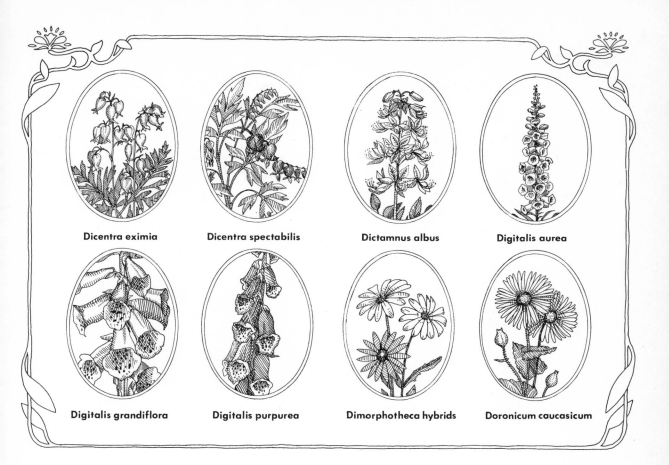

Dicentra eximia

Dicentra spectabilis

Dictamnus albus

Digitalis aurea

Digitalis grandiflora

Digitalis purpurea

Dimorphotheca hybrids

Doronicum caucasicum

ECHINOPS   **Blue globe thistle**

Perennial/Biennial
To 4 feet

Light: Sun
Water: Moderate/Scant
Bloom: Summer/Fall

Unusual plants, with lobed leaves and globes of tiny blue flowers. Plants will tolerate dry soil if necessary. Excellent as cut or dried flowers.

Suggested Variety:
  'Taplow Blue'

ECHIUM   **Bugloss**

Perennial/Biennial
To 1½ feet

Light: Sun
Water: Heavy
Bloom: Summer

With rough tongue-shaped leaves, echiums bear masses of bell-shaped flowers about 1/2 inch across, usually blue, although rose or white forms are also available. These are long-flowering plants that are well suited for dry sunny locations and soil not too rich.

EMILIA FLAMMEA   **Tassel flower**

Annual
To 2 feet

Light: Sun
Water: Moderate
Bloom: Summer

Oblong and slightly hairy leaves; scarlet flowers are in terminal clusters. Plants will tolerate a dry soil if necessary. Nice for cut flowers. Pretty accent in garden.

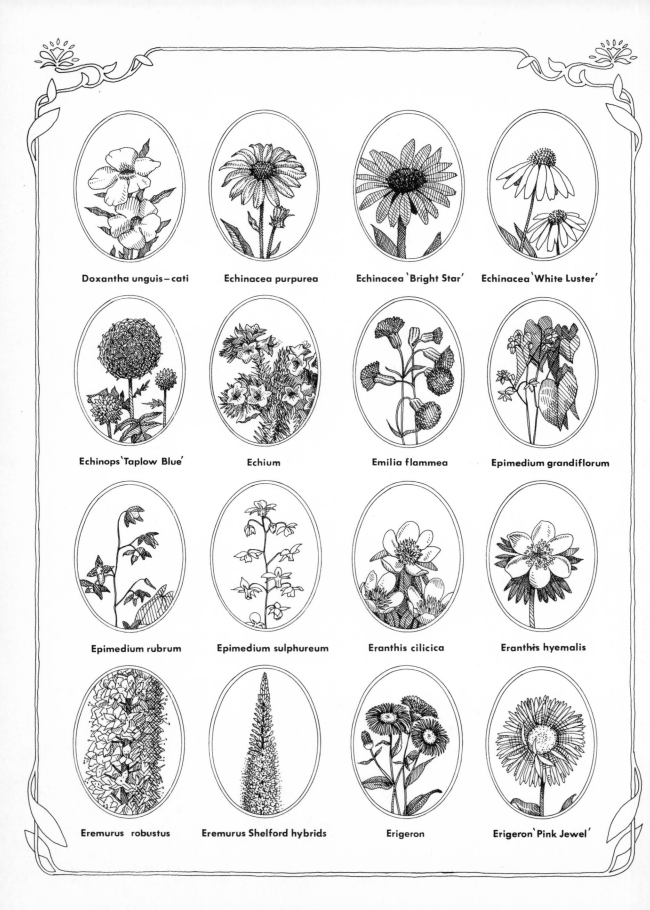

Doxantha unguis—cati

Echinacea purpurea

Echinacea 'Bright Star'

Echinacea 'White Luster'

Echinops 'Taplow Blue'

Echium

Emilia flammea

Epimedium grandiflorum

Epimedium rubrum

Epimedium sulphureum

Eranthis cilicica

Eranthis hyemalis

Eremurus robustus

Eremurus Shelford hybrids

Erigeron

Erigeron 'Pink Jewel'

EPIMEDIUM   Bishop's hat

Perennial
To 1 foot

Light: Shade
Water: Moderate
Bloom: Summer

Here are garden plants valued for their colorful heart-shaped foliage that turns reddish bronze in fall. Plants like a moist soil and thrive in a shady place. Good appeal in concentrated masses in garden.

E. grandiflorum. Heart-shaped leaves 2 to 3 inches long with spiny-toothed margins; violet flowers.

E. rubrum. Lovely red species.

E. sulphureum. A beautiful yellow form; floriferous.

ERANTHIS   Aconite

Bulb
To 1 foot

Light: Sun/Bright
Water: Moderate
Bloom: Spring

These relations of the buttercup are not true aconites, which are summer perennials. Plants are low-growing and grow well in protected areas. Plant tubers 2 to 3 inches apart and 2 inches deep. Makes a mass of color in very early spring.

E. cilicica. Scented bright-yellow 1-inch flowers; bronze-green leaves.

E. hyemalis. Similar to *E. cilicica.*

EREMURUS   Himalayan foxtail lily

Bulb
To 8 feet

Light: Sun
Water: Heavy
Bloom: Spring

This group of spectacular flowering plants is more rightly classified as tuberous. Flowers are small but there are hundreds to a spire, making quite a sight. Eremurus prefers a sandy garden soil where there is good drainage and lots of sun. After plants bloom, grow them somewhat dry as leaves die off; plants come back the following year. Good as background subjects in the ornamental garden or by themselves as a feature of the garden. Bees love them.

E. robustus. Tall plumes of white flowers; spectacular.

Suggested Variety:
   Shelford hybrids

ERIGERON   Fleabane

Perennial/Annual
To 2½ feet

Light: Sun
Water: Scant
Bloom: Summer/Fall

Bushy plants, with pink or purple flowers that have a yellow eye. Need well-drained soil that is not too rich in nutrients. Generally easily grown.

Suggested Variety:
   'Pink Jewel'

ERYTHRONIUM   Adder's-tongue

Bulb
1 foot

Light: Shade
Water: Moderate
Bloom: Spring

A group of woodland bulbs with fine dainty flowers. Pretty but not spectacular. Plant bulbs in summer or fall 3 inches apart, 2 inches deep. Plants will not tolerate extreme heat.

E. albidum. Plain or mottled leaves, white, pink, or purple flowers.

E. americanum. A yellow flowering species.

E. oregonum. Creamy-white flowers; very handsome.

ESCHSCHOLZIA CALIFORNICA
California poppy

Annual
To 2 feet

Light: Sun
Water: Moderate
Bloom: Spring

The California poppy bears bright-golden flowers and finely cut silver foliage. Plants make spectacular display in gardens. Difficult to transplant.

EUCHARIS GRANDIFLORA   Amazon lily

Bulb
To 2½ feet

Light: Bright
Water: Heavy (let dry out)
Bloom: Spring/Summer/Fall

A spectacular lily, with 2-inch scented white flowers on 2-foot stems. Plants bear flowers, rest, and then bloom again. Bloom is best when crowded. Cannot tolerate cold (60 F. minimum).

EUCOMIS PUNCTATA   Pineapple lily

Bulb
To 2 feet

Light: Sun
Water: Heavy
Bloom: Summer

A rosette of handsome leaves with a 2-foot stalk topped with hundreds of greenish white flowers that are handsome when cut. Plant bulbs in early fall about 10 inches apart, 5 inches deep. Need winter protection.

EUPATORIUM COELESTINUM
Mistflower

Perennial
To 3 feet

Light: Bright
Water: Moderate
Bloom: Summer

Plants have heart-shaped leaves and crowns of blue flowers, making quite a garden display. Grow in well-drained soil where they will spread rapidly. Good for cut flowers.

EUPHORBIA   Spurge

Perennial
To 1½ feet

Light: Sun/Bright
Water: Moderate
Bloom: Summer

Like its relative, the Poinsettia, spurge has colored bracts that look like yellow flowers. Likes well-drained soil and good sun.

E. heterophylla. Bright-green leaves have red and white coloring in summer.

E. marginata (snow-on-the-mountain). Fine ground cover, with highly decorative green and white leaves.

FELICIA   Blue daisy

Perennial
To 2 feet

Light: Sun
Water: Heavy
Bloom: Summer/Fall

A group of fine garden flowers for full sun; used as annuals in cold climates. When plants get straggly, cut back to 6 inches to force healthy growth.

F. amelloides (blue daisy). Oval leaves; beautiful sky-blue flowers. Also called *Agathaea coelestis.*

F. bergeriana. Floriferous and easily grown.

FREESIA

Bulb
To 1 foot

Light: Bright
Water: Moderate
Bloom: Winter/Spring

These plants are so beautiful and so sweetly scented that it is a shame they are so difficult to

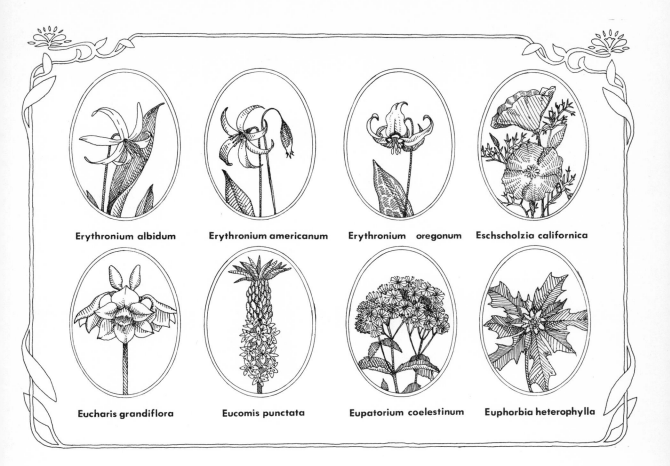

Erythronium albidum

Erythronium americanum

Erythronium oregonum

Eschscholzia californica

Eucharis grandiflora

Eucomis punctata

Eupatorium coelestinum

Euphorbia heterophylla

grow in the garden. They require well-drained soil, even moisture, and a cool situation. Flowers are white, yellow, or orange. If you have the patience, do give them a try; they are superb cut flowers.

FRITILLARIA   Crown imperial

Bulb
To 3 feet

Light: Shade
Water: Heavy
Bloom: Spring

A group of unusual but pretty flowers, with types for all regions. Plant bulbs in summer or fall 3 inches apart and 3 to 4 inches deep in a loamy soil that drains readily. Fine plants in borders or in groups. Can be left undisturbed for years.

F. imperialis (crown imperial). Purple, brick-red, or yellow-red flowers.

F. meleagris (snake's-head). Flowers are veined with purple or maroon.

GAILLARDIA ARISTATA   Blanket flower

Annual/Perennial
To 2 feet

Light: Sun
Water: Moderate
Bloom: Summer

Also called *G. grandiflora,* blanket flowers bear 3-inch blooms on slender stems: flowers are yellow or red. The plants do not tolerate heavy soils and must have loamy garden soil to grow best, as well as almost perfect drainage. Nice for the cutting garden or ornamental garden if you have the patience for them.

Suggested Variety:
   'Sundance'

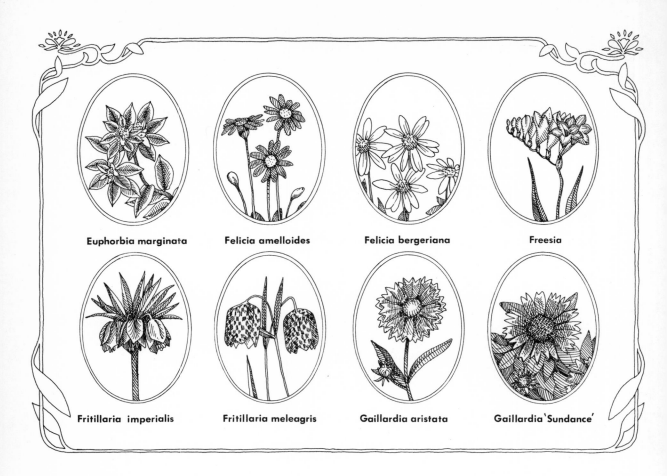

Euphorbia marginata   Felicia amelloides   Felicia bergeriana   Freesia

Fritillaria imperialis   Fritillaria meleagris   Gaillardia aristata   Gaillardia 'Sundance'

GALANTHUS NIVALIS   Snowdrop

Bulb
To 10 inches

Light: Shade
Water: Moderate
Bloom: Spring

A popular bulbous plant that blooms in very early spring; pretty and delicate, with white nodding flowers and grassy foliage. Plant bulbs in early fall 2 inches apart, 2 inches deep. Leave undisturbed for years. Do not feed.

GALTONIA CANDICANS   Giant summer hyacinth

Bulb
To 4 feet

Light: Sun
Water: Heavy
Bloom: Summer

With strap-shaped leaves and dozens of bell-shaped white flowers, Galtonia is worth its space in any garden. Blooms are fragrant and make nice display in groups. Space bulbs 1 foot apart, 8 inches deep. Dig up bulbs; tender to frost.

GAMOLEPIS TAGETES   Sunshine daisy

Annual
To 1 foot

Light: Sun
Water: Moderate
Bloom: Summer

A lovely daisy that bears many bright-yellow or orange flowers; can tolerate dry soil. Nice for a spot of color here or there and easy to grow.

GAZANIA LONGISCAPA   Gazania

Perennial
To 10 inches

Light: Sun
Water: Moderate
Bloom: Summer/Fall

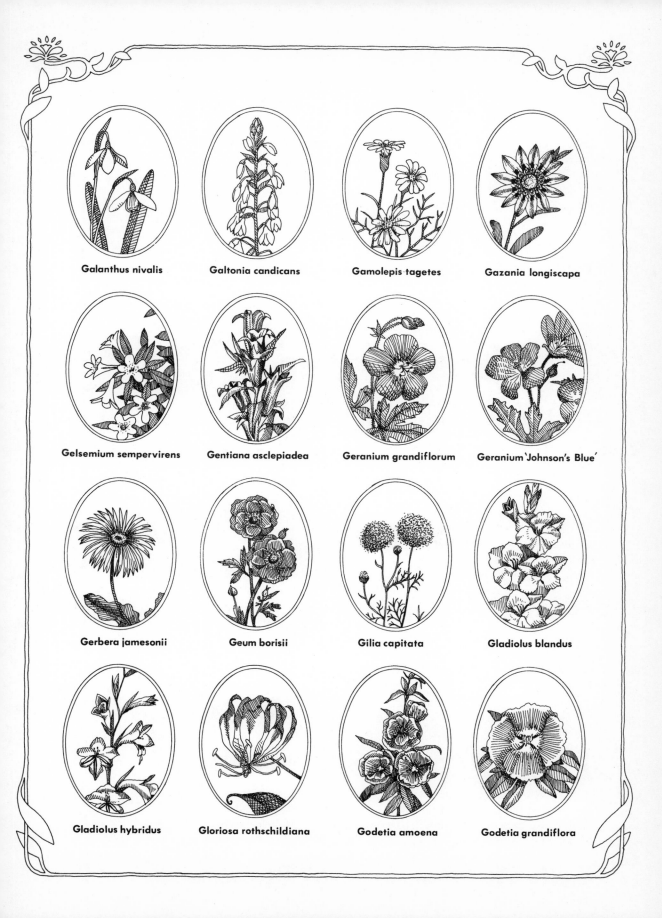

Galanthus nivalis

Galtonia candicans

Gamolepis tagetes

Gazania longiscapa

Gelsemium sempervirens

Gentiana asclepiadea

Geranium grandiflorum

Geranium 'Johnson's Blue'

Gerbera jamesonii

Geum borisii

Gilia capitata

Gladiolus blandus

Gladiolus hybridus

Gloriosa rothschildiana

Godetia amoena

Godetia grandiflora

With grasslike leaves, gazanias bear handsome large orange or yellow flowers. Plants like a very sunny place and tolerate almost any soil. Use mounds of gazanias for a different and colorful ground cover. Can be treated as an annual if sown early.

GELSEMIUM SEMPERVIRENS Carolina yellow jasmine

Vine
To 20 feet

Light: Sun/Bright
Water: Heavy
Bloom: Summer

A fine evergreen vine with shiny light-green leaves and fragrant tubular yellow flowers. Can be grown on trellis or fence and makes a beautiful cover. Needs plenty of water.

GENTIANA ASCLEPIADEA Gentian

Perennial
To 1 foot

Light: Shade
Water: Moderate
Bloom: Summer

If you are able to give gentians an acid soil, by all means grow some for their vivid blue flowers because they make a bold statement in the garden. The plants need an evenly moist soil and eventually grow into large clumps, making quite a display.

GERANIUM GRANDIFLORUM Cranesbill

Perennial
To 20 inches

Light: Sun
Water: Moderate
Bloom: Summer

A lilac-flowering geranium, with 1- to 2-inch flowers that bloom a long time. Plants thrive in almost any garden soil and are best left undisturbed for several years.

Suggested Variety:
'Johnson's Blue'

GERBERA JAMESONII Transvaal daisy

Perennial
To 1½ feet

Light: Sun
Water: Moderate
Bloom: Spring/Summer

A fine daisy, with salmon flowers 4 to 5 inches across. Blooms profusely for several months. Likes full sun, good drainage, and a somewhat acid soil.

GEUM BORISII

Perennial
To 2 feet

Light: Bright
Water: Moderate
Bloom: Summer

A handsome relative of the rose family, *G. borisii* bears bright-yellow flowers and clumps of dark-green foliage. Plants need exceptional drainage and will tolerate shade if necessary. Good color accents. Remove faded blossoms (before they set seed) for longer bloom period.

GILIA CAPITATA

Annual
To 2½ feet

Light: Sun
Water: Heavy
Bloom: Summer

Plants are covered with globes of tiny light-blue flowers and have feathery foliage. Flowers are long-lasting, and plants grow in almost any soil.

GLADIOLUS

Bulb
To 4 feet

Light: Sun
Water: Heavy
Bloom: Summer

A popular group of flowers for cutting. Grows well in most areas if dug up yearly and reset annually. Plant corms 4 to 6 inches apart, 4 to 6 inches deep. Most types need staking. Some fine dwarfs now available.

G. blandus. Grows to 2 feet. Pink flowers.

G. hybridus. The popular florist gladiolus used for cut flowers. Comes in an array of colors and flower sizes.

GLORIOSA ROTHSCHILDIANA
Glory-lily

Bulb
To 5 feet

Light: Sun/Bright
Water: Heavy (allow to dry out before watering)
Bloom: Summer

Spectacular red and orange flowers; a climber, with slender leaves. Good for mild climates; dig up yearly in cold climates. Good as pot plant, too.

GODETIA   Satinflower

Annual
To 2½ feet

Light: Bright
Water: Moderate
Bloom: Spring/Summer

A group of pretty garden plants that like cool conditions. Very showy, godetias are floriferous and provide good color almost any place in the garden. Need a sandy loam and some sun to prosper. Sometimes sold under the name Clarkia.

G. amoena (farewell-to-spring). Two-inch pink or lavender cup-shaped flowers.

G. grandiflora. Two- to 4-inch red flowers. Floriferous.

GOMPHRENA GLOBOSA   Globe amaranth
Annual
To 1½ feet

Light: Sun
Water: Heavy
Bloom: Summer/Fall

Available in tall and short varieties, plants have small round flower heads, usually purple or white. Plants tolerate hot weather and are usually easily grown.

GYPSOPHILA   Baby's breath
Perennial
To 1½ feet

Light: Sun
Water: Heavy
Bloom: Spring/Summer

Fine lacy plants with branching habit and tiny flowers. Make unique garden accent and background for more dramatic plants. Use a neutral (pH 7.0) soil and grow in full sun.

G. elegans. Feathery and pretty; scads of white or rose blooms.

G. paniculata (baby's breath). More floriferous than *G. elegans.*

HAEMANTHUS   Blood lily

Bulb
To 3 feet

Light: Bright
Water: Moderate
Bloom: Summer

Spectacular plants but cannot survive cold. Pot in spring in containers with tip above soil line. Plants rest in fall and winter; keep just barely moist. Excellent container garden plants.

H. coccineus. Coral-red flowers in early fall.

H. multiflorus. Blood-red flowers for summer.

HELENIUM AUTUMNALE   Helen flower
Perennial
To 4 feet

Light: Sun
Water: Heavy
Bloom: Summer/Fall

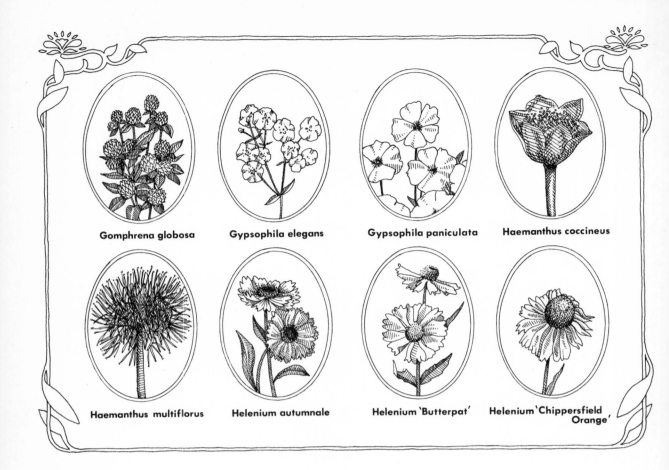

Gomphrena globosa   Gypsophila elegans   Gypsophila paniculata   Haemanthus coccineus

Haemanthus multiflorus   Helenium autumnale   Helenium 'Butterpat'   Helenium 'Chippersfield Orange'

A fine garden flower, with great clusters of bright-orange daisylike flowers, 2 inches across. Plants grow in almost any type of soil if there is enough moisture. Pinch out tips of stalks in early summer to prolong bloom.

Suggested Varieties:
  'Butterpat'
  'Chippersfield Orange'

HELIANTHUS   Sunflower

Perennial/Annual
To 5 feet

Light: Sun
Water: Heavy
Bloom: Summer

A better group of flowers than most people think. Grows easily in most gardens. Excellent for background. Plants spread rapidly, so dig them up and divide every second year in spring or fall.

H. annuus. Popular favorite with large yellow flower heads. Annual.

H. multiflorus. Thinner leaves then *H. annuus;* yellow flowers. Perennial.

HELICHRYSUM BRACTEATUM
Strawflower

Annual
To 2½ feet

Light: Sun
Water: Heavy
Bloom: Summer

A fine plant with lovely red or orange daisylike flowers. Flower petals are actually stiff modified leaves; true flowers are in center. Plants flourish in almost any soil in sun. Splendid as cut flowers and for drying for indoor winter decoration.

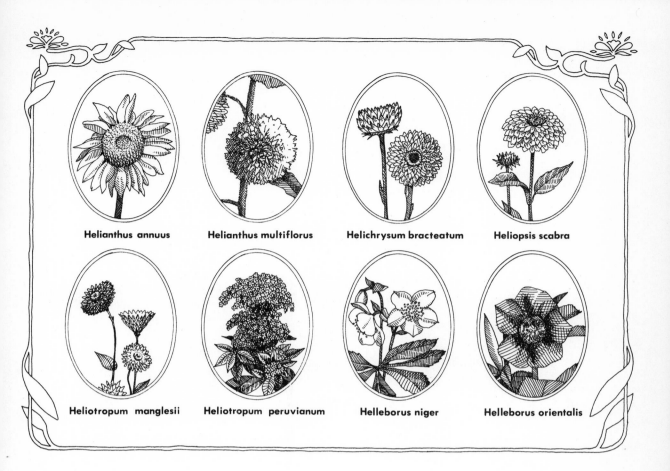

Helianthus annuus   Helianthus multiflorus   Helichrysum bracteatum   Heliopsis scabra

Heliotropum manglesii   Heliotropum peruvianum   Helleborus niger   Helleborus orientalis

HELIOPSIS SCABRA

Perennial
To 3 feet

Light: Sun
Water: Heavy
Bloom: Summer/Fall

If you want a plant that blooms over a long season and one with brightly colored yellow flowers, Heliopsis is for you. The plants do well in almost any type of soil and bloom profusely; certainly worth space in the flower garden.

HELIOTROPUM   Heliotrope

Perennial
To 4 feet

Light: Shade
Water: Scant
Bloom: Summer

The fragrant and popular heliotropes can tolerate shade and still be beautiful. Plants are easy to grow if they are not overwatered. A very good summer bedding plant for accent color.

H. manglesii. Large clusters of purple blooms; floriferous.

H. peruvianum. Scented dark-violet flowers.

HELLEBORUS   Lenten rose/Christmas rose

Perennial
To 16 inches

Light: Shade
Water: Heavy
Bloom: Winter/Spring

These plants bloom anytime, from winter to early spring, and last a long time. Plants need a shady moist place in the garden—under trees or shrubs perhaps—and an alkaline soil (pH 8.0).

H. niger (Christmas rose). Lovely green scalloped leaves and large white flowers.

H. orientalis (Lenten rose). Large 4-inch white blooms.

HEMEROCALLIS   Day lily

Perennial
To 3 feet

Light: Bright
Water: Moderate
Bloom: Spring/Summer/Fall

There are many kinds of day lilies, some short and others to 3 feet, in an array of different colors but mainly orange or yellow. The plants are extremely beautiful in masses but are not easy to grow; they require almost perfect drainage and take a good deal of time to establish themselves. Still, they are worth a try because they are so very colorful.

HESPERIS MATRONALIS   Sweet rocket

Perennial
To 3 feet

Light: Bright/Shade
Water: Moderate
Bloom: Summer

Sweet rocket's clusters of fragrant purple flowers make a good garden accent. Grow plants in any type of well-drained soil; plants tolerate some shade. Remove faded flowers to prolong blooming season.

HEUCHERA SANGUINEA   Coralbells

Perennial
To 3 feet

Light: Bright/Shade
Water: Moderate
Bloom: Summer/Fall

This plant should be grown more because it does bloom in shady locations and produces dozens of pink flowers on wiry stems. Coralbells need a rich, rapidly draining soil and are attractive in clumps. Good for borders, paths, and rock gardens.

Suggested Variety:
   'Chartreuse'

HIBISCUS   Rose mallow

Perennial
To 8 feet

Light: Sun
Water: Moderate
Bloom: Summer/Fall

Lovely relatives of the hollyhock family, with enormous flowers, some 8 inches across. Plants like sun and a rich soil kept evenly moist. Handsome vertical background for other plants; many new varieties.

H. moscheutos. Decorative toothed leaves, large pink flowers.

H. trionum. Short-lived 1-inch yellow flowers with maroon centers.

HIPPEASTRUM   Amaryllis

Bulb
To 2½ feet

Light: Shade/Bright
Water: Moderate
Bloom: Winter/Spring/Summer

The popular amaryllis has gigantic flowers, some 8 inches across, in deep red, pink, or other shades. Plants need a rich soil that drains freely and good bright light.

H. unnemannia fumariaefolia. Species type with smaller flowers.

Suggested Varieties:
   'Appleblossom'
   'Fire Dance'
   'Scarlet Admiral'

HYACINTHUS   Hyacinth

Bulb
To 2 feet

Light: Sun
Water: Moderate
Bloom: Spring

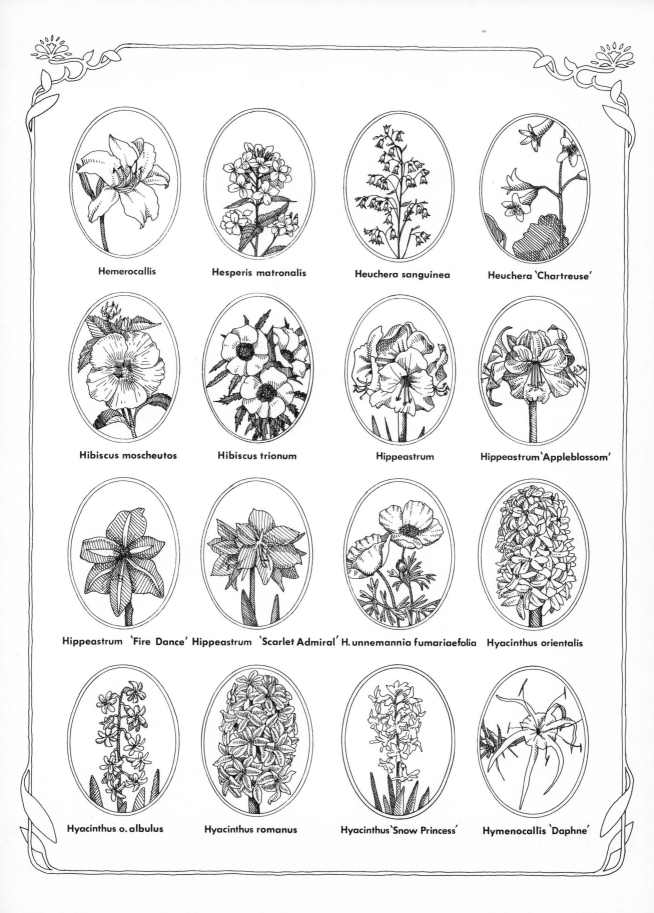

Hemerocallis　　　**Hesperis matronalis**　　　**Heuchera sanguinea**　　　**Heuchera 'Chartreuse'**

Hibiscus moscheutos　　　**Hibiscus trionum**　　　**Hippeastrum**　　　**Hippeastrum 'Appleblossom'**

Hippeastrum 'Fire Dance'　**Hippeastrum 'Scarlet Admiral'**　**H. unnemannia fumariaefolia**　**Hyacinthus orientalis**

Hyacinthus o. albulus　　　**Hyacinthus romanus**　　　**Hyacinthus 'Snow Princess'**　　　**Hymenocallis 'Daphne'**

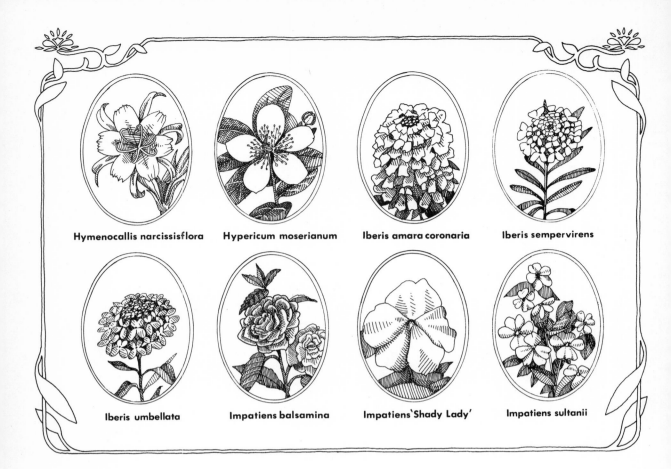

Hymenocallis narcissisflora	Hypericum moserianum
Iberis amara coronaria	Iberis sempervirens
Iberis umbellata	Impatiens balsamina
Impatiens 'Shady Lady'	Impatiens sultanii

Sweetly scented hyacinths are popular garden flowers. For most areas, plant in fall. Space bulbs 5 inches apart and 5 inches deep. Use a winter mulch and leave plants undisturbed. Make handsome display in drifts.

H. orientalis. Large blue flowers. The most popular hyacinth.

H. o. albulus. An improved variety of *H. orientalis,* more robust, with blue, pink, or white flowers.

H. romanus. Blue or white flowers.

Suggested Variety:
  'Snow Princess'

HYMENOCALLIS NARCISSIFOLIA
Spider lily

Bulb
To 3 feet

Light: Sun
Water: Heavy (allow to dry out before watering)
Bloom: Summer

Very large fragrant flowers make spider lily a desirable plant. Blooms appear on tall leafless stalks; straplike leaves may be evergreen or deciduous. Tender. Dig up and store bulbs yearly. Space bulbs 1 foot apart, 5 inches deep.

Suggested Variety:
  'Daphne'

HYPERICUM MOSERIANUM
Saint-John's-wort

Perennial
To 2½ feet

Light: Bright
Water: Moderate
Bloom: Summer/Fall

Lovely cupped golden flowers make this plant a desirable addition outdoors; grows easily in almost any soil in sun or bright light. Cut stems to ground level each year to encourage new growth.

IBERIS   Candytuft

Perennial/Annual (evergreen)
To 1 foot

Light: Sun/Bright
Water: Moderate
Bloom: Spring/Summer/Fall

These plants, with dark-green foliage and dazzling white flowers, can add much to a garden. Plants need a well-drained location and grow in almost any soil. Cut old flower stems as soon as they fade to encourage new flower stems.

I. amara coronaria. Fragrant white flowers in clusters. Annual.

I. sempervirens (evergreen candytuft). Dark-green leaves and 2-inch clusters of tiny white blooms.

I. umbellata (globe candytuft). Bushy plants; small pink flowers. Annual.

IMPATIENS   Patience plant

Annual
To 3 feet

Light: Sun/Shade
Water: Heavy
Bloom: Summer/Fall

Some varieties grow only 10 inches tall; others grow to 3 feet. Flowers are pink or red; new varieties have more vividly colored flowers, including bicolor. All patience plants do well in sandy soil in sun or shade. Use plants as bedding subjects, in borders, and as tall varieties for background material.

I. balsamina. Lovely pink flowers on tall plants.

I. sultanii. Old-fashioned pink species. Still good.

I. walleriana. Bright red-flowers on bushy plants.

Suggested Variety:
  'Shady Lady'

INCARVILLEA

Perennial
To 2½ feet

Light: Sun
Water: Moderate
Bloom: Summer

A group of overlooked plants. Pretty pink flowers. Grow well in rich loamy soil that has excellent drainage. Remove faded flowers to extend growing season.

I. delavayi. Lovely pink flowers; floriferous.

I. grandiflora. Larger flowers; more robust than *I. delavayi.*

INULA ORIENTALIS

Perennial
To 2 feet

Light: Sun
Water: Heavy
Bloom: Summer

Of easy culture, Inula bears large yellow flowers. Plants grow in almost any soil. Use in groups for bright color; good for edgings or in flower beds.

IPOMOEA PURPUREA   Morning glory

Vine
To 15 feet

Light: Sun
Water: Scant
Bloom: Summer

Lovely vining annuals, with large blue funnel-shaped flowers that last a day; decorative leaves. Plants grow fast in almost any soil. Do not feed. Start new plants each year.

Suggested Varieties:
  'Candy Pink'
  'Pearly Gates'

IRESINE HERBSTII   Bloodleaf

Annual
To 2 feet

Light: Sun
Water: Heavy
Bloom: Summer

This plant is grown for its fantastic multicolored leaves (usually red and yellow), which make a dramatic statement in a garden. Plants need good sun and will tolerate bad soils.

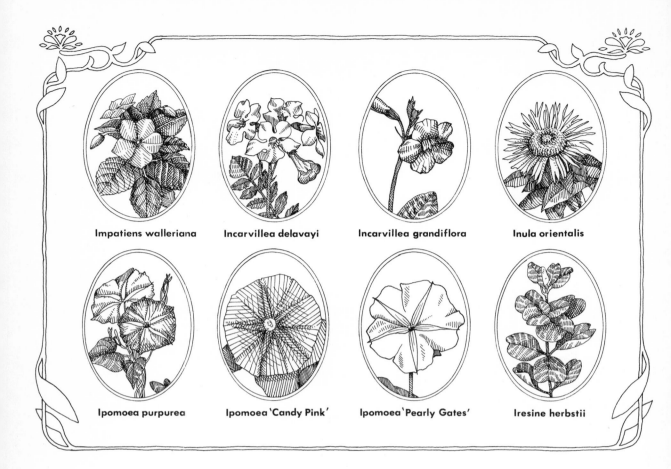

Impatiens walleriana Incarvillea delavayi Incarvillea grandiflora Inula orientalis

Ipomoea purpurea Ipomoea 'Candy Pink' Ipomoea 'Pearly Gates' Iresine herbstii

IRIS   Iris

Bulb
To 1½ feet

Light: Bright/Shade
Water: Heavy
Bloom: Spring/Summer

Three groups comprise the cultivated irises of gardens; finer flowers are hard to find. All irises like a somewhat shady to bright location, with lots of water at the roots.

I. hybrids (Dutch iris). Many varieties; fine yellow flowers.

I. reticulata. Several species in this group; blue to deep violet flowers.

I. xiphioides (English iris). White through shades of blue to violet flowers.

I. xiphium (Spanish iris). White, yellow, orange, or blue flowers.

IXIA   Corn lily

Corm
To 2 feet

Light: Sun
Water: Moderate
Bloom: Spring/Summer

Large group of handsome flowering plants, with 2-inch flowers on wiry stems. Flower color varies from red to pink, orange to yellow; all flowers usually have dark centers. Foliage is grassy and swordlike. Excellent cut flowers. Plant in fall 3 to 6 inches apart, 3 inches deep. Dig up yearly and store.

JASMINUM OFFICINALE   Jasmine

Vine (semi-evergreen)
To 15 feet

Light: Bright
Water: Moderate
Bloom: Summer/Fall

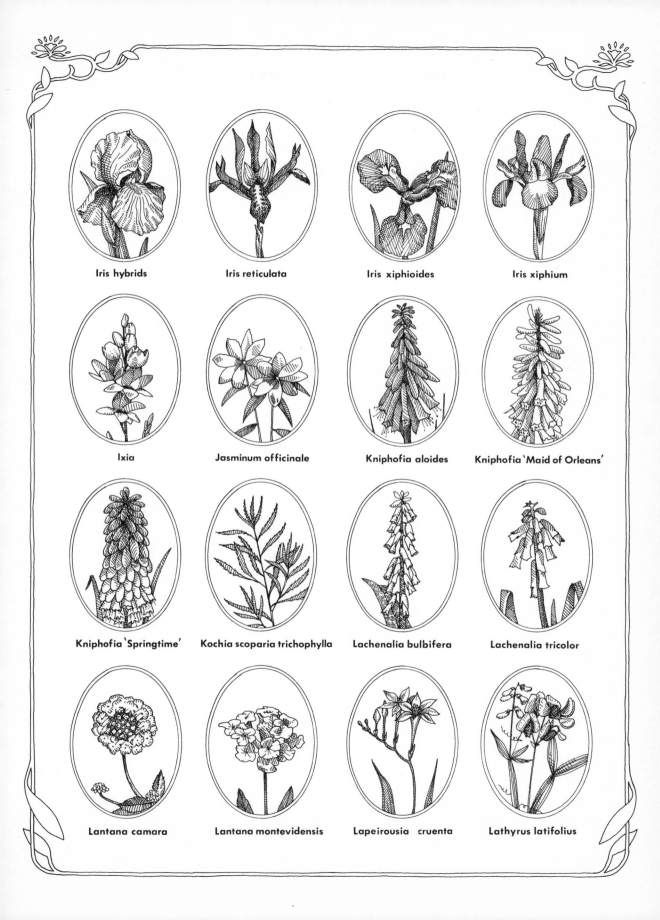

Iris hybrids

Iris reticulata

Iris xiphioides

Iris xiphium

Ixia

Jasminum officinale

Kniphofia aloides

Kniphofia 'Maid of Orleans'

Kniphofia 'Springtime'

Kochia scoparia trichophylla

Lachenalia bulbifera

Lachenalia tricolor

Lantana camara

Lantana montevidensis

Lapeirousia cruenta

Lathyrus latifolius

A lovely vine with small (1-inch) fragrant white flowers. Plants do well in almost any type of soil with even moisture and will tolerate shade if necessary and still bloom. Pinch frequently to keep well shaped and provide suitable support (trellis or pergola).

KNIPHOFIA ALOOIDES   Red-hot poker
Perennial
To 9 feet

Light: Sun
Water: Heavy
Bloom: Summer/Fall

Long gray-green leaves with coral-red flowers that become orange and then greenish yellow. Long-lasting plants that make strong vertical statement in garden. Good background plant and almost immune to insects.

Suggested Varieties:
  'Maid of Orleans'
  'Springtime'

KOCHIA SCOPARIA TRICHOPHYLLA
Fire bush
Annual
To 3 feet

Light: Sun
Water: Moderate
Bloom: Fall

An erect, much-branched plant, with numerous narrow leaves. Red flowers become purple-red in autumn. Needs good sun and will tolerate hot weather. Not fussy about soil.

LACHENALIA   Cape cowslip
Bulb
To 1 foot

Light: Sun
Water: Scant/Moderate
Bloom: Spring

Fine group of bulbous plants for spot color. Grow easily in most situations if soil drains readily.

L. bulbifera. A showy, large-flowered species, with erect, dark green, and sometimes spotted leaves. Deep-purple, red, and yellow flowers.

L. tricolor (Cape cowslip). Dark-green leaves with dull-purple spots; red and yellow flowers.

LANTANA
Annual
To 3 feet

Light: Sun
Water: Moderate
Bloom: Summer/Fall

Grow these popular plants in rich loamy soil with heavy watering. Good substitute for ground cover, and trailing types are especially handsome in baskets on patio or terrace.

L. camara. A prickly-stemmed plant. Flowers open pink or yellow and then become red or orange. Will perennialize in a warm winter climate.

L. montevidensis. A trailing variety, with rosy-lilac flowers.

LAPEIROUSIA CRUENTA
Bulb
To 1 foot

Light: Sun
Water: Moderate
Bloom: Summer/Fall

These are really lovely little border plants or are just fine in clumps by themselves where you want some vivid color. The flowers are a splendid carmine red against narrow dark-green leaves. Excellent for woodland landscapes and totally charming. Lift and store bulbs in severe winter climates.

LATHYRUS   Everlasting pea
Perennial/Annual
To 8 feet

Light: Sun
Water: Moderate
Bloom: Summer

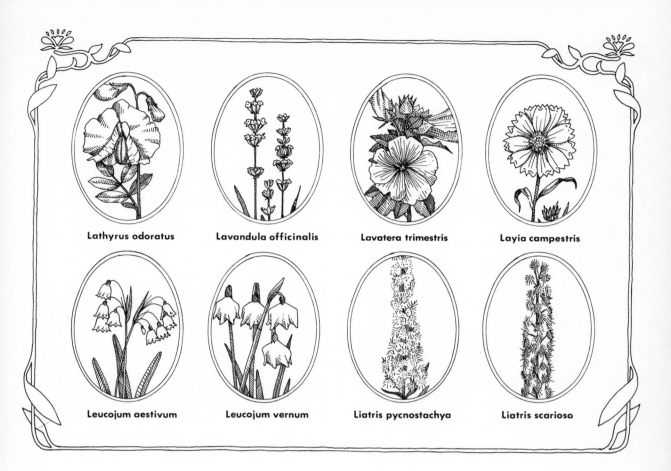

Lathyrus odoratus　　**Lavandula officinalis**　　**Lavatera trimestris**　　**Layia campestris**

Leucojum aestivum　　**Leucojum vernum**　　**Liatris pycnostachya**　　**Liatris scariosa**

Lovely plants that do well in rich loamy soils and plenty of sun. Like coolness. There are short, knee-high, and tall vining types. A good all-around group of plants for gardens, but they need some pampering to get established.

L. latifolius. Large rose-colored flowers; climbing habit. Perennial.

L. odoratus (sweet pea). A climbing pea; fragrant flowers of various colors. Excellent for window boxes or planters. Cutting back stimulates new growth. Annual.

LAVANDULA OFFICINALIS
Common lavender

Perennial
To 3 feet

Light: Sun
Water: Moderate
Bloom: Summer/Fall

A low-growing plant, with exquisitely fragrant pale gray-blue flowers. Flowers are highly valued for cutting and drying. Easily grown.

LAVATERA TRIMESTRIS　Tree mallow

Annual
To 6 feet

Light: Sun
Water: Moderate
Bloom: Summer/Fall

Roundish leaves with rose-colored flowers. Liable to attack by hollyhock rust, otherwise easily grown. Only recently available in this country and worth a try.

LAYIA CAMPESTRIS　Tidytips

Annual
To 1½ feet

Light: Sun
Water: Moderate
Bloom: Summer

A narrow-leaved plant that bears pretty yellow flowers tipped with white. Grows easily if it has sufficient sun and moderate moisture at the roots. Makes lovely mounds of color in the garden.

LEUCOJUM   Snowflake

Bulb
To 1½ feet

Light: Sun
Water: Heavy
Bloom: Spring/Summer

Lovely white blooms. Easily grown. Plant bulbs in fall 4 inches apart, 2 inches deep. Use under deciduous trees and for spot color anywhere in the yard. Leave bulbs undisturbed for years.

L. aestivum. White drooping flowers in clusters of 4 to 8.

L. vernum (snowflake). Solitary, drooping, and fragrant white flowers.

LIATRIS   Gayfeather

Perennial
To 5 feet

Light: Sun
Water: Scant
Bloom: Summer/Fall

These are tall plants with spires of pretty lavender or white flowers and make fine background accents in the flower garden. Plants need a well-drained loamy soil and otherwise will fend for themselves. Best grown in clumps to create a profusion of color.

L. pycnostachya. Pale-purple flower spires.

L. scariosa. Taller than *L. pycnostachya;* purple blooms.

L. spicata. Purple or white flowers in dense spires.

LIGULARIA DENTATA   Leopard plant

Perennial
To 2½ feet

Light: Bright
Water: Moderate
Bloom: Summer

Grown for its decorative foliage, Ligularia has broad evergreen cream-and-green speckled leaves. Makes handsome accent and is unusual in gardens. Plants grow easily in almost any soil.

LILIUM   Lily

Bulb
To 5 feet

Light: Sun
Water: Heavy
Bloom: Summer

This group of plants, which needs little introduction, has lilies for almost all regions of the country. Sun is the prime requisite for floriferous plants, and most lilies need good drainage. Excellent in clumps in any part of the garden.

L. candidum (Madonna lily). Two- to 3-inch-long pearl-white flowers that are tinged purple.

L. regale (regal lily). White fragrant flowers.

L. tigrinum. Old species superseded in quality by modern hybrids.

Suggested Varieties:
    American hybrids
    Asiatic hybrids
    Aurelian hybrid
    Candidum hybrids
    Longiflorum hybrid
    Martagon hybrids
    Oriental hybrids

LIMONIUM   Sea lavender

Perennial/Annual
To 2 feet

Light: Sun
Water: Moderate
Bloom: Summer

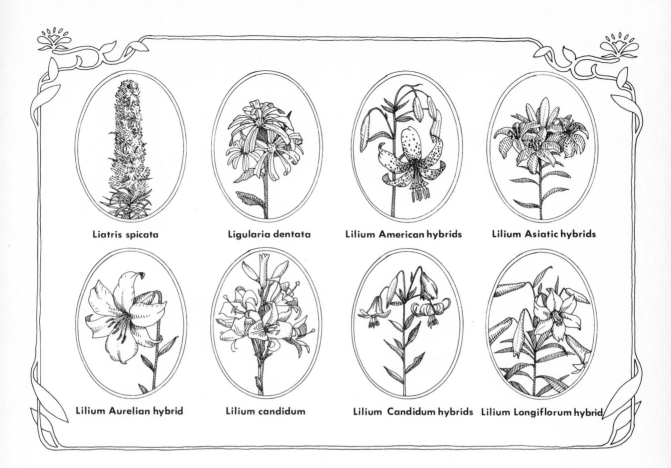

Liatris spicata | Ligularia dentata | Lilium American hybrids | Lilium Asiatic hybrids

Lilium Aurelian hybrid | Lilium candidum | Lilium Candidum hybrids | Lilium Longiflorum hybrid

A favorite group of plants for seaside plantings because they are resistant to salt spray. Plants are delicate and lacy, with small lavender flowers. Be sure soil for sea lavender drains readily. Flowers are good for cutting and last long when dried.

L. latifolium. Blue-flowered variety, with a woody base. A hardy border plant that may be raised from root cuttings. Good for cut flowers. Perennial.

L. sinuatum. Tall, with blue, lavender, or rose blooms. Annual.

L. suworowii. Branched flower clusters of rose pink. Floriferous. Annual.

LINARIA MAROCCANA   Toadflax

Annual
To 1 foot

Light: Sun
Water: Moderate
Bloom: Summer

Bright violet-purple flowers. Good for rock gardens or borders. Likes coolness and grows well in almost any soil.

LINUM   Flowering flax

Annual
To 1 foot

Light: Sun/Bright
Water: Moderate
Bloom: Summer

The small flowers of *L. grandiflorum* are superb color. Plants grow well in any light but prefer bright light. Make sure soil is well drained.

L. grandiflorum. (scarlet flax). One of the best showy annuals. Branched at base, with large rose flowers. Hardy and good for rock gardens.

L. perenne (perennial flax). Good for rock gardens or borders. Pale-blue flowers.

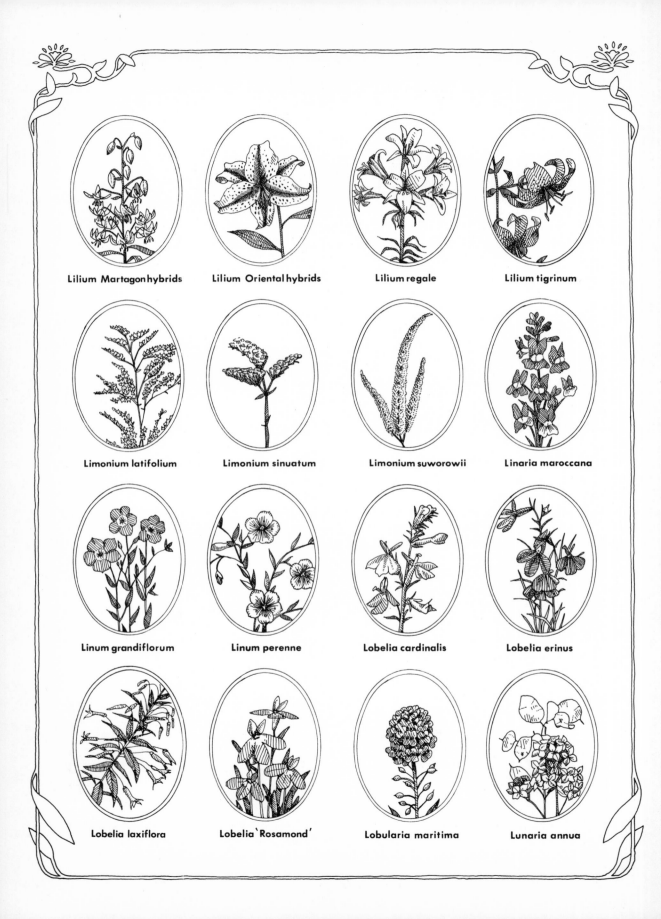

Lilium Martagon hybrids

Lilium Oriental hybrids

Lilium regale

Lilium tigrinum

Limonium latifolium

Limonium sinuatum

Limonium suworowii

Linaria maroccana

Linum grandiflorum

Linum perenne

Lobelia cardinalis

Lobelia erinus

Lobelia laxiflora

Lobelia 'Rosamond'

Lobularia maritima

Lunaria annua

LOBELIA

Annual
To 1 foot

Light: Bright/Shade
Water: Heavy
Bloom: Summer

A fine group of small plants that can be used in many ways in the garden: edges, borders, beds, and so on. Plants grow easily in regions where summers are cool, and they prefer a shady place. Use a loamy garden soil.

L. cardinalis. A red-flowering lobelia and very pretty.

L. erinus (blue lobelia). Variable in habit; lovely blue flowers. Can be grown as perennial in mild winter areas.

L. laxiflora. Hairy leaves; red and yellow flowers.

Suggested Variety:
  'Rosamond'

LOBULARIA MARITIMA   Sweet alyssum

Annual
To ½ foot

Light: Sun
Water: Moderate
Bloom: Spring/Fall

Here is a plant that blooms with tiny flowers from late spring to fall. Some varieties have white flowers, others pink or blue, and all are useful as edging plants, in rock gardens, or to provide color after spring bulbs have finished blooming. Lobularias prosper in almost any soil and the flowers are scented, making them especially desirable.

LUNARIA ANNUA   Honesty/dollar plant

Annual
To 2 feet

Light: Sun
Water: Moderate
Bloom: Spring

Violet-lilac flowers and the popular pods that look like silver dollars. Will tolerate light shade. Easily grown. An excellent dried flower.

LUPINUS   Lupine

Annual
To 3 feet

Light: Sun
Water: Moderate
Bloom: Summer/Fall

Although known for their lovely blue flowers, lupines also come in reds and pinks. Plants are tall, making nice backgrounds for the flower garden, and are especially good in areas with cool summers. Plant in loamy soil. Sometimes difficult to get growing but really handsome plants worth the challenge.

L. hartwegii. Fine yellow-flowering plant.

L. subcarnosus (Texas bluebonnet). Bright blue flowers.

Suggested Variety:
  Russel Hybrid

LYCHNIS   Maltese cross

Perennial
To 3 feet

Light: Sun
Water: Heavy
Bloom: Summer

Floriferous plants that add splendid masses of color to any garden but must have excellent drainage and lots of sun. Always desirable.

L. chalcedonica. Brilliant scarlet flowers on a stiffly erect, hairy stem. Good plant for watery areas.

L. coronaria (rose campion) (mullein pink). Purple, flesh-colored, or white bell-shaped flowers.

L. viscaria (catchfly). Large rose or white flowers. Excellent for rock garden.

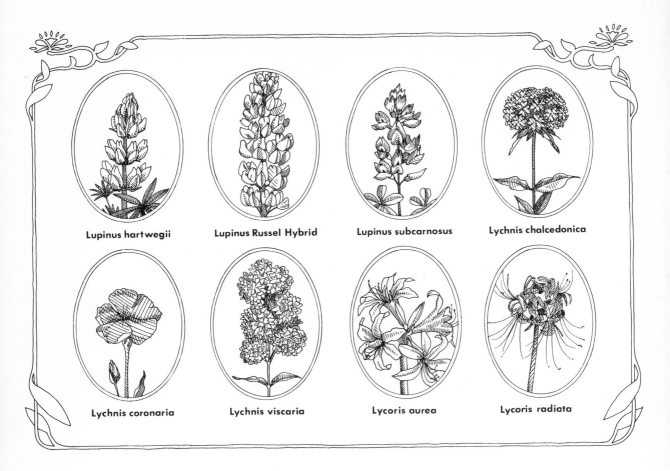

Lupinus hartwegii	Lupinus Russel Hybrid	Lupinus subcarnosus	Lychnis chalcedonica
Lychnis coronaria	Lychnis viscaria	Lycoris aurea	Lycoris radiata

LYCORIS   Golden spider lily

Bulb
To 2 feet

Light: Sun
Water: Moderate
Bloom: Summer/Fall

These are fine bulbous plants that bear showy yellow or pink flowers, large and dramatic. Plants need a well-drained sandy soil. Lift bulbs yearly and store in cool dry place.

L. aurea. Funnel-shaped and erect golden-yellow flowers. Foliage appears after flowers.

L. radiata (short-tubed lycoris). Deep-pink to nearly scarlet flowers.

LYSIMACHIA PUNCTATA   Moneywort

Perennial
To 2 feet

Light: Bright
Water: Heavy
Bloom: Summer

This erect, somewhat branching plant will grow in less than good conditions and still produce many yellow flowers. Best for shady locations, moneywort provides a nice spot of color; makes good cut flowers.

LYTHRUM SALICARIA   Purple loosestrife

Perennial
To 5 feet

Light: Sun
Water: Heavy
Bloom: Summer

Red-purple flowers make this herbaceous perennial a favorite; best where there is ample moisture. Use for borders or wherever you need color.

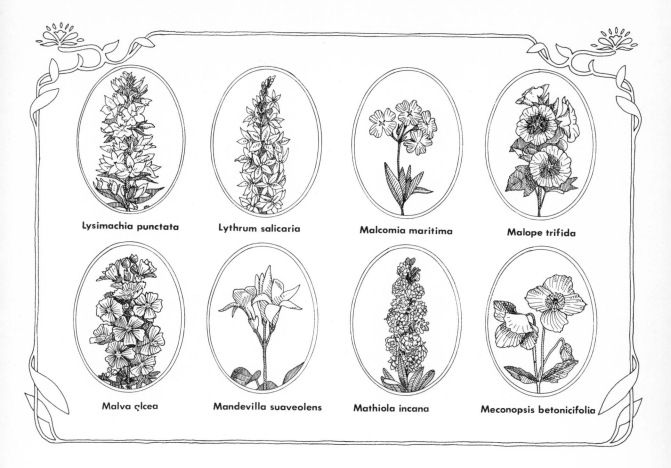

Lysimachia punctata   Lythrum salicaria   Malcomia maritima   Malope trifida

Malva çlcea   Mandevilla suaveolens   Mathiola incana   Meconopsis betonicifolia

MALCOMIA MARITIMA   Virginia stock

Annual
To 1 foot

Light: Sun
Water: Moderate
Bloom: Spring/Summer

An erect branched species, with lilac, rose, red, or white flowers. Can be kept in bloom from spring to autumn by successional sowing, starting in autumn. Easy to grow.

MALOPE TRIFIDA   Mallow-wort

Annual
To 3 feet

Light: Sun
Water: Moderate
Bloom: Summer

Bushy plant with large trumpet-shaped purple or white flowers. Plants require good drainage and a sunny location. Good for borders and bedding and excellent for cut flowers.

MALVA ALCEA   Hollyhock

Perennial
To 3 feet

Light: Sun/Bright
Water: Heavy
Bloom: Summer/Fall

With palm-shaped leaves, Malva bears handsome red flowers in masses at the top of tall stems. Plants can grow in almost any soil and make fine additions to gardens where mass is needed. Not spectacular, but worthy of space.

MANDEVILLA SUAVEOLENS
Chilean jasmine

Vine
To 20 feet

Light: Sun
Water: Heavy
Bloom: Summer

Mandevilla produces an abundance of fragrant creamy-white pink-tinged flowers. This is a very handsome deciduous climber that grows well in a loamy garden soil; likes heat and sun. With excellent color, it is a fine plant to cover walls and fences.

MATHIOLA INCANA   Stock

Annual
To 3 feet

Light: Sun
Water: Heavy
Bloom: Summer

Double or single flowers are of various colors; snowy white through pink. Hardy, sometimes biennial. Excellent cut flower and fragrant in evenings. Use wherever a vertical accent is needed. Really lovely flowers; many good varieties.

MECONOPSIS BETONICIFOLIA   Blue poppy

Perennial
To 5 feet

Light: Shade/Bright
Water: Heavy
Bloom: Summer

With sky-blue to rosy-lavender flowers and a delicate appearance, these handsome poppies are excellent garden additions. Plants like coolness, some shade, and an acid soil (pH 5.5. to 6.0). If you want an abundance of these lovely flowers, be sure to put plants where drainage is excellent.

MENTZELIA LINDLEYI   Blazing star

Annual
To 2 feet

Light: Sun
Water: Moderate
Bloom: Summer

Two or three bright-yellow flowers top the stems of blazing stars. Showy and fragrant blooms open in evening and remain until next morning. Provide a well-drained location. Good for borders or wherever some dramatic color is needed.

MESEMBRYANTHEMUM CORDIFOLIUM   Fig marigold

Annual
To 1 foot

Light: Sun
Water: Scant
Bloom: Summer/Fall

These plants have creamy white variegated leaves and purple or red flowers. Grow in almost any soil and like dryness. Good for borders and ground covers.

MIMULUS VARIEGATUS   Monkey flower

Annual
To 1 foot

Light: Bright/Shade
Water: Heavy
Bloom: Summer

Plants have bright-green leaves and multicolored 2-inch flowers. Monkey flower needs little care; it can have abuse if necessary and still prosper. Forms mounds of color. Not spectacular but worth space.

MIRABILIS JALAPA   Four-o'clock

Annual
To 2 feet

Light: Sun
Water: Moderate
Bloom: Summer

A handsome plant with fragrant funnel-shaped white, yellow, or crimson flowers striped or blotched. Blooms open in the afternoon and close in the morning. Plants grow in any well-drained soil but do require good sunlight. Fine plants for borders. Always pretty.

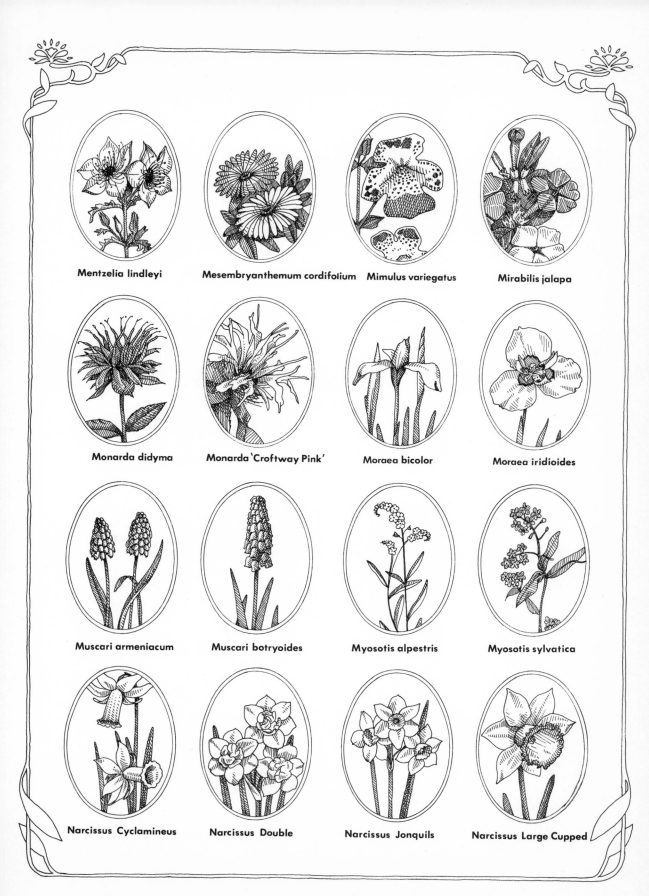

Mentzelia lindleyi

Mesembryanthemum cordifolium

Mimulus variegatus

Mirabilis jalapa

Monarda didyma

Monarda 'Croftway Pink'

Moraea bicolor

Moraea iridioides

Muscari armeniacum

Muscari botryoides

Myosotis alpestris

Myosotis sylvatica

Narcissus Cyclamineus

Narcissus Double

Narcissus Jonquils

Narcissus Large Cupped

MONARDA DIDYMA   Bee balm

Perennial
To 3 feet

Light: Sun
Water: Heavy
Bloom: Summer/Fall

A rough, hairy-leaved plant with bright-scarlet flowers. Makes a colorful display. To prolong bloom remove faded flowers before they produce seed. A very easy-to-grow plant for garden lovers.

Suggested Variety:
   'Croftway Pink'

MORAEA   Yellow moraea

Bulb
To 2 feet

Light: Sun
Water: Moderate
Bloom: Summer

Iris-type plants that are graceful and lovely and bloom a long time, one flower following another. Use in clumps by themselves for special accent in garden.

M. bicolor. Brilliant, sweet-scented yellow flowers with a black-brown blotch at base of outer segements.

M. iridioides (butterfly iris). Fanlike leaves with white flowers that have yellow or brown spots on outer segments.

MUSCARI   Grape hyacinth

Bulb
To 1½ feet

Light: Sun
Water: Moderate
Bloom: Spring

These favorites are so easy to grow that little instruction is necessary. Grow in clumps under trees or wherever some blue color is needed.

M. armeniacum. Azure to purplish blue flowers; dark-green long leaves.

M. botryoides (grape hyacinth). Deep sky-blue flowers that form little bells near top of stem. Popular.

MYOSOTIS   Forget-me-not

Perennial
To 1 foot

Light: Sun
Water: Moderate
Bloom: Spring

A group of small plants with small blue flowers. Very pretty in beds or in small islands, giving a dainty appearance. Plants require a very rich loamy soil and are not easy to grow.

M. alpestris. Azure-blue flowers with a small yellow eye.

M. sylvatica (woodland forget-me-not). Blue flowers with yellow eye.

NARCISSUS   Daffodil

Bulb
To 2 feet

Light: Bright/Shade
Water: Moderate
Bloom: Spring

Here is the group of fine flowering bulbs that everyone loves. The cup-shaped flowers come in a variety of colors and there are dozens of varieties available for all regions, all purposes. There is also a wide assortment of flower shapes. Narcissus plants look best grouped by themselves in gardens to create a stellar spring display. The plants need a loamy garden soil with lots of compost and drainage must be good.

Suggested Varieties:
   Cyclimineus
   Double
   Jonquils
   Large Cupped
   Poeticus
   Small Cupped
   Tazetta
   Triandrus
   Trumpet

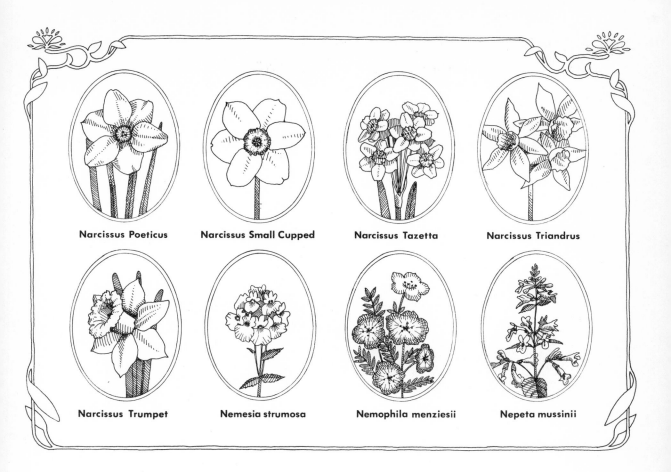

Narcissus Poeticus   Narcissus Small Cupped   Narcissus Tazetta   Narcissus Triandrus

Narcissus Trumpet   Nemesia strumosa   Nemophila menziesii   Nepeta mussinii

NEMESIA STRUMOSA   Nemesia
Annual
To 1½ feet

Light: Sun
Water: Moderate
Bloom: Summer

A very showy plant, with white, pale-yellow, orange, or rosy-purple flowers. Plants thrive in coolness and need a rich compost loam to bear abundant bloom. Difficult but good.

NEMOPHILA MENZIESII   Baby blue-eyes
Annual
To 1 foot

Light: Sun/Bright
Water: Moderate
Bloom: Spring/Summer

A spreading hairy plant with pretty flat-faced white to light-blue flowers. Plants need a well-drained soil. Excellent for bed and borders. Not spectacular, but good where blue color is needed.

NEPETA MUSSINII   Catmint
Perennial
To 1 foot

Light: Sun
Water: Moderate
Bloom: Summer

With its silver-gray leaves and pale-lavender flowers, catmint is an invaluable edging plant. It likes full sun and almost any well-drained soil.

NERINE BOWDENII
Bulb
To 1½ feet

Light: Sun
Water: Heavy
Bloom: Summer/Fall

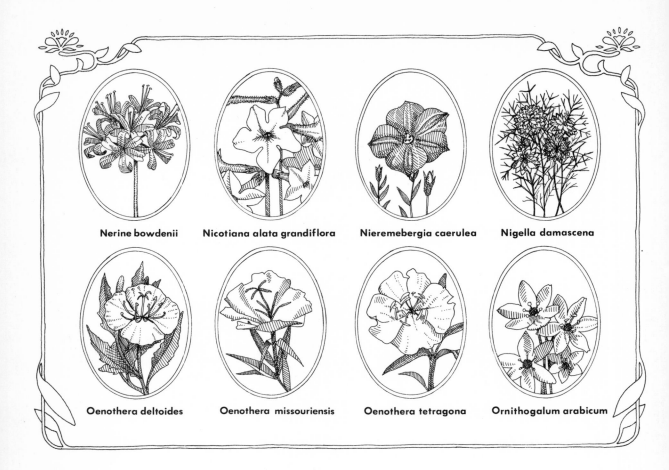

Nerine bowdenii   **Nicotiana alata grandiflora**   **Nieremebergia caerulea**   **Nigella damascena**

Oenothera deltoides   **Oenothera missouriensis**   **Oenothera tetragona**   **Ornithogalum arabicum**

A showy plant, with glossy green 12-inch leaves and large pale-pink lilylike flowers. Give heavy water during growing season. Plants for special places.

NICOTIANA ALATA GRANDIFLORA
Flowering tobacco

Annual
To 2 feet

Light: Bright/Shade
Water: Heavy
Bloom: Summer

A strong-scented plant with greenish yellow foliage and scarlet, yellow, or white flowers. Strongly scented at night; will become perennial in mild winters. Good in border and shady problem areas.

NIEREMBERGIA CAERULEA   Cupflower

Annual
To 3 feet

Light: Bright/Shade
Water: Heavy
Bloom: Summer

A much-branched, stiffly erect plant with thin stems covered with white hairs. The numerous bell-shaped flowers are about 1 inch across. Flowers are bright blue-violet with darker lines and yellow in the throat. Plants like coolness. Excellent for shady areas.

NIGELLA DAMASCENA   Love-in-a-mist

Annual
To 1½ feet

Light: Sun
Water: Moderate
Bloom: Summer

Large blue flowers and feathery foliage. A fine hardy plant for very sunny places; grows in almost any soil.

OENOTHERA   Sundrops

Annual
To 2 feet

Light: Sun
Water: Moderate
Bloom: Summer

A group of pretty flowering plants that are easy to grow in almost any situation. Floriferous and good for borders or rock gardens.

O. deltoides. A pretty plant with fragrant white flowers that turn pink and last 1 to 2 days. Flowers are 1½ to 3 inches across.

O. missouriensis. Leaves are 1 to 3 feet long; yellow flowers, 3 to 4 inches across, open in the evening.

O. tetragona (sundrops). Sometimes biennial. Erect. Yellow flowers are 1 to 1½ inches across.

ORNITHOGALUM   Star-of-Bethlehem

Bulb
To 2 feet

Light: Sun
Water: Moderate
Bloom: Summer

These plants last for weeks as cut flowers and are easy to grow in almost any situation. Different and certainly worth space in the garden.

O. arabicum. Large aromatic white flowers with black centers.

O. thyrsoides (chincherinchee). Dense white to golden yellow flowers. Long-lasting.

O. umbellatum (common star-of-Bethlehem). Satiny white flower; green-striped white outside.

OXALIS   Bowie oxalis

Bulb
To 1 foot

Light: Sun
Water: Moderate
Bloom: Summer

A fine group of free-flowering plants that like moisture and seem to thrive in sun or shade. Considered weedlike in most areas, but they offer a lot of color for little effort. Plant wherever you want a spot of color, and leave undisturbed for quick cover.

O. bowieana. A near-stemless plant with large purple bell-shaped flowers.

O. cernua (Bermuda buttercup). Stemless, with bell-shaped yellow flowers nearly 1 inch long. Can become a weed in mild areas.

PAEONIA   Chinese peony

Perennial
To 2½ feet

Light: Sun
Water: Moderate
Bloom: Summer

These spectacular flowering plants like coolness and a well-drained soil. Plant peonies in beds by themselves, or in front of shrubberies where the roots will not be disturbed, as they are apt to be in mixed borders. Highly recommended.

P. lactiflora. Handsome fragrant leaves and showy white flowers 3 to 4 inches across.

P. officinalis (common peony). Solitary red flowers up to 5 inches across.

PAPAVER   Alpine poppy

Perennial/Annual
To 1 foot

Light: Sun
Water: Moderate
Bloom: Summer

A useful group of plants with lovely color. Most bloom profusely with little care. Excellent when massed in beds by themselves. Will tolerate most

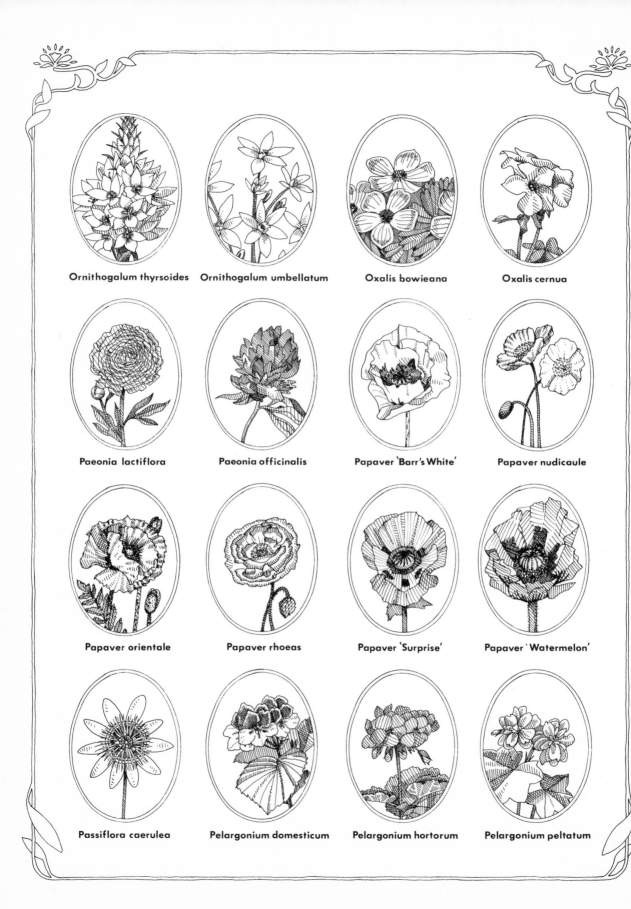

Ornithogalum thyrsoides   Ornithogalum umbellatum   Oxalis bowieana   Oxalis cernua

Paeonia lactiflora   Paeonia officinalis   Papaver 'Barr's White'   Papaver nudicaule

Papaver orientale   Papaver rhoeas   Papaver 'Surprise'   Papaver 'Watermelon'

Passiflora caerulea   Pelargonium domesticum   Pelargonium hortorum   Pelargonium peltatum

soils but must have a sunny location and almost perfect drainage.

P. nudicaule (Iceland poppy). Fragrant solitary flowers in a variety of colors. An extremely attractive border or show plant. Usually grown as an annual.

P. orientale (Oriental poppy). An erect perennial with magnificent scarlet flowers 4 to 6 inches or more across. Will not flower until the second year.

P. rhoeas (Shirley poppy). White to scarlet flowers 2 to 3 inches across. Generally grown as an annual.

Suggested Varieties:
  'Barr's White'
  'Surprise'
  'Watermelon'

PASSIFLORA CAERULEA   Passionflower
Vine
To 20 feet

Light: Sun
Water: Heavy
Bloom: Summer

A climber of great vigor with solitary, slightly fragrant, exotically colored flowers 3 to 4 inches wide and orange fruit. Excellent on walls facing south and west. Plants grow well with heavy moisture in any type of soil. Very fast-growing; unusual.

PELARGONIUM   Geranium
Annual
To 2½ feet

Light: Sun
Water: Moderate
Bloom: Summer

Popular plants that do very well in almost any garden with minimum attention. In year-round warm climates they grow all year and become shrubby plants; in most regions they are treated as annuals. As bedding plants, in borders, or by themselves, geraniums are colorful additions to the home yard. Zonal-leaved geraniums, Martha

Washington types, ivy geraniums, and scented geraniums are all part of the group.

P. domesticum (Lady Washington geranium). Popular plant available in many colors.

P. hortorum (common geranium). Pale-rose, red, carmine, or white flowers.

P. peltatum (ivy geranium). Excellent for hanging baskets because of its trailing habit. Carmine-rose or white flowers.

PENSTEMON GLOXINIOIDES
Beardtongue
Perennial
To 2½ feet

Light: Sun
Water: Moderate
Bloom: Summer

Large brightly colored red, violet, blue, or white, flowers. Plants need full sun and a well-drained soil; good protection is required through winter or plants die. Use in masses in gardens for handsome effect. Excellent as cut flowers.

Suggested Variety:
  'Firebird'

PETUNIA
Annual
To 1 foot

Light: Sun
Water: Moderate/Heavy
Bloom: Summer

Possibly the most widely grown annual, petunias are showy border or container plants with large funnel-shaped flowers in a multitude of colors; flowers bloom and bloom and bloom. Like plenty of water and sun. Some are cascading, others upright; small and large ones. A galaxy of bloom for little effort. Pinch off faded flowers to promote a second bloom in early fall. There are large and small, cascading or upright petunias.

Suggested Varieties:
  'Cherry Blossom'
  'Cherry Tart'

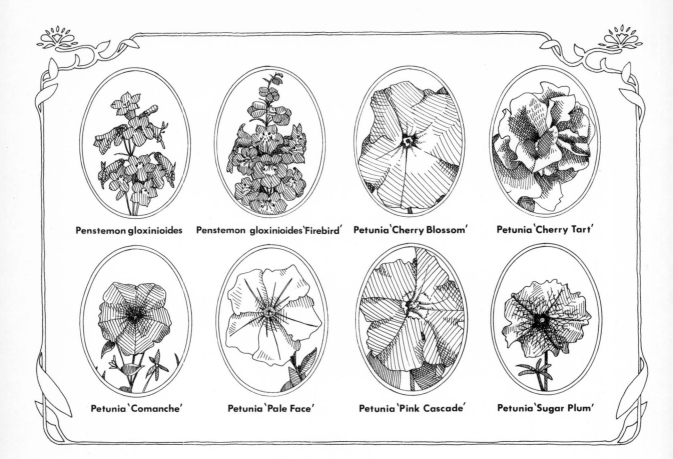

Penstemon gloxinioides   Penstemon gloxinioides 'Firebird'   Petunia 'Cherry Blossom'   Petunia 'Cherry Tart'

Petunia 'Comanche'   Petunia 'Pale Face'   Petunia 'Pink Cascade'   Petunia 'Sugar Plum'

'Comanche'
'Pale Face'
'Pink Cascade'
'Sugar Plum'

PHACELIA CAMPANULARIA California bluebells

Annual
To 1 foot

Light: Sun
Water: Moderate
Bloom: Summer

Deep-blue bell-shaped flowers with white spot at the base. Plants do best in poor soil and will tolerate dryness. Easy and handsome.

PHASEOLUS Scarlet runner bean

Vine
To 8 feet

Light: Sun
Water: Moderate
Bloom: Summer

Spectacular vining plants that need sun and well-drained soil. Plants cover areas quickly and are at their best on trellises and arbors. A delightful addition to the garden if a quick mass of color is needed, and not that difficult to grow.

P. coccineus. Flowers usually scarlet (sometimes white or scarlet and white); a tall twiner.

P.c. albus (Dutch runner bean). White blooms.

PHLOX

Perennial
To 3 feet

Light: Sun
Water: Heavy
Bloom: Spring/Summer

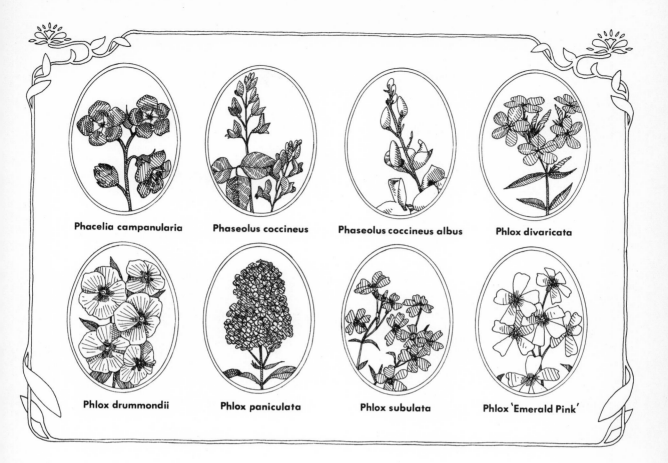

Phacelia campanularia

Phaseolus coccineus

Phaseolus coccineus albus

Phlox divaricata

Phlox drummondii

Phlox paniculata

Phlox subulata

Phlox 'Emerald Pink'

Phlox is grown by most gardeners for masses of colorful flowers. It does well in most regions with little attention. Some species are small, to 10 inches; others grow over 40 inches. There are dozens of species and varieties and certainly a phlox for your garden. Grow them—you will like them.

P. divaricata. Thin green leaves and bunches of small lilac flowers.

P. drummondii (annual phlox). A very showy phlox, with colors ranging the spectrum. Good for borders.

P. paniculata (summer phlox). Large, violet-purple flowers. Extensively used in gardens.

P. subulata (moss phlox). Purple, rose, lilac, or lavender flowers with darker centers. Small, to 10 inches.

Suggested Variety:
    'Emerald Pink'

PHYSOSTEGIA VIRGINIANA
False dragonhead

Perennial
To 4 feet

Light: Sun/Shade
Water: Moderate
Bloom: Summer/Fall

A very easy-to-grow plant, with flesh-colored or purple flowers in spines and dark-green willow-like leaves. Grows in almost any soil, in sun or shade.

Suggested Variety:
    'Vivid'

PLATYCODON Chinese bellflower

Perennial
To 3 feet

Light: Sun
Water: Moderate
Bloom: Summer

A rather pretty group of plants valued for their excellent cut flowers. Easily grown. If you have some space, try them.

P. grandiflorum (Chinese bellflower). Bell-shaped blue, pink, or white flowers on tall stems.

P. mariesii. A blue form of *P. grandiflorum,* small, to 18 inches.

PLUMBAGO

Vine
To 8 feet

Light: Sun
Water: Heavy
Bloom: Summer/Fall

These rather pretty climbers have pale-blue flowers that bloom over a long period. The plants need a well-drained soil and are dormant through the winter months. Plumbago vines make fine quick cover for walls or fences, and plants are floriferous. Also called Ceratostigma but still listed as Plumbago in most garden catalogs.

P. capensis. Beautiful small pale-blue flowers.

P. scandens (Cerastostigma plumbaginoides). Oval leaves and small white flowers in profusion.

POLEMONIUM   Charity/Greek valerian

Perennial
To 2½ feet

Light: Sun
Water: Heavy
Bloom: Summer

One of the first perennials to start growth in spring. Flowers are pretty but not spectacular, and plants need a rich soil that drains readily. Polemonium takes buckets of water. Worth a try if you have some additional space.

P. caeruleum. Hollow erect stems with bell-shaped blue or white flowers.

P. reptans (creeping Jacob's ladder). A creeping plant with drooping blue or white flowers.

POLYANTHES TUBEROSA   Tuberose

Bulb
To 3 feet

Light: Sun
Water: Moderate
Bloom: Summer

The tuberose is known for its pure-white, very fragrant, showy flowers that you can keep in bloom throughout the greater part of the year by planting the bulbs in succession. Excellent for borders and cut flowers; useful for buttonholes and bouquets. Space bulbs 6 to 8 inches apart, 4 inches deep. Lift yearly and store.

Suggested Variety:
  Pacific Giant

PORTULACA GRANDIFLORA   Rose moss

Annual
To 1 foot

Light: Sun
Water: Scant
Bloom: Summer

A red, yellow, or purple flower, 1 to 4 in a cluster. The flowers open in direct sunshine, close in shade. Good in a sunny border. Rose moss prospers in a hot dry place where other plants may not grow.

PRIMULA   Primrose

Perennial
To 2 feet

Light: Bright/Shade
Water: Heavy
Bloom: Spring

A large varied group of handsome flowering plants in dozens of colors. Has dozens of uses in the garden. Primroses are incredibly easy to grow if they have plenty of water. All grow best in an acid soil (pH 6.0) and in partial shade.

P. auricula. Fragrant yellow flowers, ½ to ¾ inches across.

P. denticulata (Himalayan primrose). Pale-purple flowers with yellow eye. Excellent garden plants

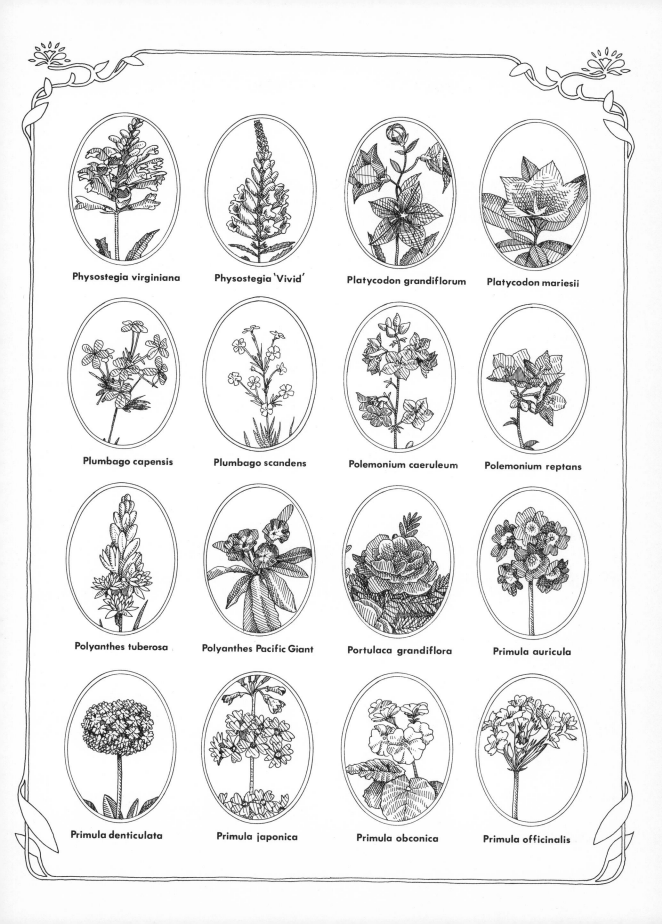

Physostegia virginiana

Physostegia 'Vivid'

Platycodon grandiflorum

Platycodon mariesii

Plumbago capensis

Plumbago scandens

Polemonium caeruleum

Polemonium reptans

Polyanthes tuberosa

Polyanthes Pacific Giant

Portulaca grandiflora

Primula auricula

Primula denticulata

Primula japonica

Primula obconica

Primula officinalis

of good constitution, suitable for wild or rock gardens.

P. japonica (Japanese primrose). Strong and sturdy growers with white, rose, or purple flowers.

P. obconica. Funnel-shaped pale lilac-purple flowers with a yellow eye, 1 inch across.

P. officinalis (P. veris) (cowslip). A standard. Very fragrant deep-yellow flowers.

P. vulgaris (true primula). Sulfur-yellow flowers blotched with dark yellow near eye, 1 to 1¼ inch across.

PULMONARIA ANGUSTIFOLIA
Lungwort

Perennial
To 2 feet

Light: Bright/Shade
Water: Heavy.
Bloom: Spring

A pretty blue-flowering plant that has a long blooming season. Plant likes some shade and a rather moist soil.

PUSCHKINIA SCILLOIDES   Striped squill

Bulb
To 1 foot

Light: Sun
Water: Moderate
Bloom: Summer

Nice small plants not too well-known. Flowers are ½ to 1 inch across and are blue or whitish, with a distinct blue stripe. Like cool conditions. Plant bulbs in fall 2 to 3 inches apart, 3 inches deep. Leave in ground all year.

QUAMOCLIT   Starglory

Vine
To 20 feet

Light: Sun
Water: Heavy
Bloom: Summer

Some very handsome vines that grow quickly and bear showy red flowers. Plants need a sandy loam and plenty of water, and they thrive in sun. Excellent for trellis or fence or walls, these vines bloom on and off throughout the summer. Handsome plants.

Q. coccinea. A twiner; fragrant scarlet flowers with yellow throat.

Q. pennata. Fernlike foliage and small bright-red flowers.

Q. sloteri. Lobed leaves and large red blooms.

RANUNCULUS ASIATICUS
French buttercup

Bulb
To 1 foot

Light: Sun
Water: Moderate
Bloom: Spring/Summer

At one time a great favorite and ranked among the most prized florists' flowers. Plants need excellent drainage. Bulbs should be lifted in winter and stored in a dry, airy place. Large flowers of various colors. Make handsome masses of color for gardens and require little care.

RECHSTEINERIA CARDINALIS
Cardinal flower

Perennial
To 2 feet

Light: Bright/Shade
Water: Heavy
Bloom: Summer

A leafy plant with red flowers; unusual and desirable for seasonal color. More often grown as a houseplant. Lift tubers and store them yearly. Needs a shady spot and lots of water.

RESEDA ODORATA   Mignonette

Annual
To 1½ feet

Light: Sun
Water: Moderate
Bloom: Summer/Fall

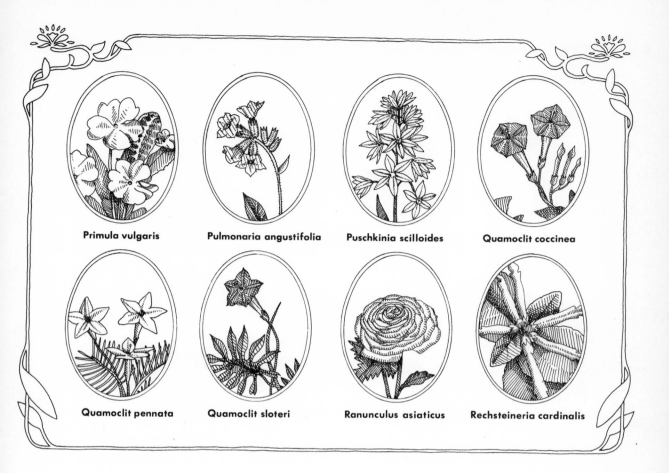

Primula vulgaris	Pulmonaria angustifolia	Puschkinia scilloides	Quamoclit coccinea
Quamoclit pennata	Quamoclit sloteri	Ranunculus asiaticus	Rechsteineria cardinalis

A very fragrant plant, with yellow-white petals, saffron anthers. Plants like some shade and coolness to be at their best. Easy and worth their space.

Suggested Variety:
  'Goliath'

ROMNEYA   California tree poppy

Perennial
To 8 feet

Light: Sun
Water: Moderate/Scant
Bloom: Summer/Fall

These are handsome plants with fragrant flowers, one bloom following another. Romneya needs a location with excellent drainage and prefers to be grown on the dry side. Striking flowers best used by themselves rather than intermingled with other plants.

R. coulteri (California tree poppy). Large fragrant white flowers.

R. c. trichocalyx. Saucer-shaped snow-white flowers with yellow centers.

RUDBECKIA   Gloriosa daisy

Annual
To 3 feet

Light: Sun
Water: Moderate
Bloom: Summer

A fine group of garden plants with large showy flowers. Once into their blooming season they provide an abundance of flowers. Rudbeckias are easy to grow in loamy garden soil and can be used as background plants or are fine for cutting. A must for all gardens; many new varieties.

R. gloriosa (gloriosa daisy). A black-eyed Susan

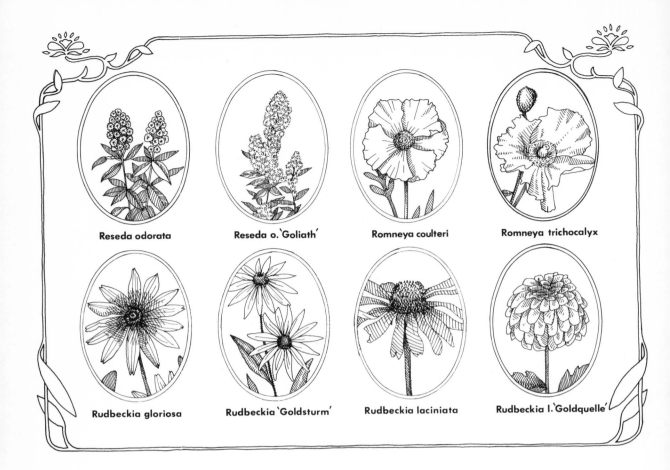

Reseda odorata   **Reseda o. 'Goliath'**   **Romneya coulteri**   **Romneya trichocalyx**

Rudbeckia gloriosa   **Rudbeckia 'Goldsturm'**   **Rudbeckia laciniata**   **Rudbeckia l. 'Goldquelle'**

with large golden-yellow flowers with a dark-brown circle.

R. laciniata (cut-leaf coneflower). Big yellow flowers marked green inside.

Suggested Varieties:
  'Goldstrum'
  'Goldquelle'

SALPIGLOSSIS SINUATA   Painted tongue
Annual
To 2 feet

Light: Sun
Water: Moderate
Bloom: Summer

Fine plants with showy, funnel-shaped, dark-purple or straw-colored flowers that are often striped. Plants like a loamy soil and sun. Make fine cut flowers.

Suggested Varieties:
  'Bolero'
  'Superbissima'

SALVIA   Sage
Annual/Perennial
To 3 feet

Light: Sun
Water: Moderate
Bloom: Summer

Seldom used but certainly worth garden space are the salvias with their tiers of flowers in red or blue. Plants need a loamy garden soil that is well drained, and although they do best in sun they also perform well in shade. Easily grown, the salvias are best used by themselves in groups.

S. haematodes. Spires of blue flowers; floriferous.

S. horminum. Tiers of purple flowers. Annual.

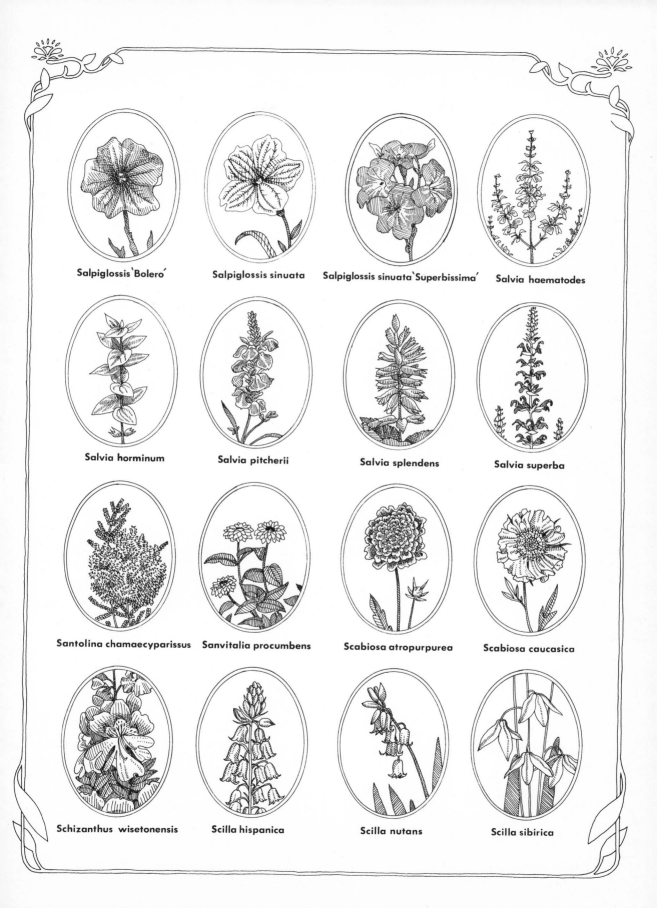

Salpiglossis `Bolero´

Salpiglossis sinuata

Salpiglossis sinuata `Superbissima´

Salvia haematodes

Salvia horminum

Salvia pitcherii

Salvia splendens

Salvia superba

Santolina chamaecyparissus

Sanvitalia procumbens

Scabiosa atropurpurea

Scabiosa caucasica

Schizanthus wisetonensis

Scilla hispanica

Scilla nutans

Scilla sibirica

S. pitcherii. Large blue flowers; branching habit. Stellar.

S. splendens (scarlet sage). A shrubby plant with red flowers. Perennial.

S. superba (violet sage). Tall stems of blue-purple flowers. Perennial.

SANTOLINA CHAMAECYPARISSUS
Lavender cotton

Perennial
To 3 feet

Light: Sun
Water: Moderate
Bloom: Summer

Bushy shrub with very crowded leaves, yellow-headed flowers very freely borne. Easily grown; needs full sun and tolerates dry soils. Santolina is probably more valued for its decorative foliage than its small flowers.

SANVITALIA PROCUMBENS
Creeping zinnia

Annual
To 1½ foot

Light: Sun
Water: Moderate
Bloom: Summer/Fall

A charming plant with flower heads (like Rudbeckia) that are bright yellow with a dark inner disk. Its creeping habit makes it a fine candidate for areas where you want low cover.

SCABIOSA   Pincushion flower

Annual
To 3 feet

Light: Sun
Water: Moderate
Bloom: Summer/Fall

An excellent group of flowers for cutting and for nice garden accents. Plants need a loamy soil that drains readily. Good in flower beds or massed by themselves.

S. atropurpurea. Crimson flowers. Excellent for cut flowers.

S. caucasica (pincushion). Pale blue flowers 3 inches across.

SCHIZANTHUS WISETONENSIS
Butterfly flower

Annual
To 2 feet

Light: Shade
Water: Moderate
Bloom: Summer/Fall

Excellent garden plants that bloom and bloom and bloom. Large flowers of varying colors, from white to reddish brown. Plants like coolness and shade from noon sun.

SCILLA   Bluebell

Bulb
To 1 foot

Light: Sun
Water: Moderate
Bloom: Spring

Good where masses of color are needed, such as under trees or shrubs. There are species for all climates, so check with your nurseryman. Most scillas are planted in fall; space bulbs 5 inches apart, 3 inches deep. Good spring color for gardens and relatively easy to grow.

S. hispanica. A popular plant; usually blue flowers, although they also can be pink, rose-purple, white, or flesh-colored.

S. nutans (English bluebell). White, purple, pink, or blue bell-like flowers.

S. sibirica. Blue bell-shaped flowers.

SCUTELLARIA BAICALENSIS   Skullcap

Perennial
To 2 feet

Light: Sun
Water: Moderate
Bloom: Summer

One-inch-long blue or purple flowers. Excellent for the front of flower borders or rock gardens. Plants need a well-drained soil; otherwise easy to grow; not spectacular, but pretty.

SEDUM SPECTABILE   Stonecrop

Perennial
To 1 foot

Light: Sun
Water: Moderate
Bloom: Summer/Fall

These are popular plants for soil conditions where nothing else will grow. The stonecrops have small pink flowers and can survive dry conditions with ease. Excellent for the rock garden or wherever you need some color.

SENECIO   Cineraria

Annual
To 3 feet

Light: Bright/Shade
Water: Moderate
Bloom: Spring/Summer

The vivid colors of cinerarias are well-known and certainly make a showy display in gardens. These plants need coolness and a loamy soil and are not as easy to grow as many other annuals. Still, their color makes them desirable. A challenge.

S. cruentus. Masses of vivid purplish red flowers.

S. elegans. Purple flowers with yellow centers.

SIDALCEA   Prairie mallow/ miniature hollyhock

Perennial
To 4 feet

Light: Sun
Water: Heavy
Bloom: Summer

Lovely plants with branching spikes of cup-shaped pink to crimson flowers. Handsome palm-shaped leaves. Plants require good drainage and lots of sun. Use in groups for a fine

accent. Mallows spread rapidly and in a few years provide an excellent display.

SILENE   Catchfly

Annual
To 1½ feet

Light: Sun
Water: Moderate
Bloom: Summer

A group of pink or lavender plants that are especially good for borders and as color islands in beds. Plants are easily grown in a well-drained soil and need sun. An overlooked plant that should be grown more.

S. armeria. Clusters of lovely pink flowers; floriferous.

S. pendula. Sparser flowers than *S. armeria;* flowers bluish white.

SINNINGIA SPECIOSA   Gloxinia

Bulb
To 2 feet

Light: Shade
Water: Moderate
Bloom: Spring/Summer/Fall

Generally grown as a houseplant, gloxinias also can be used in gardens. They have slipper-shaped red, pink, or purple flowers. Plants bloom, then rest, and then bloom again. If you have a shady cool nook, try these outdoors. Best to leave in pots. Pot one bulb to a container; leave tip barely exposed. Many excellent varieties, some with huge 7-inch flowers.

SOLIDAGO   Goldenrod

Perennial
To 3 feet

Light: Sun/Bright
Water: Heavy
Bloom: Summer/Fall

Goldenrods are not often grown in gardens, yet they make fine color accents. Plants have dense

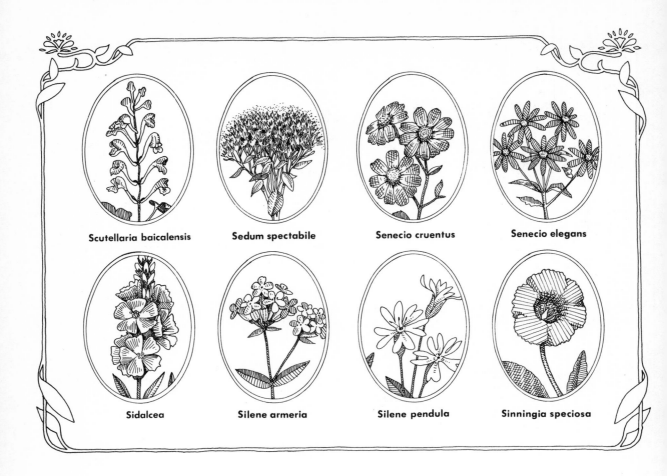

Scutellaria baicalensis

Sedum spectabile

Senecio cruentus

Senecio elegans

Sidalcea

Silene armeria

Silene pendula

Sinningia speciosa

yellow blossoms that are very appealing. Grow in any soil. Use goldenrods in flower gardens or borders.

SPARAXIS TRICOLOR   Harlequin flower
Bulb
To 2 feet

Light: Sun
Water: Moderate
Bloom: Spring

Bright cheerful flowers in vivid colors of red, yellow, or blue, with sword-shaped foliage. Excellent for rock gardens or borders and as cut flowers. Must have well-drained soil and must be kept dry after foliage has matured in summer. Plant bulbs in fall 2 to 3 inches apart, 3 inches deep. Tender.

SPREKELIA FORMOSISSIMA   Aztec lily
Bulb
To 3 feet

Light: Sun
Water: Heavy (allow to dry out before watering)
Bloom: Summer

A spectacular outdoor or indoor pot plant with 4-inch crimson-red flowers and straplike leaves. Space 8 inches apart, 4 inches deep. Must be dug up yearly. Flowers last a long time. Tender.

STERNBERGIA LUTEA
Bulb
To 1 foot

Light: Sun
Water: Heavy
Bloom: Fall

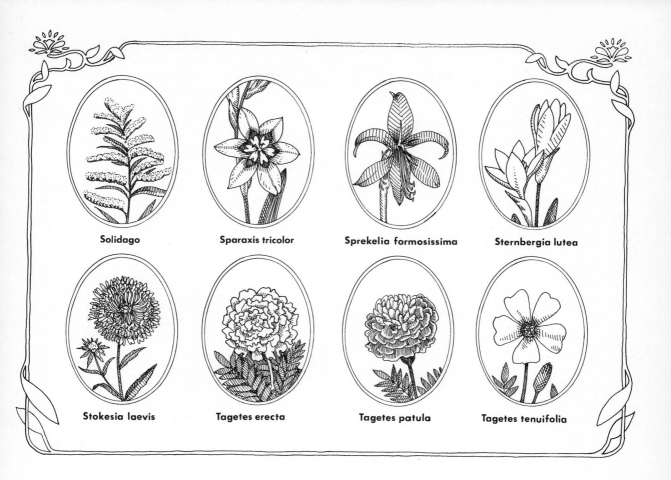

Solidago

Sparaxis tricolor

Sprekelia formosissima

Sternbergia lutea

Stokesia laevis

Tagetes erecta

Tagetes patula

Tagetes tenuifolia

These overlooked plants are graceful and pretty and resemble crocuses. The flowers are yellow-gold against dark grassy-green leaves, making a handsome picture. Plant bulbs in summer 3 inches apart, 5 inches deep. Hardy to −5 F.

STOKESIA LAEVIS   Cornflower aster

Perennial
To 1½ feet

Light: Sun
Water: Moderate
Bloom: Summer/Fall

Lovely blue flowers and a long bloom season make stokesias desirable plants. Be sure to provide excellent drainage and a loamy soil. White, pink, and yellow varieties are also available.

TAGETES   Marigold

Annual
To 2½ feet

Light: Sun
Water: Heavy
Bloom: Summer/Fall

A very useful and pretty group of garden flowers, some dwarf, some tall, but all valuable for garden landscaping. With double or single yellow or orange flowers, about 2 inches across, plants are easily grown in almost any garden soil in sunny locations. If you have space for only one kind of flower, marigolds should be your choice.

T. erecta. Large yellow flowers.

T. patula (French marigold). Yellow or orange blooms.

T. tenuifolia. Dwarf; small golden-orange flowers.

THALICTRUM   Meadow rue

Perennial
To 4 feet

Light: Sun/Bright
Water: Moderate
Bloom: Summer/Fall

Fine lacy-foliaged plants with handsome masses of tiny lavender or pink flowers. Plants need a loamy enriched soil that drains well. Excellent plants for garden beds and backgrounds. Generally easy to grow.

T. aquilegifolium. Lavender or pink flowers. Good varieties available.

T. glaucum. Fragrant and fuzzy yellow flowers.

THERMOPSIS CAROLINIANA

Perennial
To 4 feet

Light: Sun
Water: Moderate
Bloom: Summer

This Thermopsis produces pea-shaped yellow flowers on tall plants. Plants do well in loamy soil in sunny locations. Nice accents for background areas. Generally easy to grow.

THUNBERGIA   Black-eyed Susan

Vine
To 10 feet

Light: Sun
Water: Heavy
Bloom: Summer/Fall

These vining annuals offer pretty flowers over a long period and are best started yearly. Plants like moisture and good sun but are somewhat intolerant of excessive heat. Excellent for trellises, arbors, or whenever colorful cover is needed.

T. alata. Yellow flowers with black centers; twining plant.

T. gibsonii. Larger flowers than *T. alata;* flowers orange.

THYMOPHYLLA
TENUILOBA   Goldenfleece

Annual
To 1 foot

Light: Sun
Water: Heavy
Bloom: Summer

A small low-growing yellow daisy. Plants grow well in heat and need a well-drained loamy soil. Pretty garden accents.

TIGRIDIA PAVONIA   Shellflower

Bulb
To 3 feet

Light: Sun
Water: Moderate
Bloom: Summer

Large red flowers that last only a day, but each stem bears successive bloom for about 4 weeks. Plant bulbs in spring 4 inches apart, 4 inches deep; be sure soil is warm. In very cold climate dig up when leaves are mature and store for next year. Hardy to 10 F.

TITHONIA ROTUNDIFOLIA
Mexican sunflower

Annual
To 3 feet

Light: Sun
Water: Moderate
Bloom: Summer

A very showy and handsome flowering plant with bright orange-red blooms. Plants grow well in any kind of soil but need full sunlight to prosper. Use as background material, or simply grow them for their beautiful flowers.

TORENIA FOURNIERII   Wishbone flower

Annual
To 2 feet

Light: Bright/Shade
Water: Heavy
Bloom: Summer

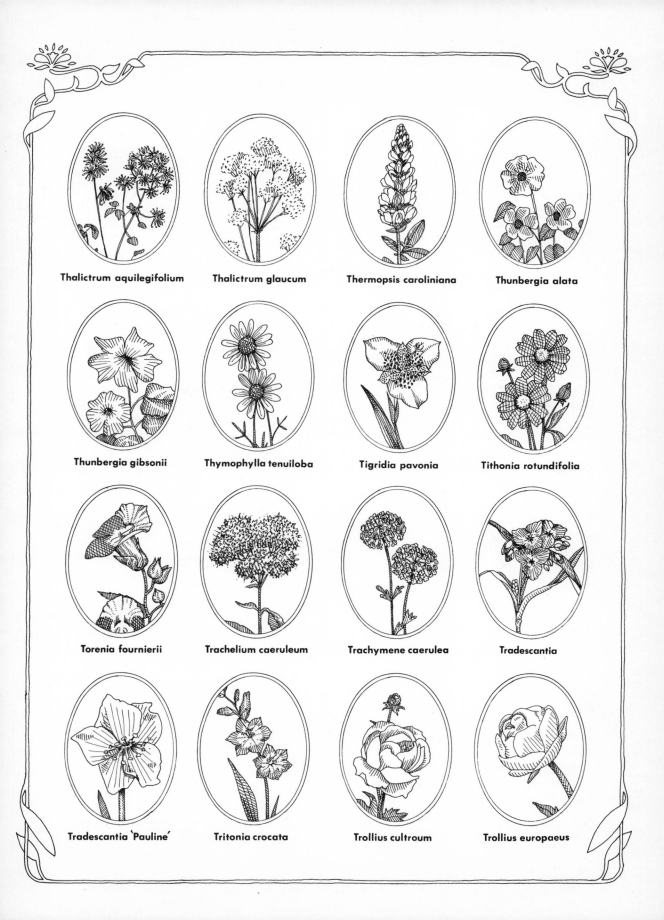

Thalictrum aquilegifolium

Thalictrum glaucum

Thermopsis caroliniana

Thunbergia alata

Thunbergia gibsonii

Thymophylla tenuiloba

Tigridia pavonia

Tithonia rotundifolia

Torenia fournierii

Trachelium caeruleum

Trachymene caerulea

Tradescantia

Tradescantia 'Pauline'

Tritonia crocata

Trollius cultroum

Trollius europaeus

With trumpet-shaped bicolor flowers and lobed leaves, the wishbone flower is a charming addition to gardens. Plants are small and attractive and require moist loamy soil and some shade. Good for garden borders or in pots on patios.

TRACHELIUM CAERULEUM

Annual
To 3 feet

Light: Sun/Shade
Water: Heavy
Bloom: Summer/Fall

A faintly fragrant blue-flowering plant that grows almost untended in any soil in partial shade or sun. The pretty clouds of blue flowers are handsome in garden beds.

TRACHYMENE CAERULEA
Blue lace flower

Annual
To 3 feet

Light: Sun
Water: Moderate
Bloom: Summer

A very pretty flowering plant with clusters of pale-blue flowers on tall stems. Plants need a sandy soil and do well only in coolness; in hot weather they do not respond well. Blue lace flowers are excellent for cutting and last a long time.

TRADESCANTIA   Spiderwort

Perennial
To 1½ feet

Light: Shade
Water: Moderate
Bloom: Spring

Popular indoor plants that are just as good outdoors, where they bear decorative leaves and handsome blue blooms. Flowers last a long time, and plants are easily grown in any soil in partial shade. Good easy-to-grow plants.

Suggested Variety:
   'Pauline'

TRITONIA CROCATA

Bulb
To 3 feet

Light: Sun
Water: Heavy
Bloom: Summer

Handsome flowers reminiscent of gladiolus. Wads of grassy foliage and flowers. Blooms in a wide choice of colors, usually orange. Good cut flower. Plant 3 inches apart, 3 inches deep. Hardy to 10 F.; in colder climates dig up bulbs and store annually.

TROLLIUS   Globeflower

Perennial
To 2 feet

Light: Sun
Water: Heavy
Bloom: Spring/Summer

Orange or yellow 2- to 4-inch flowers and palm-like leaves. Plants like plenty of water at roots and good sun; provide loamy soil. Unusual and very charming plants for gardens. Generally available only in seed.

T. cultroum. Small yellow-orange flowers.

T. europaeus. Orange blooms.

T. ledebouri. Fine orange flowers; floriferous.

TROPAEOLUM   Nasturtium

Tuber
Vining

Light: Sun
Water: Scant
Bloom: Summer/Fall

For summer and fall color it is difficult to find better color than nasturtiums. Plants grow easily in any soil and bloom profusely for months. Do not feed. Some are trailers, others are more upright; most like cool nights. Use anywhere in garden where bright color is needed.

T. majus. The most popular nasturtium; orange-red flowers. Vining.

T. peregrinum. Yellow flowers, different in shape from *T. majus.*

T. polyphyllum. Small orange flowers.

TULBAGHIA FRAGRANS   Society garlic
Bulb
To 1½ feet

Light: Sun
Water: Heavy
Bloom: Summer

Pretty lavender flowers, dozens to a cluster, that bloom for many months. Place bulbs 10 inches apart, 1 inch deep. Dig up yearly. Tender.

TULIPA   Tulip
Bulb
To 4 feet

Light: Sun
Water: Moderate
Bloom: Spring/Summer

Here is a group of universally accepted flowers for gardens that are tough to beat. There are dozens of flower forms and hundreds of colors to choose from. Some tulips bloom early, others in midseason, and many are late bloomers. Indeed, there are enough tulips to keep you growing and going all through the warm months. Generally, tulips need a well-drained somewhat sandy soil. The bulbs do best where they can be left in the ground all year round; plant bulbs 5 inches deep. Because there are so many classifications of tulips it is impossible to give cultural directions for them. Within each group there are idiosyncrasies that can only be known by working with the plants. The following is a mere sampling of tulips.

T. Kaufmanniana. One of the species of tulips with vividly colored flowers.

Suggested Varieties:
    Cottage
    Darwin
    Darwin Hybrid
    Double Early
    Lilyflower
    Parrot
    Single Early

URSINIA ANETHOIDES
Annual
To 1½ feet

Light: Sun
Water: Moderate
Bloom: Summer

Very pretty orange flowers, with feathery foliage. Plants need lots of sun and a sandy soil. Do not feed. Charming garden accents.

VALERIANA OFFICINALIS
Garden heliotrope
Perennial
To 4 feet

Light: Sun
Water: Heavy
Bloom: Summer

Plants bear clusters of fragrant pinkish white flowers. Easily grown in any kind of soil, any conditions. A good one for beginners.

VALLOTA SPECIOSA   Scarborough lily
Bulb
To 2½ feet

Light: Shade
Water: Heavy
Bloom: Summer/Fall

Spectacular red flowers make this plant a dramatic outdoor accent. Plant in early summer or fall, with nose of bulb slightly below soil. Grow in pots in garden. Must be taken indoors in late fall.

VENIDIUM FASTUOSUM
Annual
To 2 feet

Light: Sun
Water: Heavy
Bloom: Summer

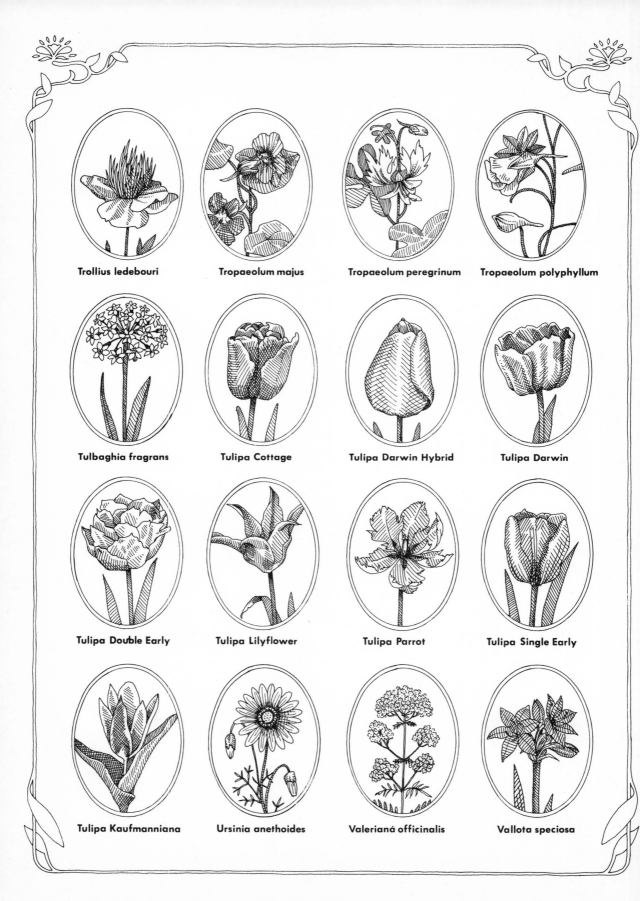

Trollius ledebouri

Tropaeolum majus

Tropaeolum peregrinum

Tropaeolum polyphyllum

Tulbaghia fragrans

Tulipa Cottage

Tulipa Darwin Hybrid

Tulipa Darwin

Tulipa Double Early

Tulipa Lilyflower

Tulipa Parrot

Tulipa Single Early

Tulipa Kaufmanniana

Ursinia anethoides

Valeriana officinalis

Vallota speciosa

Large and brilliant orange daisylike flowers and fern foliage make this a showy plant. It grows well in a sandy loam that drains freely. Good for beds or borders.

VERBASCUM   Mullein

Perennial
To 4 feet

Light: Sun
Water: Moderate
Bloom: Summer/Fall

These branched plants have fuzzy leaves and fine lavender flowers. Provide excellent drainage. Plants grow easily. Nice for background plantings.

Suggested Variety:
 'Cotswold Gem'

VERBENA HORTENSIS   Verbena

Annual
To 1 foot

Light: Sun
Water: Moderate
Bloom: Summer/Fall

A spreading plant that bears multitudes of red or lavender flowers 2 to 3 inches across. Plants need a loamy soil and good drainage. Excellent as ground cover or where islands or color are needed. A very handsome garden plant.

VERONICA   Speedwell

Perennial
To 1½ feet

Light: Sun
Water: Moderate
Bloom: Summer

These favorites have dramatic pink or blue flowers. A fine bedding plant that needs a loamy soil and sunlight. Several new varieties that bloom over a long period.

V. incana (woolly speedwell). Lovely blue flowers.

V. longifolia. Grows in clumps. Handsome. Lilac flowers in dense clusters.

VINCA ROSEA   Periwinkle

Annual
To 1 foot

Light: Bright/Shade
Water: Moderate
Bloom: Summer/Fall

Lovely plants with lavender-blue flat-faced flowers. Plants can be used for ground cover or as edging. Nice small plants for garden and relatively easy to grow.

VIOLA   Violet/pansy

Annual/Perennial
To 1 foot

Light: Sun
Water: Heavy
Bloom: Spring/Summer

Both violets and pansies belong to the genus called Viola and technically are all perennials, but some are treated as annuals. Violets bear blue flowers while the pansies come in an array of lovely colors. All the plants do well in a rich moist soil, and while full sun is recommended for them, in very hot regions some shade is necessary. The plants have many uses in the garden ranging from borders to edgings to bulb gardens, where they furnish needed color after bulbs finish blooming.

V. odorata (sweet violet). Heart-shaped leaves and fragrant dark-blue flowers make this a popular species. Many varieties.

V. tricolor (Johnny-jump-up). Purple and yellow flowers that resemble small pansies.

V. tricolor hortensis (pansy). An excellent strain with flowers in many different colors: white, blue, rose, yellow, purple, and bicolors.

V. williamsii. Lovely violet flowers.

V. wittrockiana. Brilliant red-purple flowers with purple blotches.

Suggested Variety:
 'White Czar'

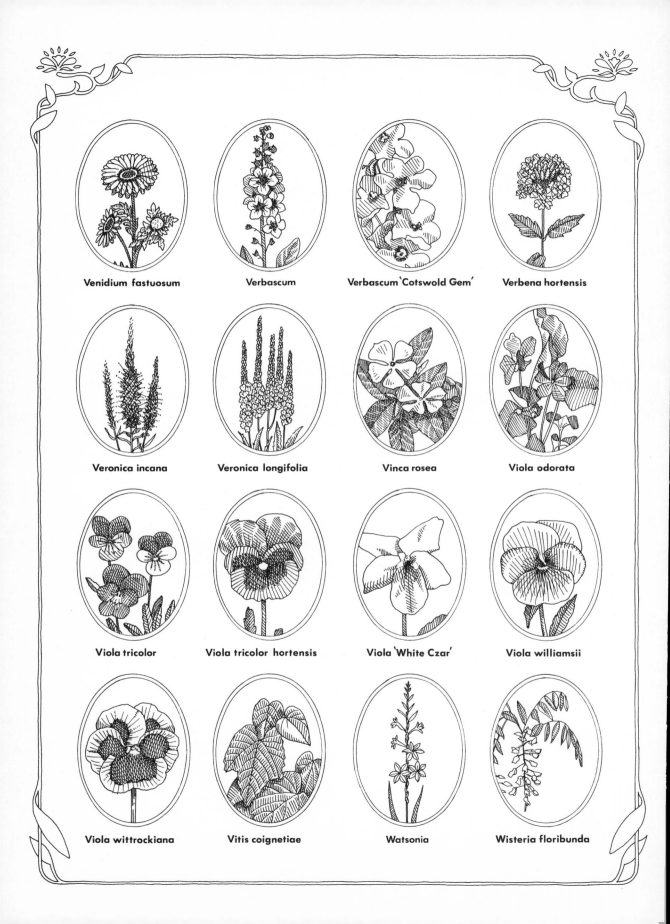

Venidium fastuosum

Verbascum

Verbascum 'Cotswold Gem'

Verbena hortensis

Veronica incana

Veronica longifolia

Vinca rosea

Viola odorata

Viola tricolor

Viola tricolor hortensis

Viola 'White Czar'

Viola williamsii

Viola wittrockiana

Vitis coignetiae

Watsonia

Wisteria floribunda

VITIS COIGNETIAE

Vine
To 40 feet

Light: Sun
Water: Heavy
Bloom: Fall

A fast-growing vine valued for its beautiful red foliage in autumn. The leaves are large and handsome. The plant is rampant so use it only where there is ample space for it such as on walls and fences.

WATSONIA

Bulb
To 4 feet

Light: Bright
Water: Moderate
Bloom: Summer

A graceful plant with branched stems and masses of 3-inch pink or red flowers. Plant bulbs in late summer or fall 6 inches apart, 4 inches deep. Lift bulbs yearly. Tender.

WISTERIA FLORIBUNDA Japanese wisteria

Vine
To 20 feet

Light: Sun
Water: Heavy
Bloom: Spring

A very popular vine with fragrant violet flowers in pendent clusters. Plants can be trained to be shrublike or treelike and need some type of support—a trellis is fine. Wisterias are not fussy about soil but they need ample water when in growth and in bloom. These deciduous vines are well liked and rightly so; in early spring they put on a spectacular display.

XANTHISMA TEXANUM Star of Texas

Annual
To 2 feet

Light: Sun
Water: Scant
Bloom: Summer

Here is an easy-to-grow, rather pretty flower with bright yellow blooms, daisylike. The plant tolerates poor dry soil and provides a good spot of color where soils are very poor. Makes fine cut flowers.

ZANTEDESCHIA Calla lily

Bulb
To 2 feet

Light: Bright
Water: Heavy
Bloom: Spring/Summer

These wonderful but overlooked plants have handsome leaves and flowers that provide splendid garden color. Plant bulbs 12 inches apart, 4 inches deep; mass in any area for a unique accent. Dig up bulbs and store yearly.

Z. aethiopica. Beautiful white flowers.

Z. elliottiana. The popular golden calla lily.

Z. rehmannii. Pink flowers; smaller than most calla lilies.

ZEPHYRANTHES GRANDIFLORA Rain lily

Bulb
To 1 foot

Light: Sun
Water: Heavy
Bloom: Summer/Fall

A fine flowering rose-pink lily for the garden; grows in masses for colorful accent. Easy to grow and blooms profusely. Plant in fall 3 inches apart, 2 inches deep.

ZINNIA

Annual
To 3 feet

Light: Sun
Water: Moderate
Bloom: Summer/Fall

Here are some fine garden flowers that even the novice can bring to bloom. Flowers are brightly colored and plants come in many heights, flower

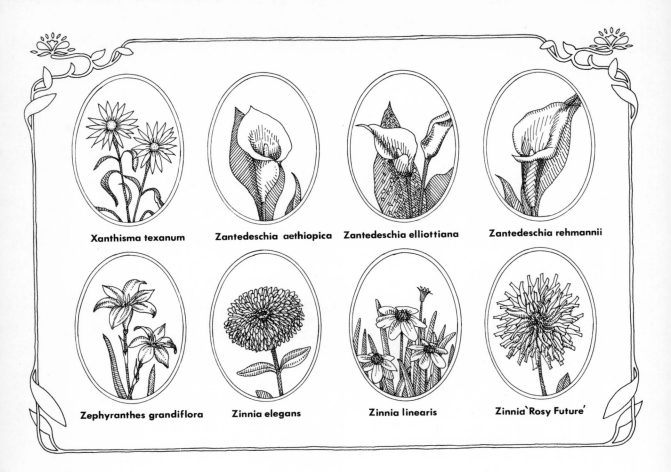

Xanthisma texanum **Zantedeschia aethiopica** **Zantedeschia elliottiana** **Zantedeschia rehmannii**

Zephyranthes grandiflora **Zinnia elegans** **Zinnia linearis** **Zinnia 'Rosy Future'**

sizes, and forms. Plants do well in any good garden soil and seem to please everyone because the flowers last a long time and are especially desirable in the late days of autumn. Used in borders, for edgings, and in flower beds, these (and petunias) are really the workhorses of many gardens.

Z. elegans: A wide range of colors available: white, pink, rose, red, yellow, orange, blue.

Z. linearis. Orange flowers; bloom late into fall.

Suggested Variety:
'Rosy Future'

common-name/botanical-name CROSS-REFERENCE CHART

ANNUALS, PERENNIALS, VINES AND BULBS

Abyssinian sword lily	(Acidanthera)	Astilbe	(*Astilbe arendsii*)
Aconite	(Eranthis)	Autumn adonis	(*Adonis autumnalis*)
Adder's-tongue	(Erythronium)	Autumn crocus	(Colchicum)
Adonis	(Adonis)	Autumn monkshood	(*Aconitum autumnale*)
African daisy	(*Arctotis grandis*)	Aztec lily	(*Sprekelia formosissima*)
Alkanet	(Anchusa)	Azure monkshood	(*Aconitum fischeri*)
Alpine poppy	(Papaver)		
Amaryllis	(Hippeastrum)	Baboonroot	(*Babiana stricta*)
Amazon lily	(*Eucharis grandiflora*)	Baby blue-eyes	(*Nemophila menziesii*)
American bittersweet	(*Celastrus scandens*)	Baby's breath	(*Gypsophila paniculata*)
American columbine	(*Aquilegia canadensis*)	Bachelor's button cornflower	(*Centaurea cyanus*)
Amur adonis	(*Adonis amurensis*)	Balloon vine	(*Cardiospermum halicacabum*)
Anemone	(Anemone)		
Annual phlox	(*Phlox drummondii*)	Basket flower	(Centaurea)

Beardtongue	*(Penstemon gloxinioides)*	Bugbane	(Cimicifuga)
Bee balm	*(Monarda didyma)*	Bugloss	(Echium)
Belladonna lily	*(Amaryllis belladonna)*	Butterfly flower	*(Schizanthus wisetonensis)*
Bellflower	(Campanula)	Butterfly iris	*(Moraea iridioides)*
Bermuda buttercup	*(Oxalis cernua)*	Butterfly weed	*(Asclepias tuberosa)*
Bishop's hat	(Epimedium)		
Black-eyed Susan	(Thunbergia)	California bluebells	*(Phacelia campanularia)*
Black snakeroot	*(Cimicifuga racemosa)*	California poppy	*(Eschscholzia californica)*
Blanket flower	*(Gaillardia aristata)*	California tree poppy	*(Romneya coulteri)*
Blazing star	*(Mentzelia lindleyi)*	Calla lily	(Zantedeschia)
Bleeding heart	*(Dicentra spectabilis)*	Camas	(Camassia)
Bloodflower	*(Asclepias currassavica)*	Candle larkspur	*(Delphinium elatum)*
Bloodleaf	*(Iresine herbstii)*	Candytuft	(Iberis)
Blood lily	(Haemanthus)	Canna	*(Canna hybrida)*
Bluebell	(Scilla)	Canterbury bell	*(Campanula medium)*
Blue daisy	*(Felicia amelloides)*	Cape cowslip	*(Lachenalia tricolor)*
Blue globe thistle	(Echinops)	Cape marigold	(Dimorphotheca hybrids)
Blue lace flower	*(Trachymene caerulea)*	Cardinal flower	*(Rechsteineria cardinalis)*
Blue lobelia	*(Lobelia erinus)*	Carnation	*(Dianthus caryophyllus)*
Blue poppy	*(Meconopsis betonicifolia)*	Carolina yellow jasmine	*(Gelsemium sempervirens)*
Border pink	*(Dianthus plumarius)*	Catchfly	*(Lychnis viscaria)*
Bowie oxalis	(Oxalis)	Catchfly	(Silene)
Brodiaea	(Brodiaea)	Catmint	*(Nepeta mussinii)*
Browallia	(Browallia)		

Chamomile	(Anthemis)		Common peony	(Paeonia officinalis)
Charity	(Polemonium)		Common star-of-Bethlehem	(Ornithogalum umbellatum)
Chilean jasmine	(Mandevilla suaveolens)		Common yarrow	(Achillea millefolium)
China aster	(Callistephus chinensis)		Coneflower	(Echinacea purpurea)
China pink	(Dianthus chinensis)		Coralbells	(Heuchera sanguinea)
Chincherinchee	(Ornithogalum thyrsoides)		Coral drops	(Bessera elegans)
Chinese bellflower	(Platycodon grandiflorum)		Coralvine	(An..gonon leptopus)
Chinese forget-me-not	(Cynoglossum amabile)		Corn cockle	(Agrostemma githago)
Chinese ground orchid	(Bletilla hyacinthina)		Cornflower aster	(Stokesia laevis)
Chinese larkspur	(Delphinium grandiflorum)		Corn lily	(Ixia)
Chinese peony	(Paeonia)		Cosmos	(Cosmos)
Christmas rose	(Helleborus niger)		Cowslip	(Primula officinalis)
Chrysanthemum	(Chrysanthemum)		Cranesbill	(Geranium grandiflorum)
Cigar plant	(Cuphea ignea)		Creeping Jacob's ladder	(Polemonium reptans)
Cineraria	(Senecio)		Creeping zinnia	(Sanvitalia procumbens)
Cladanthus	(Cladanthus arabicus)		Crown imperial	(Fritillaria imperialis)
Climbing bittersweet	(Celastrus scandens)		Cupflower	(Nierembergia caerulea)
Cockscomb	(Celosia argentea)		Cupid's-dart	(Catananche caerulea)
Common American columbine	(Aquilegia canadensis)		Cut-leaf coneflower	(Rudbeckia laciniata)
Common crocus	(Crocus vernus)		Cyclamen	(Cyclamen)
Common foxglove	(Digitalis purpurea)		Daffodil	(Narcissus)
Common geranium	(Pelargonium hortorum)		Dahlia	(Dahlia)
Common lavender	(Lavandula officinalis)		Day lily	(Hemerocallis)

Delicate lily	(*Chlidanthus fragrans*)	Flame anemone	(*Anemone fulgens*)
Dollar plant	(*Lunaria annua*)	Fleabane	(Erigeron)
Dusty miller	(*Centaurea rutifolia*)	Florist's cyclamen	(*Cyclamen persicum*)
Dutch iris	(Iris hybrids)	Flossflower	(*Ageratum houstonianum*)
Dutchman's-pipe	(*Aristolochia durior*)	Flowering flax	(Linum)
Dutch runner bean	(*Phaseolus coccineus alba*)	Flowering maple	(*Abutilon hybridum*)
Dwarf morning glory	(*Convolvulus tricolor*)	Flowering onion	(Allium)
		Flowering tobacco	(*Nicotiana alata grandiflora*)
English bluebell	(*Scilla nutans*)		
English daisy	(*Bellis perennis*)	Fountain plant	(*Amaranthus salicifolius*)
English iris	(*Iris xiphioides*)	Four-o' clock	(*Mirabilis jalapa*)
English monkshood	(*Aconitum napellus*)	Foxglove	(Digitalis)
English wallflower	(*Cheiranthus cheiri*)	French buttercup	(*Ranunculus asiaticus*)
Evergreen candytuft	(*Iberis sempervirens*)	French marigold	(*Tagetes patula*)
Everlasting pea	(Lathyrus)		
		Garden heliotrope	(*Valeriana officinalis*)
False dragonhead	(*Physostegia virginiana*)	Gas plant	(*Dictamnus albus*)
False indigo	(Baptisia)	Gayfeather	(Liatris)
Farewell-to-spring	(*Godetia amoena*)	Gazania	(*Gazania longiscapa*)
Fern-leaved yarrow	(*Achillea filipendulina*)	Gentian	(*Gentiana asclepiadea*)
Feverfew	(*Chrysanthemum parthenium*)	Geranium	(Pelargonium)
		Giant onion	(*Allium giganteum*)
Fig marigold	(*Mesembryanthemum cordifolium*)	Giant summer hyacinth	(*Galtonia candicans*)
Fire bush	(*Kochia scoparia trichophila*)	Gladiolus	(Gladiolus)
Five-leaf akebia	(*Akebia quinata*)	Globe amaranth	(*Gomphrena globosa*)

Globe candytuft	(*Iberis umbellata*)	Harvest brodiaea	(*Brodiaea elegans*)
Globeflower	(Trollius)	Hawk's-beard	(*Crepis rubra*)
Gloriosa daisy	(*Rudbeckia gloriosa*)	Helen flower	(*Helenium autumnale*)
Glory-lily	(*Gloriosa rothschildiana*)	Heliotrope	(Heliotropum)
Glory-of-the-snow	(*Chionodoxa sardensis*)	Himalayan foxtail lily	(Eremurus)
Gloxinia	(*Sinningia speciosa*)	Himalayan primrose	(*Primula denticulata*)
Goatsbeard	(*Aruncus sylvester*)	Hollyhock	(*Altheae rosea*)
Golden centaurea	(*Centaurea macrocephala*)	Hollyhock	(*Malva alcea*)
		Honesty	(*Lunaria annua*)
Golden columbine	(*Aquilegia chrysantha*)	Hyacinth	(Hyacinthus)
Golden crocus	(*Crocus chrysanthus*)		
Goldenfleece	(*Thymophylla tenuiloba*)	Iceland poppy	(*Papaver nudicaule*)
Golden lantern	(*Calochortus pulchellus*)	Iris	(Iris)
Golden marguerite	(*Anthemis tinctoria*)	Italian aster	(*Aster amellus*)
Goldenrod	(Solidago)	Ivy geranium	(*Pelargonium peltatum*)
Golden spider lily	(Lycoris)		
Golden-yellow sweet pea	(*Crotalaria retusa*)	Japanese anemone	(*Anemone japonica*)
		Japanese primrose	(*Primula japonica*)
Grape hyacinth	(*Muscari botryoides*)	Japanese wisteria	(*Wisteria floribunda*)
Grape leaf anemone	(*Anemone vitifolia*)	Jasmine	(*Jasminum officinale*)
Greek anemone	(*Anemone blanda*)	Job's tears	(*Coix lacryma-jobi*)
Greek valerian	(Polemonium)	Johnny-jump-up	(*Viola tricolor*)
Ground morning glory	(*Convolvulus mauritanicus*)	Kaffir lily	(*Clivia miniata*)
Hanging begonia	(*Begonia pendula*)	Lady Washington geranium	(*Pelargonium domesticum*)
Harlequin flower	(*Sparaxis tricolor*)		

Lantana	(Lantana)	Mariposa lily	(Calochortus)
Larkspur	(Consolida ambigua)	Marsh marigold	(Caltha palustris)
Larkspur	(Delphinium)	Mask-flower	(Alonsoa warscewiczii)
Lavender cotton	(Santolina chamaecyparissus)	Meadow rue	(Thalictrum)
Lazy daisy	(Aphanostephus skirrobasis)	Meadow saffron	(Colchicum speciosum)
		Mexican sunflower	(Tithonia rotundifolia)
Leadwort	(Ceratostigma plumbaginoides)	Michaelmas daisy	(Aster)
		Mignonette	(Reseda odorata)
Lenten rose	(Helleborus orientalis)	Miniature hollyhock	(Sidalcea)
Leopard plant	(Ligularia dentata)	Mistflower	(Eupatorium coelestinum)
Leopard's-bane	(Doronicum caucasicum)	Moneywort	(Lysimachia punctata)
Lily	(Lilium)	Monkey flower	(Mimulus variegatus)
Lily leek	(Allium moly)	Montbretia	(Crocosmia crocosmaeflora)
Lily of the Nile	(Agapanthus africanus)		
Lily of the valley	(Convallaria majalis)	Moonflower	(Calonyction aculeatum)
Lobelia	(Lobelia)	Morning glory	(Convolvulus)
Love-in-a-mist	(Nigella damascena)	Morning glory	(Ipomoea purpurea)
Lungwort	(Pulmonaria angustifolia)	Moss phlox	(Phlox subulata)
		Mullein	(Verbascum)
Lupine	(Lupinus)	Mullein pink	(Lychnis coronaria)
Madonna lily	(Lilium candidum)	Naples onion	(Allium neapolitanum)
Mallow-wort	(Malope trifida)	Nasturtium	(Tropaeolum)
Maltese cross	(Lychnis)	Neapolitan cyclamen	(Cyclamen neapolitanum)
Marguerite	(Chrysanthemum frutescens)	Nemesia	(Nemesia strumosa)
Marigold	(Tagetes)	Oriental poppy	(Papaver orientale)

Painted daisy	*(Chrysanthemum coccineum)*	Prairie mallow	(Sidalcea)
Painted tongue	*(Salpiglossis sinuata)*	Prickly poppy	*(Argemone grandiflora)*
Pansy	*(Viola tricolor hortensis)*	Primrose	(Primula)
Passionflower	*(Passiflora caerulea)*	Prince's-feather	*(Amaranthus hypochondriacus)*
Patience plant	(Impatiens)	Purple loosestrife	*(Lythrum salicaria)*
Pearl everlasting	*(Anaphalis margaritacea)*	Rain lily	*(Zephyranthes grandiflora)*
Perennial flax	*(Linum perenne)*	Red-hot poker	*(Kniphofia aloides)*
Periwinkle	*(Vinca rosea)*	Regal lily	*(Lilium regale)*
Persian centaurea	*(Centaurea dealbata)*	Rock purslane	*(Calandrina umbellata)*
Peruvian lily	*(Alstroemeria aurantiaca)*	Rocky Mountain columbine	*(Aquilegia caerulea)*
Petunia	(Petunia)	Rocky Mountain garland	*(Clarkia elegans)*
Phlox	(Phlox)	Rose campion	*(Lychnis coronaria)*
Pimpernel	(Anagallis)	Rose mallow	(Hibiscus)
Pincushion flower	*(Cenia barbata)*	Rose moss	*(Portulaca grandiflora)*
Pincushion flower	*(Scabiosa caucasica)*		
Pineapple lily	*(Eucomis punctata)*	Sage	(Salvia)
Pink	(Dianthus)	Saint-John's-wort	*(Hypericum moserianum)*
Pink-sand verbena	*(Abronia umbellata)*	Satinflower	(Godetia)
Plumbago vine	(Plumbago)	Scarborough lily	*(Vallota speciosa)*
Poppy-flowered anemone	*(Anemone coronaria)*	Scarlet flax	*(Linum grandiflorum)*
Poppy mallow	*(Callirhoë involucrata)*	Scarlet runner bean	(Phaseolus)
Porcelain ampelopsis	*(Ampelopsis brevipedunculata)*	Scarlet sage	*(Salvia splendens)*
Pot marigold	*(Calendula officinalis)*	Scotch crocus	(Crocus)

Sea lavender	*(Limonium latifolium)*
Sea pink	(Armeria)
Shasta daisy	*(Chrysanthemum maximum)*
Shellflower	*(Tigridia pavonia)*
Shirley poppy	*(Papaver rhoeas)*
Short-tubed lycoris	*(Lycoris radiata)*
Siberian wallflower	(Cheiranthus)
Sieber crocus	*(Crocus sieberii)*
Skullcap	*(Scutellaria baicalensis)*
Snake's-head	*(Fritillaria meleagris)*
Snapdragon	*(Antirrhinum majus)*
Sneezewort	*(Achillea ptarmica)*
Snowdrop	*(Galanthus nivalis)*
Snowflake	*(Leucojum vernum)*
Snow-in-summer	*(Cerastium tomentosum)*
Snow-on-the-mountain	*(Euphorbia marginata)*
Society garlic	*(Tulbaghia fragrans)*
Spanish iris	*(Iris xiphium)*
Speedwell	(Veronica)
Spiderflower	*(Cleome spinosa)*
Spider lily	*(Hymenocallis narcissifolia)*
Spiderwort	(Tradescantia)
Spring adonis	*(Adonis vernalis)*

Spring meadow saffron	*(Bulbocodium vernum)*
Spurge	(Euphorbia)
Starglory	(Quamoclit)
Star-of-Bethlehem	(Ornithogalum)
Star of Persia	*(Allium christophii)*
Star of Texas	*(Xanthisma texanum)*
Stock	*(Mathiola incana)*
Stonecrop	*(Sedum spectabile)*
Strawflower	*(Helichrysum bracteatum)*
Striped squill	*(Puschkinia scilloides)*
Summer adonis	*(Adonis aestivalis)*
Summer forget-me-not	*(Anchusa capensis)*
Summer phlox	*(Phlox paniculata)*
Sundrops	*(Oenothera tetragona)*
Sunflower	(Helianthus)
Sunshine daisy	*(Gamolepis tagetes)*
Swan River daisy	*(Brachycome iberidifolia)*
Sweet alyssum	*(Lobularia maritima)*
Sweet pea	*(Lathyrus odoratus)*
Sweet rocket	*(Hesperis matronalis)*
Sweet sultan	*(Centaurea moschata)*
Sweet violet	*(Viola odorata)*
Sweet William	*(Dianthus barbatus)*

Tahoka daisy	*(Aster tanacetifolius)*
Tassel flower	*(Amaranthus caudatus)*
Tassel flower	*(Emilia flammea)*
Texas bluebonnet	*(Lupinus subcaornosus)*
Threadleaf coreopsis	*(Coreopsis verticillata)*
Thrift	(Armeria)
Tickseed	(Coreopsis)
Tidytips	*(Layia campestris)*
Toadflax	*(Linaria maroccana)*
Transvaal daisy	*(Gerberia jamesonii)*
Tree mallow	*(Lavatera trimestris)*
True primula	*(Primula vulgaris)*
Trumpet flower	*(Datura metel)*
Trumpet vine	*(Allamanda cathartica)*
Trumpet vine	*(Bignonia capreolata)*
Trumpet vine	*(Doxantha unguis-cati)*
Tuberose	*(Polyanthes tuberosa)*
Tuberous begonia	*(Begonia tuberhybrida)*
Tulip	(Tulipa)
Tussock bellflower	*(Campanula carpatica)*
Twinspur	*(Diascia barberae)*
Verbena	*(Verbena hortensis)*
Violet	(Viola)

Violet boltonia	*(Boltonia latisquama)*
Violet sage	*(Salvia superba)*
Virginia stock	*(Malcomia maritima)*
Virgin's bower	(Clematis)
Watsonia	(Watsonia)
Wax begonia	*(Begonia semperflorens)*
White mariposa	*(Calochortus venustus)*
Wild indigo	*(Baptisia tinctoria)*
Willow bellflower	*(Campanula persicifolia)*
Winged everlasting	*(Ammobium alatum)*
Wishbone flower	*(Torenia fournierii)*
Wolfsbane	*(Aconitum vulparia)*
Woodland forget-me-not	*(Myosotis sylvatica)*
Woolly speedwell	*(Veronica incana)*
Woolly yarrow	*(Achillea tomentosa)*
Yarrow	(Achillea)
Yellow cosmos	*(Cosmos sulphureus)*
Yellow foxglove	*(Digitalis grandiflora)*
Yellow moraea	(Moraea)
Zinnia	(Zinnia)

index